Political Woman

POLITICAL WOMAN

Jeane J. Kirkpatrick

Basic Books, Inc., Publishers

NEW YORK

This book
is dedicated to the legislators
whom it describes.

Contents

Foreword

IN American public life, in elected or appointed office, women are noticeable by their absence. Why?

Why, when women in increasing numbers are asserting themselves, training themselves, seeking equal rights, equal opportunities and equal responsibilities in every aspect of American life, have so few contested successfully in the political arena? How can more women be encouraged to seek public office?

The Center for the American Woman and Politics was established in 1971, as part of the Eagleton Institute of Politics at Rutgers University, to investigate these and related questions in the belief that the future health of the American political system requires active participation by *all* segments of our society.

It is commonly assumed that women face obstacles—in entering politics, in competing for higher office, in functioning successfully as politicians—which differ in degree or in kind from those facing aspiring or practicing male politicians. To determine whether such an hypothesis reflects political and social realities, the Center for the American Woman and Politics sponsored a conference and commissioned this book.

Fifty women state senators and representatives from twenty-six states were invited to the three-day conference in May 1972, which was supported by a generous grant from the Carnegie Corporation of New York. These women, experienced politicians all, were selected on the basis of diversity and competence from nominations submitted by the various state organizations of the American Association of University Women, the League of Women Voters and the National Federation of Business and Professional Women's Clubs.

In discussion groups they debated and argued and shared anecdotes about their individual and collective evolution from political novice to seasoned campaigner to (in some instances) wielders of power and influence as chairpersons of important committees. In confidential interviews, they revealed their political struggles and ambitions, the private price they paid for being a public person, and their personal styles of functioning as competent colleagues in essentially all-male legislative bodies.

To this intensely human raw material, Professor Jeane J. Kirkpatrick has brought her professional background as a political scientist and her empathetic insight to produce what is—shockingly enough—a first, the first major study of women in American public life. In commissioning this book, the Center for the American Woman and Politics hopes to demonstrate that women can and do cope with the demands of political office; that women in politics and government constitute a legitimate and neglected field of inquiry for the social sciences, especially political science; that there is a need for more serious literature of all kinds about women's public roles; and finally that women who want to exercise political power in their own right must take the responsibility in their own hands, individually and collectively.

The Center for the American Woman and Politics finds that women politicians tend to see themselves as more honest, more hardworking, more knowledgeable about the issues, more concerned with the public interest, and more accessible to constituents than most of their male colleagues. At a time when the public opinion polls demonstrate a pervasive distrust of government and lack of confidence in political incumbents, women may have an unusual opportunity to restore faith in public institutions and the formation of public policy by putting themselves forward as candidates for office.

Ida F. S. Schmertz
Center for the American Woman and Politics
The Eagleton Institute of Politics
Rutgers University

Preface

THIS study owes its existence to the cooperation of the women legislators who attended a conference sponsored by the Center for the American Woman and Politics of the Eagleton Institute of Politics (Rutgers University). The legislators consented to fill out questionnaires, to submit to long personal interviews as their contribution to learning something more than we now know about the terms and conditions of women's participation in politics. Although, like politicians generally, most are obviously more interested in acting in and on the world than in introspection, they were, almost without exception, generous with their time and attention. That is the principal reason that I have dedicated this book to them.

There is another reason as well. In the course of interviewing, going over the tapes and transcriptions of the interviews, and making sense of these data, I came to admire these women legislators—as women who had made their way through a complicated, often discouraging obstacle course and as politicians who brought a high sense of duty, dedication, skill, balance and perseverance to political office. Democratic governments have great need of such citizens and legislators.

My initial concerns about the effects of the conference situation on the interviews proved unwarranted as it became clear that these women, who were strong enough to have resisted the various social pressures against women in public office, were obviously not going to have their perceptions or descriptions of reality altered by the experience of being together for several days and being exposed to the same speakers. The success of the interviews was also a tribute to the skill of the interviewing team that I was able to recruit. The interviewers on this project, all experienced professionals, were, in alphabetical order, Anne Brunsdale, Publications Director, the American

Enterprise Institute; Anne Collins, Assistant Professor, Educational Psychology, Catholic University; Elizabeth Douvan, Professor of Psychology, University of Michigan; Valerie Earle, Professor and Chairman of Political Science, Georgetown University; Victoria Schuck, Professor of Political Science, Mt. Holyoke College. I also did a full share of interviews. Lucia Ballantine, a member of the Executive Committee of the Center, also assisted in the interviewing. The interviewing schedule was arduous; the interviews ran between two and three hours each and were taped and later transcribed. Anonymity was assured to all respondents, and I have made a serious effort to honor that promise. While individual legislators may well recognize sentiments, words and portions of their biographies in the manuscript, the contextual information that would enable other readers to link anecdotes and opinions to a specific legislator is systematically withheld.

All of the legislators participated in group discussions at the conference. These discussions were taped and transcribed, and relevant and appropriate comments from these groups have been used.

The officers of the Center for the American Woman and Politics and of the Eagleton Institute of Politics also deserve a large share of whatever credit this project merits. Ida Schmertz, Ruth Mandel, and Donald Herzberg provided support and assistance without interference. They have been generous and supportive in all phases of the project. A grant from the Carnegie Corporation largely financed the project; naturally I should like to express my gratitude for the financial support that made this study possible. The Georgetown University Computer Center provided the machine time needed to analyze the questionnaire data, and Eric Novotony, a graduate fellow at Georgetown University, assisted in the computer analysis.

Thanks are also due good friends and advisers who read the entire manuscript and offered criticisms and suggestions: Harold D. Lasswell, Austin Ranney, Alan Rosenthal, Donald Herzberg, Elizabeth Douvan, Anne Collins, William J. Keefe, Ida Schmertz and Ruth Mandel. Through successive versions, Charlotte Fischer and Joyce Horn labored to transform my crabbed penmanship into sensible typescript. Finally, my greatest debt is to my husband, who has read this manuscript almost as many times as I, and whose criticism and encouragement were of inestimable value. He definitely qualifies as a "participant husband" (see Chapter 9, pp. 231-32).

I alone am responsible for the analysis and interpretation of data. All faults of omission and commission are, alas, mine.

Jeane J. Kirkpatrick
Georgetown University

Political Woman

Chapter I

Sex and Power

POLITICAL man is a familiar figure with a long history. As chief, prince, king, counsellor, premier, president, dictator, chairman he has led, battled, pillaged, conquered, built, judged, governed. Political man has fascinated and challenged historians and philosophers; he has been described, dissected, praised, excoriated and psychoanalyzed. It is probably not fair or reasonable to reproach the many men who have written about politics for ignoring women since women, through the modern period, at least, have had a very small share, though a very large stake, in political power.[1]

Even today, the most important and interesting question about women's political role is why that role is so insignificant. The most important and interesting question about women's political behavior is why so few seek and wield power. Women are numerous enough at the lowest level of politics—in the precincts, at the party picnics, getting out the vote, doing the telephoning, collecting the dollars— but remarkably scarce at the upper levels where decisions are made that affect the life of the community, state, nation.[2]

Half a century after the ratification of the nineteenth amendment, no woman has been nominated to be president or vice-president, no woman has served on the Supreme Court. Today, there is no woman in the cabinet, no woman in the Senate, no woman serving as governor of a major state, no woman mayor of a major city, no woman in the top leadership of either major party.[3] It is true in the U.S. today, as in the nations described earlier by Duverger, that: "While, in elections, the proportion of women voting is smaller than men, the gap between the two is very narrow and the equality of the sexes may be regarded as practically achieved. On the other hand, the proportion of women playing a real part in political leadership is ridiculously small. . . . There are hardly any women in the bodies which take political decisions and direct the state."[4]

The fact that so few American women seek and wield political power distinguishes their political behavior from that of men. This crucial difference is the reality from which this inquiry into political woman begins.[5] No doubt these differences (seeking and wielding power) have been so little examined because questions about women's participation in power processes have been so rarely raised. No doubt they have been rarely raised because the political behavior of women has been perceived as a "given." No doubt that, when raised, these questions have been given little attention because their answers have seemed self-evident. But today when success in politics depends, or appears to depend, more on social skills than on physical force, it is by no means self-evident why women should so rarely seek to participate directly and actively in political power processes. Whether women have the capacity to participate fully in the power processes of society, why they have so rarely sought to do so, and if or how they differ from men when they do so, are empirical questions which can be answered only by systematic inquiry.

Women as a Political Category

Politics is an activity carried on in the name of collectivities. The possession and use of power is always justified with reference to some collectivity (e.g., the French, the Irish, the people, the working class), and demands are made in the name of groups. The collectivities in whose name public transactions are carried out change as the bases of group identities change.

From time to time new attributes such as nationality and religion come into being, or existing attributes such as race, sex, income level, or life style are suddenly perceived as the basis of common identity. The bases of group identity at any given time tell us a great deal about a culture, for a new group can come into being only when the culture is receptive to new symbols of identity. The vogue of Marxism, for example, is in large measure accounted for by the receptivity of Western culture to symbols of identity deriving from the distribution of wealth and power. The failure of Nazism is related to the nonreceptivity of neighboring nations to racial symbols such as "Aryan." For a symbol of identity to become socially significant it is necessary either (1) that some large portion of the people who share the relevant characteristic identify with it, or (2) that some strategically placed group state such an identification and present demands in its name. (It is not necessary that those who claim the identification and state the demands actually share the relevant characteristic.) Both have occurred in the case of women. In the past decade the female sex—like youth—has become a basis of political identity. Women have become a politically relevant social group in whose name grievances are stated, claims are made, and demands put forth.

At any moment there exist in any society shared characteristics which do *not* become the bases of political action. Fat people are such a category. No demands on the public conscience and resources are made in their name despite the fact that one of their dominant physical characteristics is defined (in America) as pathological and is treated as an object of ridicule, that moral attributes—such as self-indulgence—are associated with their condition, that no cultural heroes display this despised characteristic, that medical science has never *really* focused its efforts on the problem, although tens of millions each year fall victim to its ravages.

Exactly why the fat people of the world do not unite to press for the solution of common problems and achieve common goals, while "Republicans," "Democrats," "monarchists," "Palestinians," "environmentalists," "Gay liberationists," and "French language purists" organize into political action groups is not entirely clear. Fat people will become a political group only after they decide that they have distinctive claims on public attention and public support. About the same time it will probably be noticed that they are "under represented" among holders of high public office. Until then they wait their turn, undiscovered as a politically relevant identifiable group—

as lost in other identifications as were youth and women only
yesterday.

Once a pregnant symbol of common identity has been discovered,
its existence, its grievances, and its demands seem clear. Nowhere is
this more evident than with "women," a population category which
has been transformed from possessors of particular biological
characteristics into a symbol of political identity.

*Questions about women's share of power and their political be-
havior assume that sexual differences are in some sense relevant to
politics.* One who does not make this assumption will no more concern herself about women's political behavior than students of
politics concern themselves with the voting behavior of people with
large feet, or red hair, or bald heads. But relevance does not necessarily imply the existence of exclusive concerns nor the advocacy of
common action.

Sex has so far served as the basis of common political action only
occasionally.[6] Women had a common stake in winning the vote
because they were excluded. They successfully organized and agi-
tated in the name of their sex. The vote achieved, the collective
concerns of women were, however, only rarely articulated in the
political arena. No women's vote developed. No women's pressure
group emerged. In the years since the nineteenth amendment became
the law of the land (August, 1920), women have split their votes
between parties and candidates in much the same proportions as
men.[7]

In fact, the existence of common policy commitments and political
units is almost irrelevant to women's stake in the political process.
Whether or not the various special concerns of women with mater-
nity, child care, nutrition, tax laws, and economic discrimination
constitute an adequate basis for common political action, *as citizens
and as subjects women have as large a stake in politics as other
citizens and subjects. They have, that is, as large a stake as men.*
Obviously, neither men nor women are affected only by legislation
specifically relevant to their sex. Obviously, both have a stake in
political decisions affecting all citizens. Most political officials articulate interests of specific constituencies but make policy on matters of
broad community concern.[8] Whether or not women have unique or

distinctive perspectives they have an obvious stake in determinations about "who gets what, when and how."[9]

The size, scope and effectiveness of modern government makes power a central value in modern society and the distribution of power a central focus of contention. Political power—that is, the right to make policy for the society—is the major stake in every election, revolution, coup d'état. The notion that power should be shared by those affected by it proved so compelling that it became the basis of a new conception of legitimacy, a new doctrine of who should rule. Popular sovereignty, representative government, republicanism, democracy are the names we give to political systems that found legitimacy on the broad sharing of political power, and competitive elections are the institutional practice that permit masses a voice in decisions about who should rule and to what broad ends. By the middle of this century universal adult suffrage had been achieved in virtually all democratic nations and autocrats turned to plebiscites to achieve the public relations benefits of popular participation without incurring the risks. Everywhere, *the right to vote symbolized access to political power.* The franchise constituted a kind of certificate of eligibility for political leadership. Newly enfranchised groups, classes, regions, races used the vote to move their representatives into positions of political leadership. The achievement of effective suffrage for blacks was followed by election of black representatives to Congress, state houses, city halls. Again and again newly naturalized and enfranchised immigrants used the vote to place one of their own in government. As Irish and Italian men gained the right to vote they elected more Irish and Italian men to party and public office. But when Irish women gained the right to vote, they also elected more Irish men to office.

Unlike the enfranchisement of other categories of people, women's suffrage did not importantly affect the social composition of government. One student of state governments noted the general tendency of voters to elect people like themselves, and commented, "Certain social characteristics, however, escape the constituencies' demand for conformity. The feminine half of our population is seldom represented by more than five to ten percent of the members of any state legislature."[10] The sexual identifications of women have proved a much less important influence on political behavior than have ethnic, regional, and economic identifications. Few women have even attempted to enter the decision-making bodies of government either to articulate the special interests of their sex or to participate in making policy for the community. Why that should be the case is by no means clear.[11]

Women's Low Participation: Four Hypothetical Constraints

Any serious consideration of women's participation and nonparticipation in "high" politics should begin by noting that political participation is also low among men. Milbraith estimates that only one to two percent of the American adult population can be called "gladiators,"[12] and this almost surely exaggerates the percentage of men who run for office in competitive elections. Running for office is by no means a part of the career of the average male, in America or elsewhere. But, though the number of men who seek public office is very small, the number of women is much smaller still.

It may be that women's low participation in politics is merely an aspect of their exclusion from other social processes. Certainly it is true that women are nearly as scarce at the upper levels of industry, church, and education as in politics and government.[13] The fact that so few women participate in politics at the upper levels where decisions are made cannot be fully explained by their low position vis-a-vis other values since, in a system where office holders are chosen by popular vote in competitive processes, political power is not dependent on the possession of other values. It may *help* to be rich, or influential in a large denomination, or president of a university, but none of these statures is a prerequisite to or a guarantee of gaining public office.[14]

An explanation of women's low participation must also account not only for the fact that few women wield power, but that few women seek positions of power.[15]

To account for the paucity of women in "high" politics various explanations have been offered. All the explanations must deal with two fundamental questions: whether male dominance of power processes derives from female preference or male imposition or both, and whether male dominance is natural or conventional, as the Greeks would have put it. Answers to questions about whether male dominance is rooted in nature or nurture can be combined in various ways. It can be argued that female subordination is "given" in nature and is preferred by females. Conversely, male dominance may be conventional not natural, but centuries of such domination may have led to the development of personality types compatible with continued dominance. That is, women may be socialized to prefer male dominance though such a preference is neither natural nor necessary.

Four explanations are most common. All should be treated as hypothetical since the evidence available is insufficient to either verify or disprove any one of them. These explanations postulate four types of disabilities, any one of which could, in principle, explain the paucity of women in public life. They are by no means mutually exclusive, though it is unusual to find any one person offering all four. I call them the Four Hypothetical Constraints. They are:

1. physiological constraints;
2. cultural constraints;
3. role constraints;
4. male conspiracy.

I propose to examine each briefly, in order that these postulated difficulties which are presumed to inhibit women's pursuit and exercise of power may be borne in mind as we examine the personality and role behavior of the women legislators who will serve as our guides to the broader subject of women in politics.

1. Physiological Constraints

That physiology is fate seems clear to more than a few serious observers of human social life. Though anathema to many in the women's movement, the position is not to be taken lightly nor dismissed by polemic. The notion that there are psychological differences between men and women which are grounded in their distinctive physiologies is not only persistent, but there are substantial though not conclusive data to support it.[16] Not all psychological or physiological differences are necessarily relevant to the political behavior of the sexes. We are concerned only with whether the distinctive psychological characteristics of the sexes (if such exist) effectively bar women from roles to which broad power over the community is attached.

The belief that physiology bars women from "high" politics involves several assumptions about physiology, personality and politics that should be made explicit. The most important of these are, first, that there are in fact universal female psychological traits relevant to politics and grounded in female physiology,[17] and second, that politics is a single type of activity whose distinguishing characteristics persist in diverse environments. Both assumptions are reasonable enough in principle. Most political scientists appear to believe that there are certain ubiquitous types of activity (such as authoritative rulemaking, adjudication, and enforcement) which may reasonably be called political. Indeed the discipline of political science rests on the belief that there are political activities or functions performed in all societies and that these activities can be recognized by a trained and careful observer although they take place in enormously diverse cultural and institutional contexts. While there is no exact agreement among students of the subject, there is a general consensus that the political dimension of social life is associated with power and with those institutions especially concerned with power processes. Governments are generally the most important of these agencies specialized in power processes.[18]

Power and the institutions especially concerned with its exercise have a historic and existential relation to what might be called brute force, including the ability to deprive persons of physical liberty, well–being, and usually, of life. Authority is also associated with power processes and helps distinguish political power from brute force. Authority involves leadership and legitimacy as well as force. Together, authority and force constitute the major components of political power.

For any generalization about relations between personality and political behavior to hold cross-nationally, the universal "political" factor must outweigh the differences in the politics of different kinds of political systems. The point is an important one. There are many differences in the politics of the U.S., USSR, and Argentina—to choose just three examples. Patterns of recruitment into political

office vary greatly; quite different skills are needed to win an election in Wisconsin, a promotion in the ranks of the Communist party
of the Soviet Union, and a following in the officer corps of
Argentina. In all, establishing leadership seems remote from the
process needed by the dominant male to gain ascendency over the
primal horde.[19] Many social scientists believe, however, that beneath
the elegance of Versailles, the casual courtesy of the House of
Commons, the ideologically veiled transactions in the Kremlin, the
campaign trail in Wisconsin there lie continuing struggles to achieve
and assert dominance. Hypotheses that postulate the existence of
quintessential, universal "political" activities and/or "political" personality types assume that the crucial personality requirements for
success are shared in all types of political context, and that certain
key aspects of power relations transcend variations in institutional
context.

How does all this relate to the physiology of women? The above
assumptions, or similar ones, are the basis of supposedly universal
relations among power, politics, and maleness.[20] Sigmund Freud,[21]
for whom sexual and reproductive functions had such importance,
followed Darwin in linking the origins of society to male dominance.
To Darwin's belief that the primitive form of human society was that
of a horde ruled despotically by a powerful male, Freud added new
explanations of male dominance, rooting it in sexual function, family
structure, and the psychology of male and female. *Totem and
Taboo*,[22] which presents Freud's reconstruction of the origins of
social life, describes society as rooted in force and authority, both of
which he believed to be indissoluably associated with maleness.

There is a tendency today in the women's movement to treat
Freud as an extreme example of misogyny and male chauvinism.[23]
This tendency ignores the extent to which Freud's views were shared
by his illustrious contemporaries and predecessors in science, medicine, literature and philosophy, and are embodied in culture and
social structure. Christianity, to take just one of the great world
religions, vests in men authority and governance of the family, and
(as Pope Paul VI recently reminded us) the Roman Catholic Church
as well. According to traditional Christian theology, physiology,
psychology, and moral duty fit women for the role of helpmate,

wife, and mother. Judaism and Mohammedanism, have, if anything, an even less exalted view of women's place. Traditional religions have reinforced traditional relations between the sexes.

Manipulation of male and female hormone levels of certain animals appear to provide some inconclusive evidence to support the notion that women are naturally submissive and men naturally aggressive. [24] Meanwhile, new versions of the physiological explanation have been offered. One of the more interesting of these deals neither in biology, teleology, or moral theory, but is presented, as is fitting to the times, in the language of social science.

Reflecting the new interest in linkages between biology and politics, Lionel Tiger argues, "Basically my proposition is that cultural forms result from the interaction of behavioral propensities—or inborn biological programmes—with existing social patterns and expectations in any community."[25] Like all proponents of the physiological explanation, Tiger treats culture as an intervening variable, itself a function of fundamental human needs. Men, he asserts, are programmed for leadership, decisionmaking, and force. Thus, "that females only rarely dominate authority structures may reflect females underlying inability—at the ethological level of pattern-releasing behavior—to affect the behavior of subordinates."[26] Further "even if they want to, women cannot become political leaders because males are strongly predisposed to form and maintain all male groups, particularly when matters of moment for the community are involved."[27] Also, ". . . there is a very rigid nature of the relationship between force and maleness which can be observed cross-culturally."[28] For Tiger, as for ethologists who have come before and almost surely will come after, the political role of the human male leader has its analogy in group leadership of male chimpanzees, baboons, and certain other primates.[29] Politics reflect male bonding and male dominance. Physiology assigns females to "private spheres."

Maybe. But any serious scientific effort to ground male political dominance and female political submission in the nature of things must take account of the existence of those women who have sought and achieved political leadership. The very existence of Golda Meir, Indira Gandhi, Elizabeth I, Isabella, Catherine, Cleopatra, demonstrates that female physiology is not a *necessary* disqualification for politics in the way that human biology disqualifies us for developing wings or feathers. Tiger discounts the few women prominent in politics by suggesting that male charisma may have rubbed off on them through close association with a father or brother. He offers no evidence. But, evidence is required. A physiological explanation must provide evidence that despite the existence of a few exceptions, despite broad intrasex differences, and despite variations in political systems, it remains true that women lack the psychosocial characteristics associated everywhere with political leadership.

2. Cultural Constraints

What are big boys made of? What are big boys made of?

Independence, aggression, competitiveness, leadership, task orientation, outward orientation, assertiveness, innovation, self-discipline, stoicism, activity, objectivity, analytic-mindedness, courage, unsentimentality, rationality, confidence, and emotional control.

What are big girls made of? What are big girls made of?

Dependence, passivity, fragility, low pain tolerance, nonaggression, noncompetitiveness, inner orientation, interpersonal orientation, empathy, sensitivity, nurturance, subjectivity, intuitiveness, yieldingness, receptivity, inability to risk, emotional liability, supportiveness,[30]

Today, discussions of women's political role turn quickly to the impact of cultural norms on male and female behavior. It is culture which elaborates the psychological, social, and moral implication of biological characteristics. Definitions of masculinity and femininity are learned and internalized; these definitions vary between cultures and are to some extent arbitrary. Women, it is said, learn that governing is men's business, incorporate this belief into their self-conceptions and behave accordingly.

Cultural explanation emphasizes (and it is frequently charged, exaggerates) human malleability. The extreme cultural position on sex differences takes the view that no psychological characteristics are necessarily associated with sex, that no social role (except that directly involved in reproduction) is *necessarily* associated with sex. This position was expressed two decades ago by Margaret Mead, who asserted, "Standardized personality differences between the sexes are . . . cultural creations to which each generation, male, and female is trained to conform."[31] And "I have suggested that certain traits have been socially specialized as the appropriate attitudes of the behavior of only one sex, while other human traits have been specialized for the opposite sex." She adds, with a swipe at physiological explanation, "This social specialization is then rationalized into a theory that the socially decreed behavior is natural for one sex and unnatural for the other, and that the deviant is a deviant because of glandular defect or developmental accident."[32]

The essential elements of the cultural explanation of sex role behavior are the propositions that:

1. Culture embodies norms defining the sexes and identifies behavior appropriate for each; these are perpetuated through the socialization process;[33]
2. These norms determine the identity, expectations, and demands of males and females;
3. Sex stereotypes are not necessarily derived from the physiological characteristics of the two sexes;
4. Norms are internalized regardless of their biological relevance;
5. In all modern industrial societies, specifically including the United States, cultural norms exist which arbitrarily limit women's personal development, social choices, and opportunity to share fully in the dominant values of the society.

These beliefs, widely shared in contemporary America and spreading rapidly through Europe, are the core of feminism and the women's movement. They obviously can and do serve as an explanation of the failure of larger numbers of women to seek and gain public office.

Politics, it is argued, is a good example of arbitrary cultural exclusion. While legal barriers to women's participation in political life have been abolished, cultural norms have preserved the definition of politics as "man's work." Politics *is* a male world in the sense that presidents, senators, congressmen, mayors, judges, virtually all important political actors, *are* men. And male incumbency creates an expectation of male incumbency in the same way that nurses are women creates the expectation that nurses will be, *are* women.

So politics comes to be seen as "masculine," the opposite of "feminine," and these associations are reinforced by a host of surrounding, supporting expectations. Not only is the pursuit of power conceived as incompatible with femininity, but so are the professions normally associated with political careers. Law is a "man's world" and business is a "man's world" and the trade unions are a "man's world." Simultaneously, cultural norms communicate and reinforce the expectation of women's commitment to home, family, community service. There are few links between "woman's world" and high politics.[34]

Cultural expectations concerning sex roles are complemented by a dual status system which measures women by different criteria than men. Like men, women gain status for effective, responsible performance of culturally sanctioned roles.[35] Any effort to perform roles assigned by the culture to the opposite sex is likely to result in a loss of status on the sex specific status ladder. The values on which women are expected to concentrate are those of affection, rectitude, well-being; the skills relevant to the pursuit of these values are those associated with nurturing, serving, and pleasing a family and community: homemaking, personal adornment, preparing and serving food, nursing the ill, comforting the downcast, aiding and pleasing a husband, caring for and educating the young. It is assumed furthermore that these activities will consume all a woman's time, that to perform them well is both a full time and a life time job.[36]

It is not our purpose to examine here the kind of life and satisfactions available for faithful performance of this traditional role, only to note the incompatibility of this role with the pursuit of a serious political career, and to emphasize that the pursuit of nonsanctioned goals tends to result in loss of status on the sex specific status hierarchy. A woman who becomes an engineer not only does not gain points on the male status ladder (it is for males) or on the female hierarchy (the skills and role of engineer are not measured on the female status hierarchy), she can lose points for inappropriate behavior. And politics has been deemed inappropriate for women. A woman entering politics risks the social and psychological penalties so frequently associated with nonconformity. Disdain, internal conflicts, and failure are widely believed to be her likely rewards.

Too, culture is often said to affect women's political behavior by depriving them of the self-esteem necessary for political leadership. In a culture which values the male more highly than the female, women may never acquire the confidence and autonomy required to seek power or wield it effectively.

The cultural explanation is the most widely used today to explain why so few women seek political office. It is argued that, from birth, female young are encouraged to develop a restricted and restrictive identity which links their sexual identity to the rejection of "male roles," which discourages the development of skills needed for "male" elite roles, which penalizes nonconformity by calling into question the "femininity" and the identity of the nonconformer.

That this is a time of cultural revolution is widely recognized. That the cultural norms described above are weakened and in flux can hardly be doubted. The concerted attack on these norms by the women's movement itself demonstrates the weakened condition of traditional culture. There is no longer such unanimity or such certainty that girls should be nurses instead of doctors, school teachers instead of college professors, that the roles of wife and mother are a full-time, life-time job, that the pursuit of what has been men's work is necessarily incompatible with femininity.[37] Today, the penalties of nonconformity to traditional roles are neither as great nor as certain as in the past. Weakened but not dead, traditional culture may nonetheless prove strong enough, it is argued, to maintain politics as a male preserve for at least another generation.

The greatest problem with the cultural explanation of differences in the personalities of males and females is that many differences are observed cross culturally. One study, for example, found that of 96 cultures studied, 82 percent emphasize nurturance in the socialization of girls, while 87 percent emphasize achievement (orientation to standards of excellence), and 85 emphasize self-reliance in the socialization of boys. The authors of the study conclude, "The observed differences in socialization of boys and girls are consistent with certain universal tendencies in the differentiation of the adult sex role." And add, "Most of these distinctions in adult role are not inevitable, but the biological differences between the sexes strongly predispose the distinction of role, if made, to be in a uniform direction."[38] Sex role is determined by socialization and socialization by culture, but cultures are, in some respects, themselves a response to human biological characteristics. (No culture is free, for example, to ignore the need to produce and care for young.) Only insofar as culture is arbitrary in its definitions of sex roles and socialization, does culture rather than physiology constitute an explanation of those definitions.

3. Role Constraints

Both the physiological and cultural explanations see the personality of women (and men) as the principal cause of the scarcity of women in politics. Explanations that emphasize social role to account for women's scarcity in politics deemphasize personality. The motives and temperament of individuals are seen as less important than the role system which defines and limits opportunities for social action.[39]

Obviously culture and role are closely related. In an integrated society culture reinforces social structure by defining and justifying goals, shaping modes of thinking and feeling, providing the cognitive map which locates each aspect of the social structure in relation to the whole and orients the individual within the structure. Social structure reinforces culture by providing roles consistent with culturally approved identities, goals, norms, and beliefs. Culture is the most important determinant of role choice. It provides individuals with a statement of social expectations. Culture provides identity and motives; roles provide opportunities for action. Each culture answers the question, "What is a woman?" in a distinctive fashion. In stable societies, the roles available to women illustrate, elaborate and reinforce the definitions. Those who explain women's low participation in "high politics" chiefly in terms of roles are also sensitive to cultural factors. But the two explanations differ in emphasis.

Role refers to a position in the social structure and its associated set of coherent norms. In any social structure, roles are complementary, as the norms that support them are complementary. Men's roles and women's roles complement one another and structure relations between the sexes. Incumbents are aware of their roles and consciously adapt their behavior to role requirements.

As with the associated cultural norms, there is a degree of flux surrounding sex roles in contemporary America, and the trend is toward broadening the number and variety of roles available to women. Still, traditional conceptions of role and role conflict are strong and are apt to remain so for some time.

Traditionally, there has been broad agreement among women and men about the incompatibility of women's "primary" role and other roles in society (especially those involving autonomy and the exercise of power). Thus the role of wife/mother and professional have typically been seen as incompatible. Both roles have been defined as full-time, life-time jobs. This presumed incompatibility between wife/mother roles and professions (such as law) associated with politics has discouraged women from acquiring the training needed to become decisionmakers.

Judgments concerning the compatibility and incompatibility roles inhere in the culture, and are embodied in social structure. Obviously, not all roles are mutually incompatible; everyone is an incumbent of multiple roles. One may be, for example, son, husband, father, friend, colleague, lawyer, legislator, Republican activist, stamp collector, and golfer without contradicting presumptions of role incompatibility. To the contrary, each of these roles may reinforce the other: a legal practice will support an attractive wife and children as well as a political career; the wife and children and friends and colleagues will enhance one's image and aid one's efforts to win office; the Republican activism will provide institutional support for a political career; golf and stamp collecting will provide acceptable relief from a demanding schedule. It is a familiar male resumé.

It is different for the attorney's wife. To begin with, she isn't an attorney. Let us say that she attended a liberal arts college and married soon after graduation. Two years of office work while her husband was in law school helped keep him there, but did not enhance her professional qualifications. Three beautiful babies enriched their lives but did not augment her professional qualifications. Years of service in the Church and the Red Cross broadened her acquaintances, but did not necessarily lay the groundwork for a successful political career.

It does seem clear that the transition from the roles of housewife and mother to the role of political decisionmaker is not easy and has not been frequently attempted. The roles of housewife, mother, lawmaker do not have what Eulau and Sprague have called "professional convergence."[40] Two professions are said to converge when they have common role requirements as, for example, law and politics—both require the ability to develop and articulate positions, to "represent" others. Many observers are convinced that social structure effectively precludes women's significant participation in power.

The nurturant skills associated with traditional women's roles seem less relevant to political role requirements. The traditional role system makes it difficult for a woman to begin a political career before middle age; makes it difficult for her to change her place of residence; makes it difficult for her to develop the skills and acquire the experience needed for a political career.

4. Male Conspiracy

This explanation of women's nonparticipation in power sees women as oppressed, barred from power by a ruling class bent on maintaining its hegemony. That ruling class is the men of the world. As Shulamith Firestone put it, relations between the sexes constitute "the oldest, most rigid class/caste system in existence, the class system based on sex—a system consolidated over thousands of years, lending the archetypal male and female roles an undeserved legitimacy and seeming permanence."[41]

Alfred Adler, the Vaertings, Viola Klein, Helen Hacker, Kirsten Amudsen, and many others have argued that "feminine" traits turn out, on close inspection, to be characteristics typical of subject peoples and are rooted not in biology but in power—or more accurately, in lack of power. Duverger concluded his important cross-national study, *The Political Role of Women*, by stating "There is no more an inferior sex than there are inferior races or inferior classes. But there is a sex, and there are classes and races, who have come to believe in their inferiority because they have been persuaded of it in justification of their subordinate position in society."[42]

This explanation of women's political role conceives cultural and role systems as effective instruments of male domination. Culture rationalizes and justifies male rule in terms of the dominant values of the community. Culture serves power; social structure embodies and protects it.

Many have been struck by the resemblance between the situations of women and blacks. More than a few have noted, too, that women's participation in radical political movements has not resulted in the liberation of women. It is observed that women demonstrate many of the characteristics of an oppressed group—lack of education and relevant professional skills, peer prejudice, economic discrimination, low self-esteem and aspirations. In addition, they are said to be more emotional than rational, more dependent than autonomous, more volatile than persistent, more predisposed to be governed than to govern. They are, we are assured, happy and content in their status because it represents the natural order of things. Feminists point out that in an age which has abandoned a belief in natural law, natural order, and especially natural hierarchy, only women are still widely believed to have a natural station (at the right hand of a dominant male) and natural duties (to serve, support and nurture him).

To many radical feminists, culture is ideology, social structure is conspiracy, the enemies are males, and females are the most oppressed political caste in history. From this perspective the women's movement is analogous to other movements of oppressed peoples. Its goal is the overthrow of an oppressive system, its method is struggle.

However, the belief that men bar women from power for the same kinds of reasons that ruling classes so frequently seek to preserve their privileged position is by no means limited to the revolutionaries. Many reformists who aim not at destroying society but at securing for women a larger share of the existing order are convinced that men tend to behave like any other group with a vested interest in the status quo, that men seek to preserve their positions of power and privilege by barring women from access to positions of influence.[43]

Many women—and a few men—believe that the existing role system was devised by men for men. It is noted that society has never barred women from breadwinning roles, but only from economic roles that are profitable and respectable. It is noted further that men do not bar women from taking part in politics, but only hamper their efforts to participate in power.

The Study

These four hypothetical constraints should be kept in mind as we explore the lives and careers of some very unusual women who *do* participate in political decisions which have significance for broad collectivities.

The study reported in this book cannot tell us why more women do not seek and attain positions in significant decisionmaking processes, but it will eliminate some hypotheses and illuminate others. By observing women acting in political arenas, we can at least establish that a creature who could reasonably be called "Political Woman" exists; we can learn something about her characteristics, her development, and her political experiences.

The study of women in American politics poses special problems. The most serious is the scarcity of women at the upper levels of politics. If we are to observe women as participants in power processes, then we must identify an arena in which decisions are made that have significance for a larger collectivity and in which women are sufficiently numerous that they can be studied not as idiosyncratic actors, but as examples of a class. It is unlikely that rank and file party workers, among whom women are very numerous, normally participate in such decisions. Where power is greater, the number of women sharply declines. The 1972 elections, often hailed as a giant step forward for women, saw the elimination of the lone woman in the Senate and brought only 14 women into the House. [44] The number of women mayors is similarly small.[45] The "women's" positions at the upper levels of both political parties frequently have more to do with public relations than with power. Where is one to look? The answer, I believe, is in the legislatures of the fifty states. [46]

Often mistakenly attacked as incompetent and inefficient, as the weak link in the chain of American governmental institutions, state legislatures are nonetheless important political arenas; and the legislators are participants in significant political decisions. Supporters and detractors of state legislators alike agree that the role and power of these bodies must remain significant. In all but a few states, service in a legislature requires serious commitment to politics and public life. As James David Barber has pointed out, there is an important dividing line between citizen politics and public office holding. Becoming a state legislator "represents a change of disruption of one's normal role in job, home, and community, rather than a minor complement to this role."[47] Legislators must run for office and defeat an opponent. Frequently they must also change their place of residence for a portion of each year. Legislators therefore can be considered members of the "political class."

Men dominate state legislatures as they dominate all other political institutions in this and other societies. But women have served in state legislatures since 1921 and although they have constituted only five to ten percent of state legislators, they are sufficiently numerous to provide a useful perspective on the kinds of women who make a commitment to political life, the kinds of circumstances that facilitate such commitments, the kinds of special problems encountered by women in political life and the modes of adaptation available to them. (After the November, 1972 elections there were 457 women in state legislatures out of a national total of over 7,700 state legislators.) The focus of this study is on the contemporary scene, on forty-six women currently involved in legislative careers. The forty-six legislators chosen for this study were included not only becaus they were women, but because they were judged by competent observers to be effective legislators.[48] Although they comprised about one-seventh of all women serving in state legislatures in 1971, they do not constitute a statistically representative sample of women legislators. They are rather examples of women who have served more than one term, who are believed to have made a significant commitment to public life, and who are effective in their respective legislatures. The women on whom the study is based were chosen from legislators recommended by state legislative representatives of the American Association of University Women, the Business and Professional Women's Clubs, and the League of Women Voters. All were interviewed in May, 1972 as they attended a conference sponsored by the Center for the American Woman and Politics of the Eagleton Institute (Rutgers University). The study utilizes data from questionnaires and lengthy personal interviews with 46 women representing 28 states. Of these, 21 were Republicans and 25 Democrats. All had served more than one term. In addition, forty male legislators attending the Eagleton Institute's Legislative Seminar (July, 1972) completed the same questionnaire that had been distributed to the women. Like the women, these men do not constitute a statistically representative sample of any larger population, but were drawn from 26 states in all regions and comprise a broadly representative group of *effective* legislators who had served more than one term. Comparable data on both women and men legislators are available only for those topics covered in the self-administered questionnaires. On the many aspects of legislative experience covered in face-to-face interviews with women legislators, published studies provide information on male legislators.

This is a book on political participation, with emphasis on legislative recruitment, socialization, and role performance. But it is also a book about people. The women legislators with whom we are concerned have multiple identifications; they are Republicans and Democrats, members of particular families, Catholics, Protestants, and Jews; westerners, midwesterners, southerners. They occupy multiple roles; they are wives, mothers, widows, church workers,civic leaders. Some are also lawyers, businesswomen, and ranch managers. This study will deal not just with their roles as legislators but with their lives as legislators. It will seek to connect their political roles with their social roles and to examine the ways in which these intersect, conflict, and reinforce one another. Finally, this study looks at the personalities of these women legislators and attempts to discover what kinds of women manage the personal, social, and professional problems believed to exist for women who occupy political roles. Focusing on these women who successfully occupy men's jobs in a man's world illuminates the various personal and institutional barriers which inhibit wider participation by women in politics and in the other processes which shape their lives.

NOTES

1. I am *not* using "political man" to refer to the political dimension of human activities as did Seymour Martin Lipset, *Political Man* (Garden City, N.Y.: Doubleday, 1960) or Robert E. Lane, *Political Man* (New York: Free Press, 1972). I am using "political man" in the sense in which it is used by Harold D. Lasswell, to describe the personality type who emphasizes power in relation to other values. This usage refers to elite rather than mass behavior. See, *inter alia*, Harold D. Lasswell, *Psychopathology and Politics* (Chicago: University of Chicago Press, 1930); *Power and Personality* (New York: W. W. Norton, 1948); *Politics: Who Gets What, When, How* (New York: McGraw-Hill, 1936); *World Politics and Personal Insecurity* (New York: McGraw-Hill, 1935); *Power and Society*, with Abraham Kaplan (New Haven: Yale University Press, 1950). The influence of Lasswell's work on this study will be evident at many points.

2. In many states, women outnumber men as precinct chairmen and political club presidents; this is not a recent phenomenon. In his 1958 book on Wisconsin politics, Leon Epstein commented, "Women officers in general deserve some special comment because

they are so numerous. . . . Nevertheless, even where numerous, the number of women holding party office probably understates the degree of activism by women. Male chairmen
interviewed in selected counties have readily granted that women—especially wives of
business and professional men—do most of the party's get-out-the-vote work." Leon D.
Epstein, *Politics in Wisconsin* (Madison: University of Wisconsin Press, 1958), pp. 88-89.
The Wisconsin pattern is by no means unique.

3. For a comprehensive catalog of what women have *not* done in politics, as well as a
description of their participation, see Martin Gruberg, *Women in American Politics*
(Oshkosh, Wisc.: Academia Press, 1968).

4. Maurice Duverger, *The Political Role of Women* (Paris: UNESCO, 1955), pp. 75-76.

5. Betty Friedan echoed the predictions of her feminist antecedents when she said in a
recent article: "Women—the last and largest group of people in this nation to demand
control of their own destiny—will change the very nature of power in this century." These
are bold words; yet, half a century after the nineteenth amendment was ratified, voting
studies tell us that the electoral behavior of women is becoming ever more like that of men,
but that even now women are slightly less involved, more intolerant, less informed, less
efficacious, and less likely to vote than men. See, *inter alia*, Angus Campbell, Philip E.
Converse, Warren E. Miller, and Donald E. Stokes, *The American Voter* (New York: Wiley,
1960), pp. 474-493; Gabriel A. Almond and Sidney Verba, *The Civic Culture* (Boston:
Little, Brown, 1965), pp. 387-401; Fred I. Greenstein, "Sex Related Differences in Childhood," *Journal of Politics* 23 (1961); Fred I. Greenstein, *Children and Politics* (New Haven:
Yale University Press, 1965). Also Morris Jacob Levitt, *Political Attitudes of American
Women: A Study of the Effects of Work and Education on Their Political Role* (Ann Arbor,
Mich.: Dissertation, University Microfilms, 1960). Earlier studies which make the same or
related points are Charles E. Merriam and Harold F. Gosnell, *Non-Voting* (Chicago: Univer-
sity of Chicago Press, 1924), pp. 109-120; Paul J. Lazarsfeld, Bernard R. Berelson, and
Hazel Gaudet, *The People's Choice*, 2nd ed. (New York: Columbia University Press, 1948),
pp. 241-244; Ralph Nafziger, Warren Engstrom, and Malcolm Maclean, "Mass Media and an
Informed Public," *Public Opinion Quarterly* 15 (Spring 1951): 105-114.

6. Jessie Bernard emphasizes that women are not an "interest group" like the others.
Women and the Public Interest: An Essay on Policy and Protest (Chicago: Aldine-Atherton,
1971), pp. 31-34.

7. In presidential elections of the last two decades women and men split their votes in
the following fashions: 1952, for Eisenhower, men 53%, women 58%; 1956, for
Eisenhower, men 55%, women 61%; 1960, for Nixon, men 48%, women 51%; 1964, for
Goldwater, men 40%, women 38%; 1968, for Nixon, men 43%, women 43% (for Wallace,
men 16%, women 12%); 1972, for Nixon, men 63%, women 62%. *The Gallup Opinion
Index*, Report No. 90 (December 1972): 10.

8. As one women's movement spokeswoman recently put it: "It is through politics,
after all, that one gets the rules and regulations, the important legislation that determines
wages and working conditions, that guarantees access and opportunities, and that provides
for the necessary service enabling women as well as men to fully develop and utilize their
talents and skills." Kirsten Amudson, *The Silenced Majority: Women and American Democracy* (Englewood Cliffs, N.J.: Prentice-Hall, 1971), p. 12.

9. The phrase is, of course, Lasswell's. Lasswell, *Politics: Who Gets What, When, How.*

10. Thomas R. Dye, "State Legislative Politics," in *Politics in the American States: A
Comparative Analysis*, Herbert Jacob and Kenneth N. Vines, ed. (Boston: Little, Brown,
1965), p. 167.

11. The "Report of the President's Commission on the Status of Women" (1963), put
the question this way: "That few women have high positions is not because of legal bars
against them, the Committee on Civil and Political Rights acknowledged. . . . Women do not
try to attain high office, either because they are unaware of possibilities open to them, or

because they are reluctant to strain traditional social patterns and attitudes. Men's failure to appreciate women's leadership abilities is also a factor. But an element of prejudice undoubtedly plays a role when appointments are made, and it excludes women from public opportunities for which they may be fitted." Margaret Mead and Frances Balgley Kaplan, *American Women* (New York: Scribner's, 1965), p. 158.

12. He raises the estimate to 5-7 percent when campaign workers as well as candidates are included. Lester W. Milbraith, *Political Participation* (Chicago: Rand McNally, 1965), p. 21.

13. A recent *Fortune* survey of the 1000 largest industrial companies and of the 50 largest nonindustrial businesses revealed that of some 6500 officers and directors earning more than $30,000 per annum, only *eleven* were women. Wyndham Robertson, "The Ten Highest-Ranking Women in Big Business," *Fortune*, April 1973, pp. 81-89.

14. The relative autonomy of the political structure vis-à-vis wealth or social status has been debated in many studies of community power. I am convinced that the "pluralist" model most closely describes the American reality. See especially R. Dahl, *Who Governs? Democracy and Power in an American City* (New Haven: Yale University Press, 1961), and Nelson Polsby, *Community Power and Political Theory* (New Haven: Yale University Press, 1963).

15. Commenting on the contrast between women's importance in local politics and their scarcity in the legislature, Leon Epstein suggested: "Since this pattern resembles American experience generally, the absence of women in the Wisconsin legislature may be explained in large part by their usually assumed reluctance actively to seek partisan office," Epstein, *Politics in Wisconsin*, p. 105. This reluctance is widely noted by students of politics and is, obviously, real. Its origins are another matter.

16. For reviews of the literature on this subject see Judith Bardwick, *The Psychology of Women: A Study of Bio-Cultural Conflicts* (New York: Harper & Row, 1971). See also Josef E. and Amreur Scheinfeld, "Sex Differences in Mental and Behavioral Traits," *Genetic Psychology Monographs* 77 (1968): 169-299; Eleanor E. Maccoby, ed., *The Development of Sex Differences* (Stanford: Stanford University Press, 1966); Julia A. Sherman, *On the Psychology of Women: A Survey of Empirical Studies* (Springfield, Ill.: Charles C. Thomas, 1971); and Judith M. Bardwick, ed., *Readings on the Psychology of Women* (New York: Harper & Row, 1972). Kirsten Amundsen takes the opposite view in *The Silenced Majority*, p. 18. So do, *inter alia*, Naomi Weisstein, "Psychology Constructs the Female," in *Women in Sexist Society*, ed. Vivian Gornick and Barbara K. Moran (New York: Basic Books, 1971), pp. 207-224; Nancy Chodorow, "Being and Doing," in *Women in Sexist Society*, ed. Gornick and Moran, pp. 259-291. See also Maccoby, *Development of Sex Differences*.

17. For an interesting discussion of this question, see Helene Deutsch, *The Psychology of Women*, vol. 2 (New York: Grune & Stratton, 1949), p. 2.

18. Other (perhaps all) institutions in a society involve power relations and the exercise of influence by superordinates over subordinates. Government is distinguished from other institutions, such as family or economy, because of its scope and its monopoly of legitimate force.

19. Note that many scholars have advanced the view that women played the crucial role in civilizing these primal hordes. See, *inter alia*, Robert Briffault, *The Mothers* (New York: Macmillan, 1927); Helen Diner, *Mothers and Amazons* (Garden City, Doubleday [Anchor], 1973); Mary Beard, *Women as a Force in History* (New York: Macmillan, 1946).

20. Note, however, that as Mary Beard points out, it is only since the seventeenth century that "political writers were fond of locating the origin of the state in a primeval gathering of men who, in order to secure protection of life and property, formed a permanent union and surrendered a part of their "original" liberty. Beard, *Women as a Force*, p. 287.

21. Note, however, that Helene Deutsch, the foremost Freudian spokes*man* (sic) on

women's psychology takes a much narrower view of the biological determinants of femininity than she is generally believed to hold. Deutsch, *The Psychology of Women*, vol. 2, pp. 1-16, *passim*.

22. James Strachey, ed., *The Standard Edition of the Complete Psychological Works of Sigmund Freud*, vol. 13 (London: Hogarth Press, 1953), pp. xv-161.

23. Others also emphasize Freud's misogyny. See, for example, Philip Rieff's *Freud: The Mind of the Moralist* (New York: Viking, 1959), pp. 173-185.

24. For example, David A. Hamburg and Donald T. Lunde, "Sex Hormones in the Development of Sex Differences," in *Development of Sex Differences*, ed. Maccoby; A. A. Ehrhardt, R. Epstein, and J. Money, "Fetal Androgens and Female Gender Identity" in "The Early-treated Adrenogenital Syndrome," *Johns Hopkins Medical Journal* 122 (1968): 160-167; F. Neumann and W. Elger, "Physiological and Psychical Intersexuality of Male Rats by Early Treatment with an Anti-endrogenic Agent," *Acta Endocrinologica*, 1965, Supplement 100. Interesting evidence that differences in maternal responses to male and female infants is rooted in the stimulus and response provided by the young infant is presented in Howard A. Moss, "Sex, Age and State as Determinants of Mother-Infant Interaction," *Readings on the Psychology of Women*, ed. Judith M. Bardwick (New York: Harper & Row, 1972), pp. 22-29. But there is also evidence that there is an important cultural factor in sex differences in aggression. See Jerome Kagan and H. A. Moss, *Birth to Maturity* (New York: Wiley, 1962); Leonard Berkowitz, *Aggression, a Special Psychological Analysis* (New York: McGraw-Hill, 1962).

25. Lionel Tiger, *Men in Groups* (New York: Random House, 1969), p. 58.

26. Ibid., p. 74.

27. Ibid., p. 75.

28. Ibid., p. 81.

29. But not all primates conform to his pattern. For a discussion of evidence to the contrary see Weisstein, "Psychology Constructs the Female," pp. 219-221. See also, for a very unfavorable review of Tiger's study, M. H. Fried, "Mankind Excluding Woman," *Science* 165 (1969): 884.

30. Judith M. Bardwick and Elizabeth Douvan, "Ambivalence: The Socialization of Women," in *Women in Sexist Society*, ed. Gornick and Moran, p. 225, also reprinted in *Readings*, ed. Bardwick. See also S. L. Bern and D. J. Bern, "Case Study of a Non-Conscious Ideology: Training the Woman to Know Her Place," in *Beliefs, Attitudes and Human Affairs*, ed. D. J. Bern (Belmont, Calif.: Brooks/Cole, 1970); K. Broverman, Donald M. Broverman, Frank Clarkson, Paul S. Rosenkrantz, and Susan R. Vogel, "Sex-Role Stereotypes and Clinical Judgements of Mental Health," *Journal of Consulting and Clinical Psychology* 34, no. 1 (1970): 1-7; Arthur H. Thomas and Norman R. Stewart, "Counselor Response to Female Clients with Deviate and Conforming Career Goals," *Journal of Counseling Psychology*, pp. 352-357; and Nancy K. Schlossberg and John J. Pietrofesa, "Perspectives on Counseling Bias: Implications for Counselor Education," *The Counseling Psychologist* 4, no. 1: 44-53.

31. Margaret Mead, *Sex and Temperament* (New York: New American Library [Mentor Books], 1950), p. 191.

32. Ibid., p. 203.

33. An interesting recent article on socialization into sex roles is Lenore J. Weitzman, Deborah Eifler, Elizabeth Hokado, and Catherine Ross, "Sex-Role Socialization in Picture Books for Pre-school Children," *American Journal of Sociology* 77 (May 1972): 1125-1130.

34. Cynthia Fuchs Epstein makes a parallel argument in her book on women in the professions: "Women learn early that most professional jobs are men's jobs and do not think about the possibility that a woman might decide to take one of them." *Women's Place: Options and Limits in Professional Careers* (Berkeley: University of California Press, 1970), p. 51.

35. Note that the "Most Admired Woman" list always includes more famous wives than women noted only for individual achievement. However, there are always representatives of the latter. The 1972 list was as follows: Mrs. Richard Nixon, Mrs. Golda Meir, Madame Indira Gandhi, Mrs. Dwight D. Eisenhower, Mrs. Aristotle Onassis, Rep. Shirley Chisholm, Queen Elizabeth II, Senator Margaret Chase Smith, Mrs. Joseph Kennedy, Mrs. Martin Luther King. Obviously, many famous wives are also known and admired for their personal accomplishments; a good example is Eleanor Roosevelt, who, between 1948 (when Gallup records begin) and 1961, led the "Most Admired" lists 13 of 14 times. *The Gallup Opinion Index*, Report No. 91 (January 1973): 25-28.

36. In *Male and Female*, Margaret Mead's 20-year-old description of the stereotype of the approved woman seems valid today. "A woman, to receive equal recognition (as her successful husband) should be intelligent, attractive, know how to make the best of herself in dress and manner, be successful in attracting and keeping first several men, finally one, run her home and family efficiently so that her husband stays devoted and her children all surmount the nutritional, psychological, and ethical hazards of maturation, and are successful too; and she should have time for 'outside things,' whether they be church, grange, community activities, or Junior League." Margaret Mead, *Male and Female* (New York: New American Library, 1955), p. 228.

37. Traditional norms have also communicated to girls that if they had the misfortune to be forced into the breadwinner role, they would enter such "women's" roles as charwoman, nurse, or teacher. See, *inter alia*, Lynne B. Igilitzin, "Sex-typing and Politicization in Children's Attitudes: Reflections on Studies Done and Undone" (Paper delivered at the meeting of The American Political Science Association, Washington, D.C., 1972).

38. Herbert Barry III, Margaret K. Bacon, and Irvin L. Child, "A Cross-Cultural Survey of Some Sex Differences in Socialization," *Journal of Abnormal and Social Psychology* 55 (1957): 327-332. See also Beatrice B. and John M. Whiting, "Task Assignment and Personality: A Consideration of the Effect of Herding on Boys" (Paper presented at the Social Science Conference, University of East Africa, Dar-es-Salaam, 1968); "Egoism and Altruism," Children of Six Cultures, Part I, *Egoism and Altruism* (forthcoming) cited and discussed in Chodorow, "Being and Doing." *op. cit.* Also Elino Haario-Mannilo, "Sex Differentiation in Role Expectation and Performances," *Journal of Marriage and Family* 29, no. 3 (August 1967): 568-578; Mark G. Field and Karin I. Flynn, "Worker, Mother, Housewife: Soviet Woman Today," *Readings*, ed. Bardwick, pp. 218-231; Morris Zelditch, Jr., "Role Differentiation in the Nuclear Family," in *Family Socialization and Interaction Processes*, ed. Talcott Parsons and Robert F. Bales (New York: Free Press, 1955).

39. Mirra Komarovsky pioneered inquiry in sex role constraints in the forties. See, e.g., "Cultural Contradictions and Sex Roles," *American Journal of Sociology* 52, no. 3 (November 1946): 184-186. See also Komarovsky's recent study of contradictions in male conceptions of sex roles, "Cultural Contradictions and Sex Roles: The Masculine Case," *American Journal of Sociology* 78 (January 1973): 873-884. Also Cynthia Fuchs Epstein, *Women's Place*; Eleanor E. Maccoby and Carol Navy Jacklin, "Sex Differences and Their Implications for Sex Roles" (Paper presented at the American Psychological Association Annual Meeting, Washington, D.C., August 1971); Shirley S. Angrist, "The Study of Sex Roles," *Journal of Social Issues* 25, no. 1 (1969: 215-232; Alice S. Rossi, "Barriers to the Career Choice of Engineering, Medicine, or Science Among American Women," *Readings*, ed. Bardwick.

40. Heinz Eulau and John D. Sprague, *Lawyers in Politics: A Study of Professional Convergence* (Indianapolis, Bobbs-Merrill, 1961).

41. Shulamith Firestone, *The Dialectic of Sex: The Case for Feminist Revolution* (New York: William Morrow, 1970), p. 16. See also Carol Hanisch, "Male Psychology: A Myth to Keep Women in Their Place," *Women's World* 1 (July-August 1971): 2.

42. Duverger, *Political Role of Women*, p. 130. See also Alfred Adler, *The Practice and*

Theory of Individual Psychology (London: Kegan Paul, 1924), Mathilde and Mathias Vaerting, *The Dominant Sex, A Study in the Sociology of Sex Differences* (London: Allen and Unwin, 1923); Viola Klein, *The Feminine Character* (New York: International Universities Press, 1964); Helen Hacker, "Women as a Minority Group," *Social Forces* 30 (September 1951); Amudsen, *The Silenced Majority*, pp. 42-52.

43. A sense of the sometimes bitter disagreements between reformists and revolutionaries of the women's movement is conveyed by Kate Millet's criticism of the suffrage movement:

> The chief weakness of the movement's concentration on suffrage, the factor which helped it to fade, disappear, and even lose ground when the vote was gained, lay in its failure to challenge patriarchical ideology at a sufficiently deep and radical level to break the conditioning processes of status, temperament, and role. A reform movement, and especially one which has fixed its attention on so minimal an end as the ballot, the sort of superficial change which legislative reform presents, and which, when it has attained this becomes incapable even to putting it to use, is hardly likely to propose sweeping radical changes in social attitudes and social structure, in personality and institutions. Marriage was preserved nearly intact, despite women's new legal rights within it. The 'home' was still creditable enough to be refurnished in gleaming colors in the ensuing period of reaction.

Kate Millet, *Sexual Politics* (Garden City, N.Y.: Doubleday, 1970), pp. 84-85.

44. The 1972 elections, which saw the defeat of the only woman serving in the Senate (Margaret Chase Smith, R-Maine), returned nine incumbents and five newcomers. Only one incumbent, Louise Day Hicks (D-Mass.), was defeated. The incumbents returned to the House were Ella T. Grasso (D-Conn.), Patsy T. Mink (D-Hawaii), Margaret M. Heckler (R-Mass.), Martha W. Griffiths (D-Mich.), Lenor K. Sullivan (D-Mo.), Shirley Chisholm (D-N.Y.), Bella S. Abzug (D-N.Y.), Edith Green (D-Ore.), and Julia Butler Hansen (D-Wash.). The newcomers were Patricia Schroeder (D-Colo.), Marjorie S. Holt (R-Md.), Elizabeth Holtzman (D-N.Y.), Barbara C. Jordan (D-Tex.), and Yvonne Braithwaite Burke (D-Calif.).

45. *Women in the Public Service* (Women's Division, Republican National Committee, Washington, D.C., 1972), p. 187, reports that at the time of publication 20 cities had women mayors.

46. Useful studies of women in politics that focus on other levels of the political process are Amudsen, *The Silenced Majority*; Gruberg, *Women in American Politics*; Frieda L. Gehlen, "Women in Congress: Their Power and Influence in a Man's World," *Trans-Action*, October 1969, pp. 36-40; Marie Barovic Rosenberg, "Political Efficacy and Sex Role" (Paper prepared for meeting of the American Political Science Association, Washington, D.C., 1972); and Emmy E. Werner, "Women in Congress: 1917-1965," *Western Political Quarterly* 19, no. 1 (March 1966): 16-30.

47. James D. Barber, *The Lawmakers: Recruitment and Adaptation to Legislative Life* (New Haven: Yale University Press, 1964), p. 221.

48. For a full description of the sampling and interview procedures, see the appendix, "A Note on Methodology," pp. 254-61. For a description of the Conference attended by the women on whom this study is based, see *Women State Legislators*, Report from a Conference, May 18-21, 1972. Center for the American Woman and Politics, Eagleton Institute of Politics, Rutgers University, New Brunswick, N.J.

Chapter II

The Participant Style: Backgrounds

ONE answer to the question, "what kinds of women run for state legislatures?" is: *all* kinds. Beautiful and plain, young, old and middle aged, fat and thin, rich and poor, housewives, lawyers, secretaries, pragmatists and idealists are all found in this sample.

They represent districts as diverse as this nation's geography: ranching country, farm belt, mining towns, white suburbs, black inner cities, small Southern towns, Mormon communities, middle-sized New England cities. They were born in the large houses of New York bankers, in the duplexes of working class Catholic neighborhoods, on farms, in tenements. They grew up in upper, middle, and lower class homes. Despite this diversity, there are patterns of common experience and activity. An average legislator, constructed from the median characteristics of our sample, would look something like this:

She is a fairly attractive, forty-eight-year-old mother of two nearly grown children. Although she has a college education she has rarely worked outside the home. She lives in the small town where she was born and is financially supported by her reasonably successful husband, who has encouraged her to run for office. Running for office was an extension of many years of volunteer community service.[1] While no one background and no one pattern of experience was shared by all the women legislators, the biographies of many

29

include these same key elements: a small town background, geographic stability, middle class, participant parents, higher education, community service.[2]

Why did this woman, who is in so many respects an average woman, decide to run for office? The question is as fascinating as it is difficult to answer.

What kinds of experience predispose a woman to get involved in politics? Legal access is only a facilitating factor, never a cause. Behind every race for public office lies a decision to spend time, energy, and effort and to risk disapproval and defeat. Behind the decision to become a candidate there is usually a desire to influence events, a belief in the possibility of influencing events, some knowledge of politics and politicians, and some base, or potential base, of community support. The absence of any of these elements constitutes a serious political handicap. Yet few people have the motivation to influence public affairs, a sense of personal efficacy, a relatively high level of political information and skills, and a social identity around which others can rally. Almost everyone everywhere is uninterested in and uninformed about politics; women, public opinion polls indicate, are even less informed and interested than men, even more inclined to live in a world dominated and limited by personal concerns. This chapter will identify some early experiences relevant to later political participation in the effort to discover personal characteristics relevant to public performance.[3]

Geographical mobility is one of the striking characteristics of modern America, but stability is the predominant experience of the legislators. The organization of modern industry, the exigencies of economic depression and opportunity, and the restless search for something better keep many Americans on the move. The more frequently they move, the less likely they are to establish roots in a community. Among the many consequences of geographical mobility is an attenuation of community ties. Identification with a place comes easiest and strikes deepest with long familiarity. Caring about schools, parks, sewers, and local government is closely related to having a stake in the future of a community. So is participation. It is not surprising to a student of political behavior to find that the women legislators had deep roots in the communities in which they grew up.[4] Over half of them grew to maturity in the place they were born; fewer than a third moved more than once while they were growing up.

Growing up in environments familiar from long exposure, they had time to learn their way around—to learn the informal rules by which people lived, to internalize the norms of the community, to come to know the structures of power and the identity of incumbents. Their environments were manageable, knowable in another sense, too. Three-fifths of the legislators grew up in small towns or in the country, fewer than a sixth in large cities. These women thus provide new confirmation for the accumulating evidence that the small towns of America (and to a lesser extent, rural communities) have served as breeding grounds of civic spirit, social responsibility, and the participant style.[5] Donald Matthews commented that "Main Street has changed since the turn of the century but it still supplies far more than its share of United States Senators."[6] It also contributes more than its share of female legislators to the state houses of America.

Social class is another important determinant of the experiences and opportunities one encounters while growing up. The class of one's parents frequently determines not only the parents' power and prestige, but their child's opportunities and sense of possibility. The impact of class on an individual is neither uniform nor inevitable. It varies with temperament, parental aspirations, and opportunity. An upper class family does not guarantee ambition, lower class background does not necessarily produce apathy and low aspirations. But they help.[7] The women legislators confirm existing findings: they are less likely to come from the lower classes, most likely to be middle class or upper class in origin. But no class background is necessarily disabling. They were drawn from all classes. About one in three describe their parents as belonging to the working class, another third as middle class, and the remaining third say that they came from upper or upper middle class families.

Educational and occupational backgrounds of parents confirm these classifications. Approximately half their fathers had not gone beyond high school, and more than half of these had no more than a primary school education. Approximately one-fourth had finished college. One-sixth had achieved professional degrees. Their fathers were bankers, truck drivers, engineers, policemen, businessmen, auto mechanics, physicians, farmers, college professors, coal miners, ministers, meat cutters. Small scale independent enterpreneurs, professional men, tradesmen, and manual workers were numerous among them. Neither the father's education nor occupation provides a reliable key to the development of active, public spirited daughters. But what of the mothers? It is maternal aspirations which are believed to be most important to the ambitions and success of offspring. Over half of these mothers had not gone beyond high school; only 13 percent had graduated from college. One-third of the mothers worked outside the home while the legislator was a child. It is clear that in these families economic need was the principal spur to the mother's employment. Occupations such as domestic worker, factory worker, filing clerk, salesperson, are rarely engaged in for self–fulfillment. Half the mothers of those with a lower class and one-third of those of middle class backgrounds worked outside the home. Perhaps the third of those from upper middle class homes worked more because of personal choice than the family's need for money. Whatever the motive that prompted an outside job, it is probably significant that one out of three of the legislators had mothers who shouldered part or all of the burden of supporting the family, or who, at any rate, was regularly involved in economic functions independent of home and family. Few of these mothers could be said to have provided their daughters with a model of feminine professional achievement, but many, as we shall see, provided a model of participant behavior.

Socio-economic characteristics such as family income and social status are significant for children to the extent that they affect their development. In rural and small town America, especially in the earlier part of the century, the effects of social and economic status were diminished by the theory and practice of egalitarianism, individualism, and social mobility. The absence of a female equivalent of Horatio Alger has not prevented some American girls from developing ambitions and aspirations for better things. The belief that one may shape one's own life and circumstances is a major premise of modern life. Girls as well as boys may dream of golden futures and plan accordingly. Several routes are available to upward mobile girls. They may rise in fame and fortune by way of a successful husband. They may rise through their own achievements. They may rise through the achievements of their children. They may rise through some combination of personal and family achievement. Upward social mobility is a striking characteristic of these legislators. It is both personal and familial. The legislators' educational levels are substantially higher than those of their parents; so are those of their husbands. Their family incomes reflect a socio-economic status higher than that of their parents; their political position is evidence of influence greater than that of their parents. Not all the women legislators are upwardly mobile. A few were born at the top of the socio-economic heap, but most were personally upward mobile. They confirm and illustrate the findings of Douvan and Adelson that upward mobile girls are active, self-confident, self-accepting, interested in achievement, realistically successful, and secure in their femininity.[8] They also indicate that Edward Shils' description of American politicians as an upward mobile group holds for women as well as men: "In the United States politicians have an unusually high degree of social mobility. Politicians, more than any other profession, represent the realization of the idea of the poor boy who takes advantage of an open society and rises to the top."[9]

In this society, as in other technologically advanced modern nations, there is an intimate relationship between education and personal achievement. The schoolroom is not only the arena in which childhood achievement can be most effectively and impressively demonstrated; but academic achievement also frequently lays the foundation for successful achievement in later life. Because so many roles in society are filled on the basis of specialized skills, education is one of the surest routes to success. Ambitious parents desire good educations for their children; ambitious children desire good educations for themselves. The women legislators on whom this study is based are substantially better educated than their parents. Four-fifths have more than a high school education; over half have a college education; a third have graduate or professional training.[10] The superiority of their educations as compared with those of their mothers far exceeds the general increase in educational levels between these generations. Their educations also exceed the norms for women of their generation. Since higher education requires personal commitment, its acquisition is proof of ambition, motivation, and impersonal interests. Graduate and professional training constitute clear-cut evidence of a girl's interest in professional roles. For many of these legislators, completion of college evidences personal drive and professional ambition. Almost four-fifths of those of lower class backgrounds completed college and in so doing indicated their drive for personal achievement. Upward mobility is also reflected in the occupations and incomes of the legislators and their spouses. Their incomes turn out to be far higher than the national average, and relatively higher than those of their parents.

More important than locale or socio-economic class are the values, beliefs, and behavior patterns acquired in growing up. Transmitted from generation to generation, values, identifications, and beliefs prepare children for the roles they will fill as adults. Through social learning and internalization, children acquire the values, beliefs and roles associated with citizenship in a society; they are prepared for both subject and leadership roles.

In a society such as ours, the most important agent of political socialization is the family. In the family a child acquires the identifications that link her to larger groups. She comes to think of herself as a Smith or a Lombardi, a Catholic or a Jew, a Texan or New Yorker, as New Englander or Westerner, as American or French. She develops feelings about her capacities and effectiveness as she learns what she can or cannot do. She develops habitual ways of confronting and dealing with reality. The identifications and expectations acquired in the process of growing up become the framework for adult perspectives and behavior. Attitudes of inclusiveness and exclusiveness develop and become the foundation for identification with community, party, state and nation. A child growing up in a family that is preoccupied with personal affairs, distrustful of the outside world, hostile to all who are different, uninterested in larger, more remote, more abstract questions of community well being, is unlikely to identify her future with an inclusive group such as party or community, unlikely to become deeply interested in community problems and issues, unlikely to become involved in community affairs.

Frames of attention, habits of concern, patterns of identification and involvement, habits of participation are known to be in large part learned. Through example, precept, and numberless cues, parents teach their children how to relate to others, how to cope with problems, what to hope for. Either an activist orientation or a passive perspective are imbided with mother's milk and family conversation. Both leadership and membership are learned behavior. A sense of political efficacy comes easily to a child who has grown up among adults who speak and act as though they thought it possible to influence public events.

It is not surprising therefore that many of the women legislators in this study had parents who were active in their communities. Like the legislators studied by Wahlke, Eulau, Buchanan, and Ferguson, [11] and the political activists described by Milbrath and others,[12] many of these women grew up in homes where activity in politics was a normal mode of adult behavior. Mothers as well as fathers were politically active. Fathers as well as mothers were active in church affairs. Church activities and political activities both involve a presumption that one can achieve desirable objectives through collective action.

Forty percent of mothers were active in politics and over 50 percent of fathers. These levels of activity are many times higher than those found in the general population. They indicate homes where identifications with larger groups were the norm, where public affairs were a habitual subject of concern. In such homes a sense of efficacy is learned along with the basic facts of public life. A girl growing up in a family where the mother as well as father was involved in public affairs would never "learn" that politics is men's business.

A home with participant parents links a child to the "center" of the civic communications network where information about public affairs is readily available, where identifications with the body politic are easily formed. And as Milbrath and others have concluded, "persons near the center of society are more likely to participate in politics than persons near the periphery."[13] Naturally such a home environment stimulates an early interest in politics. Reports like the following graphically illustrate the familial character of political involvement.

For me it was my father's and uncle's influence. My uncle would take me into the Statehouse on George Washington's Birthday, and when they would have openhouse and the governor would shake hands with the citizenry. For many years he took me in there to wait in line and meet the governor and shake hands. And he would take me to all the historical places.

My father was always helping candidates. He always would work at the polls and I was always very involved in that. He took me to political rallies, and after classes I would go directly to a polling place instead of going home, to pass out literature for whatever candidate he was supporting and I would decorate my bicycle with candidate stickers, then I would be conveniently outside a church for people to see.

So one of those warm October days I was in the seventh grade and I remember talking to two people and I said, "Someday, I will run for political office."

Another comments, "I suppose I have had politics in my blood all of my life." She used to watch her uncle, the Senator, campaign for office. "The main point was that no one knew he was campaigning. He'd pay sombody a call and sit out on the front porch with someone and rock and drink lemonade, and talk about whatever the host was interested in. I would play out in the yard with the children. It looked like we were just paying a social visit. What we were really doing was campaigning."

Douvan and Adelson have reported that "Parent membership is strongly related to adolescent membership and to all forms of social activity."[14] They tell us, too, that parent memberships and social activity are also related to ego development, to achievement orientation, to a perspective on the future, to the internalization of group norms, to the development of positive attitudes toward authority, and to the development of leadership potential. The biographies of these women legislators confirm the findings of Douvan and Adelson.

But, involved and active parents are not a necessary prerequisite to the development of politically active daughters. Half the legislators had parents who were active in community affairs, half did not. The latter group developed participant habits and leadership skills without an active parental model. Many had already developed a participant style during adolescence. Three-fourths of all the women legislators were active in extracurricular affairs at school. The activist impulse was apparently unaffected by the type of school attended, by class, background, or color. Lower class parents were less likely to be active in politics or church affairs than middle of upper class parents, but many of their daughters had already become active in school affairs by adolescence.

The relation between high school social participation, personality, and politics is significant and intriguing. Harrison Gough found that students who participated in extracurricular affairs were more self-disciplined and tolerant, self-assured and socially effective, more optimistic and goal oriented.[15] These are traits believed to be characteristic of both men and women who participate in democratic politics.

The record of these women in school extracurricular activity suggests that by late adolescence and early adulthood they had already developed a sense of competence and self–confidence necessary to participation and leadership. The experience of participation further developed their social skills and reinforced their sense of personal efficacy.

Furthermore, they exhibited these capacities and predispositions at a period when many of their female contemporaries were withdrawing from achievement goals, from intellectual endeavor, and from roles that were potentially competitive with men.[16] At a time when most American girls were concerned and preoccupied with femininity and with sex roles, these young women maintained their interest in public goals and continued their involvement in more public activities. The implications of this development pattern are very important.

Parents and teachers generally expect that girls will share the same achievement goals as boys up to puberty. After that, subtle and not so subtle cues communicate to girls a potential conflict between their specifically feminine goals and achievement unrelated to feminine goals. At the same time that biological maturation emphasizes a girl's sexual identity, she is frequently confronted for the first time with widespread expectations that she will withdraw from the race for public and professional achievement and concentrate instead on the achievements associated with a sex-specific feminine role. At this stage, girls' withdrawal from pursuit of the dominant values of this achievement-based society proceeds apace. To survive this developmental stage with personality and achievement goals intact requires a strong ego, a high level of personal integration, and strong feminine identifications. These later serve as the basis of unconflicted un-neurotic participation in public life.

So far only women legislators have been considered. The data presented tell us a great deal about the women who serve in our state legislatures, but nothing about how women differ from men. Comparable information is available on the forty male legislators who participated in the Eagleton Institute's Legislative Seminar in the summer of 1972. As already indicated, these men do not constitute a statistically representative sample of men in American legislatures. But they were drawn from twenty-six states in all geographical regions and are good examples of *effective* state legislators. They differ in various respects from the women: they are younger, more of them have statewide reputations, more have professional training, all have been continuously employed. This is all the more reason to believe that those characteristics that they share with the women are common to American legislators and not specifically associated with the experience of either men or women.

The number and extent of these shared characteristics is significant and suggestive. Like the women, the male legislators have deep roots in their communities. About two-thirds grew up in the communities where they were born. Few moved about as children. Most lived in small towns and rural areas. Even more than the women, the male legislators are an upward mobile group. Two-fifths come from lower class backgrounds,[17] but two-thirds now have income in excess of $20,000. Like the women, most of the men come from families where the parents were active in church and community affairs. They, too, were inveterate participants while young. All but one was active in extracurricular activities in school and college.

In spite of the many differences in the experiences of boys and girls, the legislators considered in this study turn out to have shared many of the experiences most relevant to politics. Obviously living a long time in one place, being upward mobile, having parents who join and participate, taking part in extracurricular activities do not *cause* political activity. There are men and women who have all these characteristics who never run for public office. But growing numbers of studies of political participation indicate that the background characteristics shared by these male and female legislators play an important part in molding the kinds of people who later make their way into democratic political arenas.

NOTES

1. She bears a striking resemblance to the hypothesized rural legislators described by Leon Epstein "who have deeper local roots, less formal education, and more political experience, and are older and less likely to have professional or business-managerial occupations . . . ." Leon Epstein, *Politics in Wisconsin* (Madison: University of Wisconsin Press, 1958), p. 99.

2. Maurice Duverger, *The Political Role of Women* (Paris: UNESCO, 1955), finds similar characteristics typical of European women who run for office. So does Ingunn Norderval Means, "Women in Local Politics: The Norwegian Experience," *Canadian Journal of Political Science*, September 1972, esp. pp. 376-388.

3. I do not raise questions here about the backgrounds of these legislators because I assume that their legislative behavior is not necessarily or importantly influenced by these backgrounds. Neither do I assume that their class, income, occupation, or habits of their parents is necessarily relevant to their later involvement in politics. They may be. Studies of political participation establish positive statistical correlations between participation and certain demographic, social, and economic backgrounds. The most useful of these studies is Lester Milbrath, *Political Participation* (Chicago: Rand McNally, 1965). But there is no reason to believe that any background characteristic or even any combination of such characteristics *causes* anyone—male or female—to devote significant portions of her time and energy to politics. Certainly, however, there is good reason to believe that early life experiences may be relevant to adult political behavior, good reason to believe that some childhoods are better breeding grounds than others for the inclinations, opportunities, and skills needed for full participation in democratic politics; good reason, then, for surveying the life histories of political actors as a part of our effort to understand the development of political woman.

4. The same relationship between candidacy and roots in the community was noted by Epstein in *Politics in Wisconsin*, p. 107, and Frank J. Sorauf in his book on the Pennsylvania legislature, *Party and Representation* (New York: Atherton, 1963), p. 74; and is reported in Malcolm E. Jewell and Samuel C. Patterson, *The Legislative Process in the United States*, 2nd ed. (New York: Random House, 1972), p. 71. See also Milbrath, *Political Participation*, p. 133.

5. See Page Smith, *As a City Upon a Hill: The Town in American History* (New York: Knopf, 1956), for a description of the extent to which American small towns have provided the nation with leadership in many fields.

6. *U.S. Senators and Their World* (Chapel Hill: University of North Carolina Press, 1960), p. 17.

7. A good discussion on the relation between political participation and social status is Milbrath, *Political Participation*, chap. 5. See also Jewell and Patterson, *Legislative Process*, p. 73; William J. Keefe and Morris Ogul, *The American Legislative Process: Congress and The States* (Englewood Cliffs, N.J.: Prenctice-Hall, 1968), pp. 121-132.

8. Elizabeth Douvan and Joseph Adelson, *The Adolescent Experience* (New York: Wiley, 1966), pp. 72-77.

9. Edward A. Shils, "The Legislator and His Environment," *University of Chicago Law Review* 18 (Spring: 1951): 581. Also Leon Epstein finds high mobility characteristic of Wisconsin legislators in *Politics in Wisconsin*, pp. 112-113; so do John C. Wahlke, Heinz

Eulau, William Buchanan, and Leroy C. Ferguson, *The Legislative System: Explorations in Legislative Behavior* (New York: Wiley, 1962), pp. 489-490; and Sorauf, *Party and Representation*, pp. 75-81.

10. These education levels do not compare unfavorably with legislators generally. While education varies by state, state legislators are much more highly educated than the populations they represent. About half of the state legislators in eight states reported by Jewell and Patterson, *Legislative Process*, p. 80, are college graduates.

11. Wahlke et al., *Legislative System*.

12. Milbrath, *Political Participation*, p. 43. Patricia Goren Bach reports the same pattern of parental activity in "Women in Public Life in Wisconsin," Alverne Research Center on Women, unpublished manuscript, p. 9.

13. Milbrath, *Political Participation*, pp. 113-114.

14. Douvan and Adelson, *Adolescent Experience*, p. 338.

15. Harrison Gough, "Predicting Social Participation," *Journal of Social Psychology* 35 (1952): 227-233; see also Robert E. Lane, *Political Life* (New Haven: Yale University Press, 1958), p. 117.

16. Judith M. Bardwick, *The Psychology of Women* (New York: Harper & Row, 1971), pp. 104-106. Also J. S. Coleman, *The Adolescent Society* (New York: Free Press, 1961). See also Judith M. Bardwick and Elizabeth Douvan, "Ambivalence: The Socialization of Women," in *Readings on the Psychology of Women*, ed. Judith M. Bardwick (New York: Harper & Row, 1972), p. 454; Julia A. Sherman, *On the Psychology of Women: A Survey of Empirical Studies* (Springfield, Ill.: Charles C. Thomas, 1971), pp. 17-21.

17. Constantini and Craif also report that male activists in California's parties more frequently come from lower class backgrounds than do women. Their findings on differences between male and female educational levels, age, and personality also parallel those reported here. Edward Constantini and Kenneth H. Craif, "Women as Politicians: The Social Background, Personality, and Political Careers of Female Party Leaders," *Journal of Social Issues* 28, no. 2 (1972): 221-222.

Chapter III

Participant Woman: Values, Life Styles, and Personalities

Life Styles

THE women on whom this study is based have a complex relation to conventional society. On the one hand they appear to be thoroughly conventional women whose lives conform to traditional values, but they are also profoundly nonconformist. To seek power, to compete and work with men, to leave a husband and a home for legislative sessions is very unconventional behavior. This pattern of conforming almost completely to traditional values and roles is fascinating and suggestive.

What are the traditional role requirements of a female adult? She should marry and be a good and faithful wife, have children, care for them, and raise them to be law-abiding, responsible citizens. She should make and keep a home for a family, take an interest in her community, support her church. She should be a loyal American who respects her country's ideals and institutions. She should be well-groomed and reasonably well-dressed, work hard at "useful" endeavors, and conform to regional, ethnic and religious requirements concerning alcohol and tobacco.

Naturally life styles vary with region, age and class, but there were many similarities in the lives of these women and they are significant for their political roles. Except for the important fact that most

41

spend a great deal of time away from home campaigning, making speeches, attending legislative sessions, the life styles and values of these legislators are profoundly traditional. In adult life as in child-hood the legislators are integrated into their communities. Most of the legislators have lived more than twenty years in their present communities. Few have moved frequently. They married and had children—though few have had more than two. Only seven have ever been divorced. Most take the responsibility for housekeeping and childcare. Few have much paid household help or expect much help from their husbands. Their husbands earn comfortable incomes and take the principal responsibility for supporting the family.

These are women who live "correct" lives. Discretion is both highly regarded and practiced. Repeatedly they comment that in public life the appearance of virtue is an independent good. Personal reputa-tions are carefully guarded—in dealings with other legislators, in housing arrangements, in travel, in campaigning.

In personal styles these women legislators are neither flamboyant nor mousey; very few would be regarded as either aggressive or abra-sive by most Americans.

Without exception they are conventional in dress and appearance. Most could blend easily into the social landscape of any traditional community. The most far-out political liberals among them were social conservatives: no wierd life styles, no granny glasses, no bra burners, no noisy profanity. *In appearance and style these women are as conservative as a group of male politicians.*

The Participant Style: The Adult Years

Employment histories of the female legislators reflect the same prior-ities expressed in their political careers. Those priorities give first place to the family responsibilities that keep mothers at home while children are young. Most of the legislators have worked outside their homes during some part of their adult lives. But only five have been continuously employed. Many have the erratic employment records so common among women who attempt to combine traditional wife and mother roles with outside employment.

Their professional backgrounds are more diverse than those of a comparable group of men. This difference is, of course, highly relevant to the different routes by which men and women most frequently come to public office. The women's occupational experience is in most, though not in all, cases less directly relevant to their roles and functions as office holders. These legislators have worked as nurses, secretaries, office managers, real estate agents, missionaries, saleswomen, social workers, journalists, administrators, and lawyers. Family income figures suggest that several have worked more from interest, ambition, and energy, than out of economic necessity. (Three-fourths report family incomes over $20,000.) Few have had true careers other than politics and homemaking.

The fact that their husbands provided financial support left most free not to work outside the home, and gave them adequate time to pursue an interest in community affairs and politics. It should not surprise us that almost none of these women had strong vocational commitments other than politics. A consuming professional commitment would doubtless preclude the organizational involvements that generally precede a political career and lay the groundwork for it, preclude running for office and serving in the legislature. Public service (and politics) is a distinctive vocation which may or may not involve a "job" and remuneration. Nearly three-fourths of these women agree that women have more time to be involved in politics than men. Many of them prefer community service to paid employment—the traditional choice. For obvious reasons those who were most regularly employed were somewhat less active in community affairs.

Before they were office holders, most of these legislators were volunteers.[1] Tocqueville's insight into the affinity between membership in voluntary associations and participation in politics is confirmed and illustrated in the biographies of these women.[2] They have a habit of pursuing community goals through collective action. Membership in civic and other "do-good" organizations rests on two predispositions: a tendency to identify public problems as private concerns, and a tendency to seek solutions through cooperative action. Some people, confronted with the more impersonal remote problems that confront their towns, churches, states, turn their attention else-

where, some despair, others take solitary actions aimed at their ame-
lioration—sending a letter to an editor, writing a book. The collective
community action solution is distinctive. People who run for office
usually have a habit of collective action before they decide to become candidates. Joining with others in activities directed to some
relatively impersonal goal is the opposite of withdrawing into family
and personal concerns, a tendency attributed to women by Maurice
Duverger, among others, to explain the low levels of political activity
of European women:

> This withdrawal into a small restricted group—this semi-exclusive concentra-
> tion on a microcosm, are in direct conflict with an interest in politics where
> problems must be stated in general terms, where everything must be taken into
> account, where an awareness of the "macrocosm" is vital.[3]

These women legislators are veritable models of participant citizenship. They display the typical American tendencies to act, to join.
Active in their churches, schools, civic associations, business and professional groups, political groups, they show a strong predilection for
purposive social activity and group oriented achievement. Half of
them were members of three or more nonpartisan voluntary organizations; another third belonged to one or two such groups. The few
who were currently members of no organizations had been in the
past. Sixty percent were active members of their churches, attending
services at least once a week. A similar proportion was currently
active in civic associations and clubs, and in business and professional
organizations. About forty percent were active in the League of
Women Voters; affiliation with this group played a key role in the
political careers of several. The fact that there were more former
than present members of school groups reflects the age of the legislators. And they were more than members. Many had been officers of
the groups to which they belonged. Several held state and national
leadership positions.

The sociability of these women is further reflected in the fact that
more than half were also members of social clubs. They liked to
relax, as well as work, with others.

Their type of sociability is not the gregariousness that masks an
inability to be alone, a dependence on others for guidance, stimula-

tion, approval. There is nothing frantic or driven about their participatory styles. Fulfillment, rather than escape, is the mood of their interpersonal relations.

Altogether these women resemble in their habits of participation the profiles of other democratic politicians of a comparable level. They resemble a group of Norwegian female office seekers of whom a composite profile is described as "a capable and energetic woman, a middle-aged mother and homemaker, who has to some extent compensated for her lack of educational or occupational distinction through organizational gregariousness."[4]

They resemble, too, the female equivalents of Pennsylvania legislators described by Frank Sorauf. But instead of the Moose-Elks-fire company of his Republicans or the Knights of Columbus, Odd Fellows, and ethnic groups of his Democrats, the women's pattern of membership was PTA, Civic Club, League of Women Voters, social club or some close variation thereof. Their record for sociability and participation approximates that of other politicians elsewhere. They provide additional documentation of Milbrath's point that "Sociable personalities are more likely to enter politics than nonsociable personalities . . . ."[5]

The psychological and social ingredients of successful group activity include fairly open ego, an attitude that is "warm rather than frigid, inclusive and expanding rather than exclusive and constricting."[6] There is a need to be sensitive to different kinds of people, to find areas of agreement, to harmonize conflicting tendencies, to cooperate, and to do all this in the absence of intimacy, full understanding or love. Purposive socializing, crucial to many activities including democratic politics, is very different than establishing intimate relations. Women, particularly, are sometimes believed to have problems in establishing functional, cooperative, personal relations oriented toward impersonal goals. The legislators in this study have this capacity in quantity. Their predilection for group activity suggests that they are specialists in purposive socializing; that it is a preferred mode of interpersonal relations, not because they are incapable of intimate relations—most have sustained marriages for many years—but because such limited personal relations are more consistent with their goal-oriented, community-oriented styles.

Personalities

Obviously no forty-six persons have identical personalities. Some legislators were talkative, articulate, outgoing, some were retiring, some were outspoken, some conciliatory, some quickly established authority in their discussion groups, some declined to participate much. However, far more striking than the personality differences of these women were their personality similarities. Taken collectively, these similarities probably constitute the personality requirements for successful female participation in elective politics.

Identifications

Following Harold Lasswell's formulation, we can say that the self consists of the ego and all its identifications.[7] It is these identifications that link an individual to people, places and traditions, and transforms a biological entity into a citizen. Basic identifications are the earliest acquisition of an infant, but the process of internalizing relations between the self and others continues throughout a lifetime. A stable environment speeds and reinforces the process of acquiring identifications. The capacity to care about people and places is grounded in early identifications, just as the capacity to function as a parent or a friend is grounded in one's childhood experience of family.

The legislators in this study are remarkably similar in self-structure. All but three are characterized by strong identifications with their localities, their families, the institutions through which they work, and the future of all these.

Identification with a place, a particular community, is probably the most effective basis for a continuing concern with its problems and prospects because this identification is the subjective link between the fate of the community and the fate of the individual. Once this psychological link is forged, the individual feels community problems as personal concerns. Experience in public-spirited, do-good activities and organizations reinforces these psychological connections. In these legislators, strong identification with home and place serves as the foundation for participation in communal and political life.

Since membership in the female sex is believed to be a substantial handicap in politics, one might expect to find these women to be dissatisfied and ambivalent about being a woman. Such expectations are confounded, however, by overwhelming evidence to the contrary. One of the most striking facts about these legislators is that they have strong sexual identifications. Symptoms of conflict and ambivalence are almost totally absent.

It makes theoretical sense that to compete and work successfully with men, women would need secure feminine identifications. Otherwise competition would produce anxiety, and anxiety, in turn, produce behavior that is either too aggressive or too submissive. It is only superficially paradoxical that women need strong feminine identifications in order to fill a "male" role. Successful non-conflicted, non-neurotic, nonconformity requires inner strength. And that kind of strength requires a high level of integration and self-acceptance.

Research on girls' development indicates that upward mobile girls frequently have strong identification with their mothers—presumably because such mothers have high aspirations with which the girls can identify and because the mothers, not being breadwinners, are not responsible for the status of the family fortunes. Identification with her mother anchors a girl's femininity. This finding helps explain one way that girls can simultaneously develop strong achievement goals and a strong feminine identity.

It is significant, too, that almost all of the legislators are married and have children. Bardwick and Douvan comment that "Success in the traditional tasks is the usual means by which girls achieve feelings of esteem about themselves, confidence and identity." [8] The assumption is that marriage and motherhood complete the process of sexual maturation for many women.

This study offers little evidence on developmental sequences. But it provides eloquent testimony on the subjective compatability of femininity and political careers. Forty-six strong-minded women rarely agree about anything, but all affirmed that women need *not* sacrifice their femininity to succeed in politics.

The interviews encouraged the expression of ambivalence and hostility toward both male and female status. They probed behavior in

competitive situations and in depth feelings about power and conflict. They elicited comment on the comparative situations of men
and women. A great deal of shrewd comment resulted—some of it
emphasizes the advantages enjoyed by men, but not one interview
suggests that the legislator regrets being a woman or would rather be
a man. These women are not only content to be women, but most
positively like women. They see advantages in their condition and
attribute various good qualities to their sex. All of them believe
women in public office can be just as logical and rational as men;
four-fifths are convinced that the country would be better off if
women had more to say about politics.

Values

In a democracy one should expect to find that those elected to office
are persons who share the dominant values of the community and
who conform to the community's standards of good behavior. Persons with very deviant values, persons who do not conform to accepted conventions—who do not behave as most people believe a
man or a woman should—will rarely be judged appropriate leaders or
decisionmakers.

A recent study of sex-related differences in political behavior spec-
ulated that "High motivation and *deviance from conventional norms*
[my emphasis] would seem to characterize these members of the
fairer sex."[9] Yet, the values these women expressed in more than
two hundred hours of interviews are traditional values. They emphasize the obligations of a woman to her husband and especially to her
children. They reflect a broad consensus on the priorities of a woman's obligations to her family. They express concern for good schools
and good government. They affirm the values that motivate parents
to give hundreds of hours to the PTA, the 4-H Clubs, the Scouts.

The values of these women legislators are those for which American society is famous. They emphasize social virtues—participation,
cooperation, sociability, and achievement. Their values are oriented
to family *and* community. Personal and social identifications are
integrated and harmonious. There is no hint of incompatibility of

family roles and citizen roles. Exclusive, defensive family-centered attitudes which so frequently make fortresses of Mediterranean families are entirely absent. *Family obligations have priority for these women, but they are linked to the community by way of inclusive identifications.*

Community service and cooperative endeavor are central values. The obligation of a citizen to take part and to help out is affirmed repeatedly, and clearly indicates that for these women the partici pant style is associated with duty and obligation as well as with personal inclination. The obligation to participate was obviously internalized early and occupies a high place in their value hierarchies, a position second only to family. This "social imperative" coexists with other community-oriented values. With a single exception (who probably is not long for politics) these legislators have a generally high opinion of others and, like the Founding Fathers, have a "decent respect for the opinions of mankind." Their generalized confidence in the decency and fairness of other people is complemented by a general confidence in the institutions of the society.

Achievement ranks high among their values. These women have a strong attraction to the achievement ethic as a just principle of social organization and as a personal creed. They believe in hard work and practice it. Again and again they assert that work can overcome obstacles. Community problems can be solved by work; anti-woman prejudice can be overcome by work; elections can be won by work; respect of one's colleagues can be gained through work; legislation can be passed with work; multiple roles can be juggled successfully if one is willing to work. They both embody and articulate the work ethic. Liberal, conservative, black, white, young, old shared commitment to personal achievement and a belief that effective work is rewarded. Such commitment to personal achievement in the public sphere is not believed to be characteristic of American women generally.

Studies have shown that some bright, achievement-oriented women tend to become anxious in competitive achievement situations (Matina Horner has labeled this tendency "the tendency to avoid success")[10] because of a presumed incompatibility between achievement and femininity. These legislators may be deviant both in the extent of their achievement drives and their sense of freedom in the pursuit of these goals. They feel free to work hard and to be effective.

The fact that they are conventional women who share the dominant values of their communities does not mean that they are mindless or spineless conformists. Quite the contrary.[11] A strong sense of purpose coexists with traditional values and achievement goals. Most are strongly inner directed, and show an unusual awareness of their values and the relation of these values to their lives. Having made traditional social values their own, they evidence strong commitment to them. They are thoughtful women with individual purposes and tenacious views about public and private affairs.[12] This sense of purpose guides many of them into public office. It is also a foundation for the autonomy that makes it possible for them to run for office. Public service has become a personal value for most. Being for the most part strong, inner-directed women, they carried their personal visions of public good into the political thicket.

The combination of conservative personal style and values with deviant role behavior is doubtless one of the keys to their political success. Skillful combination of a conventional style with unconventional role behavior no doubt makes the latter more acceptable to voters. In democratic political life, voter approval is the prerequisite for all other accomplishment.

Cognitive Styles

It may be, as David Gutman argues, that relatively more women are characterized by "the 'autocentric' ego styles in which the order of events is seen as related to the self," and relatively more men by the "allocentric ego style, in which the order of events is seen as having a direction and logic of its own."[13] It may be that American women tend to be less analytic, more holistic; less manipulative, more contemplative; less objective, more emotional; less rational, more impulsive. But the evidence on both the distribution and the causes of such characteristics is mixed and sparse.[14]

There is no lack of data on the cognitive styles of these women legislators. With very few exceptions these legislators display characteristics most frequently associated with men.[15] Boundaries between ego and events are clear, no effort is made to personalize the environment, events are perceived and described as independent of the self. There are no evidences of diffuse ego functioning.

To the contrary, in accounts of their political lives all these legislators except four demonstrated stable self-conceptions clearly differentiated from their environments and not contingent on the continuous confirmation of others. They demonstrate, too, a capacity to analyze and appraise interactions and contexts and to place themselves in social processes. It is true that a good number speak of themselves as part of a family unit without differentiating the interests and identities of the various members of the family. Otherwise, however, their descriptions of social processes reflect clear distinctions between self and others. They are practiced in analyzing people and interpersonal relations, are skilled and comfortable in maintaining functional, instrumental relations with others, but their analyses and relations are humanized by empathy and warmth. Their characteristic approach to political and social problems is more rational and analytic than emotional; and they bring to politics the pragmatic problem-solving orientation widely believed to be characteristic of American politics. Problems are analyzed contextually. There is little tendency to abstract, universal thought. Their inclusive identifications and broad social experience tend to promote the development of an orientation to concrete problems, just as social isolation and alienation breed abstract, universalistic and utopian thought. While it is sometimes believed that identification with a locality and concern with local affairs lead to a "parochial" (therefore narrow, limited and mean) perspective, in fact, warm personal relations and social concern can only be generalized, not abstracted.

Whether their rational, analytical, manipulative, cognitive style preceded or followed the long involvement in public affairs cannot be inferred from the available data. However, it almost certainly helps these women function effectively among their male political associates.

Self-esteem

Successive studies of politics and personality have identified self-esteem as a personality trait with special significance for politics.[16] The legislators in this study exhibit all the qualities associated with self-esteem: feelings of personal worth, competence, strength, self-control, autonomy. They know themselves to be competent and capable. Again and again in interviews they expressed confidence in their ability to achieve objectives, confidence in their ability to win approval and cooperation from others, confidence in their ability to solve problems. That is to say they have confidence in their intrinsic worth, their stability and self-mastery, their social skills and intellectual abilities.

Self-confident self-control is an important component of high self-esteem. A person who lacks secure internal controls lives in fear of herself. Afflicted by anxieties and ambivalence, such a person will not be able to mobilize her energies to achieve goals because too much effort is expended fighting the internal struggle. One who feels herself threatened by anarchic impulses also feels threatening. Fear of the self—of being too destructive, too violent, too ambitious, too lustful, too dependent—undermines self-esteem at the same time that it fosters fear of others.

People who are fearful of themselves are also likely to be withdrawn and solitary. The effort to control threatening impulses consumes both time and energy and leaves little opportunity or inclination for socializing. The person of uncertain self-control "knows" that, however she may appear to others, she is "really" potentially unstable and unreliable. What reason, then, is there to believe others are different? The self threatened by internal anarchy is unlikely to have confidence in the reliability and benevolence of others.

Self-esteem is also closely associated with a sense of adequacy and efficacy. Adequacy relates to one's resourcefulness and vulnerability, efficacy to one's competence. Both are necessary to goal achievement. A person who feels highly vulnerable to attacks from others minimizes social contacts with those believed to be potentially threatening. Such a person avoids situations of conflict and competition because she lacks the optimism necessary for such encounters, and feels the risk of the encounter to be too great. To compete for leadership one needs to believe in one's capacities; one needs an ego strong enough to risk defeat. Democratic competition screens out those who cannot "take the heat" by forcing officeholders through the ordeal of public competition. She who cannot stand to be attacked, who cannot stand to lose, who cannot speak out in her own behalf, cannot achieve public office—at least not for long.

The American Voter asserts that "It is the sense of political efficacy that . . . differs most sharply and consistently between men and women," with men "more likely than women to feel that they can cope with the complexities of politics and to believe that their participation carries some weight in the political process."[17] It is significant that the women in this study display a notably high sense of political efficacy. They do not doubt their ability to influence events in desired directions.

The questionnaires and interviews explored many aspects of the legislators self-evaluation: level of competence, adequacy, comfort in coping with oneself, with families and colleagues; with social, intellectual, and moral challenges. The results were consistent and persuasive. Overwhelmingly, the legislators feel comfortable in their self-control (70 percent said that they do not worry much about their abilities). A generalized expectation of success gives them optimism and confidence. They have experienced repeated success but also know how to fail. Overwhelmingly they say that defeat does not destroy them, that they can risk, and overcome without much difficulty the disappointment of losing. They think well of themselves, well of their sex, and believe that others share their opinion.[18]

Like the "participants" described by Lester Milbrath, "They feel personally competent; they know themselves and feel confident of their knowledge and skills; their ego is strong enough to withstand blows; they are not burdened by a load of anxiety and internal conflict; they can control their impulses; they are astute, sociable, self-expressive, and responsible."[19]

They remind us, too, that "High self-esteem fosters a particular coping style—active, exploratory, manipulative. For the person with high self-esteem the world is malleable. It invites and rewards exploration, accomplishment, curiosity, involvement, attempts at mastery."[20]

Personality and Politics: A Comment

Obviously, professions have different requirements. Rossi, for example, has identified personality traits found to be particularly characteristic of scientists: an extremely low sociability, low concern for and a general "apartness" from others; high intellectual ability, extreme independence, intense channeling of energy in one direction.[21] Obviously, the women in this study are ill suited for such roles, not because they lack intellectual ability, but because they are very sociable people who display neither "apartness" nor "extreme independence." If Rossi's characterization is correct—and it is based on a good deal of suggestive evidence—then the same qualities needed by a man or woman for politics would disqualify them for science.[22]

If a person who finds group endeavors and organizational participation distasteful wanders into politics, it is doubtful that she would stay long; democratic politics shares with communal activities a need for continuous interaction among participants—meeting, talking, persuading, compromising. Verba and Nie's recent study indicates that there are significant differences between "communal" and "campaign" activities (especially in their relationship to conflict) and that some of the people attracted to one type of activity do not engage in the other,[23] but, they also assert, the two types of activity have much in common. The candidate for public office normally engages in both at some point in his or her career.[24] Politics is a highly social, very permeable profession whose requisites for success are largely identical with the characteristics of these legislators.

According to many qualified observers of sex differences in contemporary culture, the dominant cultural stereotypes define strength and autonomy as masculine traits. Bardwick and Douvan, for example, identify as part of the "traditional masculine personality qualities—objectivity rather than subjectivity, aggression rather than passivity, the motive to achieve rather than the fear of success, courage rather than conformity and professional commitment, ambition and drive."[25]

Yet most of these women are strong, active, and goal-oriented achievers who are thoroughly integrated into their communities,[26] and who have won their communities' seal of approval. Almost all were elected in tough contests with male opponents.

This apparent paradox—violating cultural norms and winning widespread approval—is intriguing and important.[27]

Characteristics of Legislators Compared: Women and Men

Like the women, the men legislators in this sample are also conventional in values and life styles. Almost without exception, they marry and stay married. They have children and remain in their communities. They go to church, support their schools and professional associations, and work in nonpartisan civic associations. They are, in short, pillars of their communities.[28]

The respects in which these male and female legislators differ are those directly relevant to traditional sex roles. The men have more education; 70 percent have professional degrees. Most are lawyers. All have been continuously employed. The male legislators have more children and enter politics earlier; 60 percent had more than two children and almost 90 percent first ran for the legislature when they were under forty. Among women, two-thirds had only two children, and three-fourths first ran for the legislature after they were forty. It will surprise no one that most men and few women had children under ten when they first ran for public office.

In spite of the many differences in the experiences of boys and girls and men and women, the legislators considered in this study turn out to be remarkably similar in many aspects of their lives most relevant to politics. The same social experiences seem to contribute to the development of politically active males and females. Many of the same personality patterns characterize both. Observable differences between them apparently derive more from social roles than from inherent predispositions. I am not suggesting that there are no differences between men and women relevant to politics, only that these data indicate that certain types of social and personality characteristics are found in both male and female legislators.

These characteristics do not cause them to run for office. There are many men and women who join civic organizations, go to church, share the dominant values of the community, marry, have children, have high self-esteem and a high sense of efficacy without running for public office. To understand how and why these women came to run for political office, it will be necessary to identify the circumstances in which they moved from being active to actually becoming a candidate. This is the step few women take. Many women are active, few become candidates. Relatively more men take the step from local party activity to candidacy for public office. Perhaps the crucial differences between women's and men's situations and motives lie at the point of entry into public office holding. Perhaps not. The next chapter will be devoted to an examination of entry into the political class, the seekers for and wielders of power.

NOTES

1. Thomas Dye reports that state legislators generally are "joiners." See Thomas R. Dye, "State Legislative Politics," in *Politics in the United States: A Comparative Analysis*, ed. Herbert Jacob and Kenneth N. Vines (Boston: Little, Brown, 1965), pp. 168-169. See also Frank J. Sorauf, *Party and Representation* (New York: Atherton, 1963), p. 79. Patricia Gorence Bach reports the same pattern of multiple organizational memberships in "Women in Public Life in Wisconsin," Alverne Research Center on Women, unpublished manuscript, p. 13; this type of sociability and political participation has been documented in many studies. Katz and Lazarsfeld found that "gregariousness" as measured by membership in organizations and number of friends was closely related to political participation. Elihu Katz and Paul J. Lazarsfeld, *Personal Influence* (New York: Free Press, 1955), pp. 287-289. Most recently, it is documented in Sidney Verba and Norman Nie, *Participation in America: Political Democracy and Social Equality* (New York: Harper & Row, 1972).

2. Alexis de Tocqueville, *Democracy in America*, ed. J. P. Mayer and Max Lerner, pt. 2 (New York: Harper & Row, 1966), chaps. 5, 6, 7, pp. 485-499.

3. Maurice Duverger, *The Political Role of Women* (Paris, UNESCO, 1965), p. 128.

4. Ingunn Norderval Means, "Women In Politics: The Norwegian Experience," *Canadian Journal of Political Science*, September 1972, p. 379.

5. Sorauf, *Party and Representation*, p. 79; Lester W. Milbrath, *Political Participation* (Chicago: Rand McNally, 1965), p. 75.

6. "The Democratic Character," in *The Political Writings of Harold D. Lasswell* (New York: Free Press, 1951), p. 495.

7. For a systematic formulation of Lasswell's conception of the social self, see Harold D. Lasswell and Abraham Kaplan, *Power and Society: A Framework for Political Inquiry* (New Haven: Yale University Press, 1950), pp. 3-15.

8. Judith M. Bardwick and Elizabeth Douvan, "Ambivalence: The Socialization of Women," in *Readings on the Psychology of Women*, ed. Judith M. Bardwick (New York: Harper & Row, 1972), p. 56.

9. M. Kent Jennings and Norman Thomas, "Men and Women in Party Elites: Social Roles and Political Resources," *Midwest Journal of Political Science* 12, no. 4 (November 1968): 475.

10. Matina S. Horner, "Femininity and Successful Achievement: A Basic Inconsistency," in *Feminine Personality and Conflict* (Belmont, Calif.: Brooks/Cole, 1970), p. 54.

11. On this question of the similarity of character structures of leaders and masses, Robert Lane commented: "The question arises of whether leaders whose personality characteristics differ from those of their constituents will validly represent their constituents." Robert Lane, *Political Man* (New York: Free Press, 1972), p. 30.

12. A fascinating and important study by DiPalma and McClosky demonstrates that "Those who preponderantly conform to majority attitudes are by substantial margins better adapted socially and psychologically than those who preponderantly reject them . . . . They exhibit greater self-esteem and less anxiety than the deviants, and are less motivated by aggression and inflexibility." Giuseppe DiPalma and Herbert McClosky, "Personality and Conformity: The Learning of Political Attitudes," *American Political Science Review* 64, no. 4 (December 1970): 1054-1073.

13. David Gutmann, "Female Ego Styles and Generational Conflict," in *Feminine Personality and Conflict,* p. 77.

14. See Eleanor E. Maccoby, ed., *The Development of Sex Differences* (Stanford: Stanford University Press, 1966) for a review of research on this topic. See also Eleanor E. Maccoby, "Women's Intellect," in *The Potential of Women*, ed. S. M. Farber and R. L. Wilson (New York: McGraw-Hill, 1963); Erik Erikson, "Reflections on Womanhood," *Daedalus*, Spring 1964; H. A. Witkin, R. B. Dyk, H. F. Faterson, D. R. Goodenough, and S. A. Karp, *Psychological Differentiation* (New York: Wiley, 1962).

15. Gutmann, "Female Ego Styles and Generational Conflict" in *Feminine Personality and Conflict.*

16. An excellent analysis of the links between self-esteem and politics is Paul M. Sniderman, "Personality and Democratic Politics: Correlates of Self-Esteem" (Ph.D. diss., University of California at Berkeley, 1971).

17. Angus Campbell, Philip E. Converse, Warren E. Miller, and Donald E. Stokes, *The American Voter* (New York: Wiley, 1960), p. 490. Note, however, that *The American Voter* has recently come under attack by feminists. Robert D. Hess and Judith V. Torney report no differences in boys' and girls' sense of political efficacy in *The Development of Political Attitudes in Children* (Garden City, N.Y.: Doubleday [Anchor], 1968), p. 213.

18. A recent report on persons active at various levels of California politics reported similarly high levels of self-confidence among both women and men, and on the basis of an Adjective Check List for personality diagnosis, it concluded that both male and female leaders were "usually capable, outgoing, socially skilled, and persistent persons," adding, "the female leaders try harder and worry more," and further suggesting that female political leaders suffered from "fretful uncertainty about themselves and their situation, which is accompanied by a greater degree of anxiety and readiness for psychological change." Constantine and Craik, "Women as Politicians: The Social Background, Personality and Political Careers of Female Party Leaders," *Journal of Social Issues* 28, no. 2 (1972): 226. The woman legislators in this study do *not* display either high levels of anxiety or fretfulness. I am tempted to suggest that Constantine and Craik have mistaken female flexibility (willingness to seek counseling) and capacity for self-criticism for fretful anxiety.

19. Milbrath, *Political Participation*, p. 89.

20. Sniderman, "Personality and Democratic Politics," p. 123.

21. Alice Rossi constructs this profile in "Barriers to the Career Choice of Engineering, Medicine, or Science Among American Women," in *Readings on the Psychology of Women*, ed. Bardwick, p. 78.

22. See the timely, interesting, and valuable essays by Max Weber, "Politics as a Vocation" and "Science as a Vocation," reprinted in H. H. Gerth and C. Wright Mills, eds., *From Max Weber: Essays in Sociology* (New York: Oxford University Press, 1946), pp. 77-156.

23. Verba and Nie, *Participation in America*, pp. 56-81.

24. Ibid., p. 201.

25. Bardwick and Douvan, "Ambivalence," p. 55.

26. These women remind us that autonomy is not associated with anomie and isolation, but is most often a product of successful social adjustment. On this point, see DiPalma and McClosky, "Personality and Conformity."

27. This is consistent with the description of girls' nonconformity: "When girls resist parental authority, they may be more likely to do so quietly—if you will, covertly, perhaps deviously—while maintaining a lady like conformity." Elizabeth Douvan and Joseph Adelson, *The Adolescent Experience* (New York: Wiley, 1966), p. 114.

28. The women in this study also closely resemble in these respects the women in Werner's study of women legislators serving in 1963-1964. They, too, had generally married, reared children, had more than a high school education, and first entered state legislatures in their late forties. Emmy E. Werner, "Women in the State Legislatures," *Western Political Quarterly* 21, no. 1 (March 1968): 46.

Chapter IV

Deciding to Run

HOW does a woman decide to run for office? Is it just another way of being involved in community affairs? Is the decision to run for the state legislature like deciding to run for president of the PTA or the League of Women Voters? How can a woman campaign successfully against a man without irritating too many voters?

And why? Why spend one's time in politics instead of the Red Cross or the Garden Club? Why go to all the effort to run and to serve? Are the reasons these forty-six women decided to run for the legislature similar or different?

How does a party decide to nominate a woman for the legislature? How much resistance is there? Why does it happen so infrequently?

The decision to run for the state legislature involves a person and a situation. This chapter explores the motives and circumstances of the forty-six women on whom this study is based when they first decided to run for the legislature.

Pathways to State Power

There is no single pathway by which the women in this study moved from private life to holding legislative office any more than there is one route by which men become lawmakers. Legislating differs from many other occupations in its lack of specific education and training. As a recent manual for legislators pointed out, "Unlike many professions, no formal program exists which a citizen may follow to learn how to become a legislator."[1] No course of study, examination, licensing board attest one's qualification. Nor is it necessary to make a long advance commitment. A woman who wants to be a physician should decide early in her college years (if not before) in order to take the biology and chemistry courses required for admission to medical school, which is followed by four to ten years of education and apprenticeship. Early commitment and long preparation are required of other professions as well. One important reason why there are few women in these high status professions and many in relatively unskilled jobs is that, expecting (and expected) to be wives and mothers rather than breadwinners, they fail to make an early career commitment and undergo the required training. Later, when they need or want to work, they are qualified only for jobs without demanding requirements.

To become a legislator it is only necessary to win an election. This does not mean that standards for lawmakers are lower than for physicians. Only that the qualifications are very different. In a democracy the job of the legislator is to represent constituents in making—and not making—laws. The chief qualification is therefore acceptability to the electorate. In principle the lack of other fixed requirements should make the job of lawmaker relatively more accessible to women. However, the absence of specific requirements does not mean that one background is as good as another. The notion that politics and government are men's business, for example, has deep roots in the American political tradition (as in most other political traditions). It is reinforced by a long standing custom of electing businessmen, lawyers, and other professionals and entrepreneurs to the legislatures. Americans have tended to believe that law is especially good training for politics and, while there is obviously no direct route from the law school to the state house, lawyers are more numerous in many legislatures than members of any other occupational group.[2]

Since law has until recently been a male profession reinforced by discriminatory law school admission policies, one very simple, clear deterrent to women's running for public office is that tradition and opportunity discouraged all but a few from entering the profession from which most candidates are recruited.[3]

But that is only one deterrence. Women have also been few in the other occupations—farming, the real estate business, journalism, insurance—from which legislators generally come. Women legislators have usually been recruited from a single, deviant, occupation: housewife. Regardless of their educational background, almost all the women in this study moved to the legislature from the role of full-time housewife. This is an unusual, unfamiliar, sex-specific pathway to political office, one virtually unexplored by political scientists.

From Homemaker to Lawmaker: Alternative Routes

There are two main routes from homemaker to lawmaker—the community volunteer route and the party worker route. They are not mutually exclusive, but, in fact, each of these women tended to specialize in one or the other activity. For purposes of clarity, I will emphasize their distinguishing characteristics.

The Volunteer Route

Noting the absence of women from the Wisconsin legislature, Leon Epstein commented, "It is striking that election to public office at this level is seldom taken as an alternative to activity in the League of Women Voters or in local party organizations."[4] Many of the women in this study did precisely that: they took election to the legislature as an alternative to (more accurately, a type of) community service. The distance from nonpartisan activity to political candidacy is less than might be supposed; both consist of group activity oriented to public goals. And though some argue that politics is distinguished from volunteer activity by the level of conflict and consensus, democratic politics is not all conflict, and nonpartisan civic activities are not necessarily conflict free. The nonpartisan activist is not infrequently deeply involved in issues and causes that divide the community: school bonds, church buildings, community development, even Red Cross drives stimulate controversy and opposition. So the move into politics is not necessarily one from consensual to conflict oriented activities. It may or may not be; and it may or may not be perceived as such.[5]

Verba and Nie find that civic and campaign activity differ "in their relationship to conflict."[6] On the other hand, Bardwick and Douvan assert that "many women professionalize their voluntary or club activities, bringing qualities of aggression, competitiveness, and organizing skills to these 'safer' activities."[7]

Why does a woman decide to change her principal focus of activity from volunteer effort to the legislature? There are, it turns out, various reasons. For most, the motives which led them to run for the legislature were the same as the motives that made them community volunteers: an awareness of public problems needing attention and a feeling of personal responsibility for those problems. Most made the switch from community volunteer to legislative candidate out of the conviction that by working through politics they could more effectively achieve the public goals to which they were committed. Describing their decisions to run, these community leaders explained, "it seemed the best way to contribute something to your own community," adding:

Politics became for me where things happened. This is where it is. This is the course. Out of this field flow all the streams that affect people's lives. You can't just leave it to other people.

I think it is one of the most important offices because it is so close to the grass roots.

After years of working with the Urban League and civil rights groups, I just knew something more had to be done.

I knew I could keep busy and make a contribution doing what I was doing, but I know very well you can have a lot more clout if you're doing it as a legislator, and it is true.

I had become familiar with state problems and anxious to have something done about some of them and thought that I could make a greater contribution in the legislature.

I knew that the things I had been working toward, the changes I wanted to see, could be best accomplished in the legislature.

In some cases intense interest in a specific policy spurred the move from community activity to candidacy. For one it was deep concern about public health policy on which she had long worked at the community level; for another it was keeping the schools open; with a third, reorganization of local government was the spur.

Some see their previous community service as a "preparation" and "education" for legislative service.

The idea seemed to me the end of a logical progression, as though I had been preparing for it for years. I seemed to be the right person at the right place at the right time with the right kind of experience to do the job.

I had been active in the Farm Bureau, the Red Cross and polio drives and other community service activities. I was active with the Future Farmers of America and the Boy Scouts. And then I got really involved in the problems relative to the housing and health codes. In a community, different problems and opportunities come up and each year you see something else that merits your attention and it becomes a way of life. Then when a chance to work on the things you care about in the legislature comes along, you are ready for it.

The timing of the transition from a nonpartisan community volunteer worker to candidate is important. Most frequently it occurred at a point when these women had more time and fewer family obligations. Community volunteer work can be done without dislocating one's family life and need create no problems for a wife and mother. Not so the legislature. One study of state government commented that "For most state legislators the political career is only a part-time occupation. Politics being a sideline, the decision to run for legislative office is not a 'big decision' comparable to choosing a nonpolitical occupation or profession."[8] This may be true for most legislators. But not for most married women. Few legislators live in state capitals. For most there are months during which they are at home only on weekends; for all, there are long hours at the capital, many evenings away from home. Being a legislator requires a lot of time. It is not surprising that most women made the decision to run at a point when they felt they either had or were about to have free time.

The community volunteer brings to political candidacy the social and personal resources accumulated in her years of civic service. For this reason, women who have achieved prominence as civic leaders can frequently move into the party structure at a fairly high level— perhaps directly into legislative candidacy.

In his study of the Pennsylvania legislature, Frank Sorauf noted that legislators were most frequently drawn from occupations "which create public contacts on which to build a political career. The lawyer, auctioneer, insurance salesman, farm implement dealer, to mention but a few, establish in their business or profession the wide circle of acquaintances so necessary for political success."[9] Membership and leadership in volunteer community affairs also provide the wide acquaintance so necessary for political success. The woman who serves as high level officer in the League, the PTA, and similar service organizations meets others with similar interests and meets them under circumstances that recommend them to one another. She has an opportunity to make good impressions and to develop good personal relations with many, an opportunity to develop a reputation for leadership, for effectiveness, for disinterested public service. Volunteer activities provide an opportunity to develop a taste for public life and many of the skills needed for it. A woman active in a civic organization learns how to run a meeting, how to plan one, how to develop an agenda and recruit support for a position. She learns how to "operate" in a public context, how to win and lose. Most important, holding responsible office and performing well enables a woman to test her capacities, to explore her abilities, and to experience the self-confidence that comes with doing a job well.

Self-esteem and participation frequently go hand in hand. The person with sufficient confidence to join others in group activities finds that confidence reinforced as she takes on new assignments and performs well. Participation in volunteer organizations (or in politics) provides women with an arena to test and develop skills, to win approval and confidence. Women not employed outside the home have little chance to "prove" themselves in a job and enjoy the approval of fellow workers. The importance of this relationship between performance, approval, and self-esteem in adults is often underestimated.

In a society such as ours, achievement needs are frequently as important for women as for men. Men satisfy achievement needs through successful job performance. But women with strong achievement needs may not be able to satisfy them through the complicated affectional relations of a family. The affection they get from family may be important to their self-confidence, but irrelevant to a feeling of competence. But the psychological gratifications of successful performance in volunteer organizations is very similar to professional success. A former president of the League of Women Voters put it this way:

> After many years in the League, it seemed a natural thing to move into political affairs. I never had any problems talking on an issue or selling anybody

on an issue, but the whole concept of selling myself was something that I had never really done. I had always had doubts about my own abilities and through the years in the League I was convinced of my capabilities. Serving as president, speaking a lot in public, increased my self-confidence enormously.

Volunteer work can also lead to a reputation for leadership. The woman with such a reputation moves into politics with the basic resources necessary to political success; leadership, influence, and name recognition are the currency of politics. Under the proper circumstances this currency can be converted into votes. It is not surprising, therefore, to find that political parties are willing to accept as candidates women (and men) who have not worked their way up the political hierarchy, but have instead developed a reputation for community activity.

Some of the community volunteers had already run for another public office before they decided to enter partisan politics. From PTA activist to candidate for the school board is a short step taken by many who get deeply involved in school affairs. Others of these women had run in nonpartisan elections for membership on library boards, constitutional conventions and town councils. Those who had already been elected to public office came to the legislative race knowing what it was like to look for votes and to serve as a representative.

Moving from community activity to the state legislature has important implications for the focus of attention. The women who come out of the PTA, the League of Women Voters and such organizations are oriented to local problems. Their focus of attention expanded (rather than changed) to include the state level. They bring to politics a problem-solving orientation rather than an ideological one, and stand in sharp contrast to persons who get involved at the state and local level out of a desire to influence national politics.

The Party Worker

In a democracy politicians are always self-made. Even the scion of a distinguished political family must prove himself a worthy heir to family charisma (a principle sometimes best illustrated in the breach). One version of the political success story concerns the person who starts at the bottom and works up, but nobody knows how frequently political careers develop that way. Political scientists do not know how many state legislators, governors, congressmen, senators were, for example, precinct leaders. We know that some were not. One-fifth of the legislators in this study held no position and apparently took no part in party affairs up to the time they ran for office. Most party workers do not become candidates for public office. Leon Epstein reminds us that potential candidates for public office constitute a small portion of the mass-membership party, that "The essence of such a party is that it contains activists who because of choice or circumstances, are unlikely to run for public office."[10]

The diversity of modern party activity attracts—indeed requires— diverse personality types with diverse needs and skills: bureaucrats, theorists, agitators, socializers. Socializers—male and female—run the dinners, luncheons, beer busts, bull roasts, picnics and coffees that are part of the life of every active party organization. Organizers plan and direct precinct organizations, fund drives, registration campaigns. Candidates run for office. Somebody runs the mimeograph machines, types the copy, collects the dollars, washes the dishes. In most party organizations women do most of the mundane chores. Over four- fifths of the women legislators and an equal percent of the male legislators agree that generally the women do the dirty work while men wield the power. But the women in this study were not content to occupy themselves in activities unrelated to power.

They did not remain at the lowest levels of party operations. About half held local party positions, an equal number held county level party office, and nearly that many played roles in state or national parties. Half had already run for public office. Their positions were responsible but not top level. Experience in these positions served the same stimulating, confidence-building functions as volunteer service. Repeatedly in the interviews, someone would comment that filling a lower party office, or successfully accomplishing some party task had given her new confidence in her abilities. A black representative comments that after two terms in a local party office, "I built up my confidence that I could go somewhere in politics." Another legislator confesses that until she served on a partisan board, "I just never thought I could get elected to anything or that I should every try. Then after I had served for a while I began to feel more qualified and more confident."

The timing of the decision to run for the legislature was again most frequently related to the age of children and the decline of family responsibilities. But among the party activists relatively more women decided to run while they still had young children.

There is no special pattern of party activities that seems most likely to lead to running for the legislature. The common thread is activity itself. The biographies of these women, as of other politicians and activists, leave no doubt that involvement stimulates involvement, that participation stimulates participation, and that running for one office stimulates running for another. One woman put it this way: "Well I had served four years on the County Board and I suppose once you have had a taste of public office and found it fascinating, I suppose everybody is tempted to go the next step higher when the opening comes."

Another confesses that after a term on the City Council: "I was really bitten by the bug and thought politics was so fascinating and it sounds corny but I really wanted to work for good government."

In the same vein another commented: "Politics is just something like a disease, once it gets into your blood you can't do anything about it."

About half had *not* previously run for office before they became candidates for the legislature. Among these were women who had been deeply involved in the organization and management of the party. One, for example, had served as campaign worker, precinct leader, president of the Democratic Women's Club, then served two terms on the executive level of the State Federation of Democratic Women. She managed a friend's successful campaign for Congress and then became the party manager for her county—a very responsible position which involved sitting in on party committees, running meetings, and keeping party lists up to date.

Not many of these women had such varied and extensive experiences before they first ran for office. A more typical party history is that of one legislator who, soon after she was married, joined the Republican Women's Club in the town to which she had just moved. She remained in the Club for the next few years, serving several times as chairman of the membership committee. Later she became active in the County Republican Association and was twice elected its president. From there it was a short step to the state federation where she again served as a committee chairman. More recently she served on the state platform committee and as a delegate to her national convention. Another common party background is that of a Legislator whose first party post was that of vice precinct chairman—an office she held for 15 years, after which she became ward chairman, a member of the county candidates screening committee and the voter registration committee. She also served for more than ten years as delegate to the state convention. In another legislative career, one woman served seven years as precinct chairman and ward leader, six years on the executive committee of the county organization, and five years as state committeewoman before she became a candidate for legislator.

An apprenticeship in the party does not guarantee party support for nomination to the legislature. Whether or not the party welcomed a woman's candidacy depended on the attitudes of party leaders toward women candidates in general, and toward that woman in particular, and on the competition for the nomination. The step from party worker to legislative candidate is not necessarily an easy one.

Party activists are frequently thought of as oriented more to national and state politics than to local politics, but in making their move to the legislature very few of these women were concerned primarily with national problems. They were oriented more to issues than personalities, but state and local issues concerned them most deeply. They were more concerned with problems than ideology and with specific problems rather than abstract ones. Perhaps this is a reflection of women's famous orientation to the concrete. Perhaps it was a consequence of experience in local organizations. Whatever the cause, most of the women focused more on local and state affairs than national politics. Their principal goals in running for office were public service and a desire to influence decisions on issues in which they had an interest. In addition, several were interested in developing a political career and some thought of running as a way of serving the party.

For many of these women party activity served as the principal training ground for candidacy. It provided an arena in which to learn about as well as to affect policies, gave training in organization and leadership, and an opportunity to develop and to exercise skills; it reinforced interest in public problems and provided a vehicle for relating public problems to private lives.

Volunteer community service and volunteer political work alike provide women without special professional or educational training for a legislative career an opportunity to acquire experience, skills, and reputations that qualify them for public office. This aspect of volunteer work is frequently overlooked and underemphasized. For many women the personal benefits derived from volunteer work are as important as the benefits derived by the community from their activities.

The Decision to Run

How many people want to serve in a state legislature? Some studies indicate that there are frequently more seats than candidates. Sorauf, for example, notes that in well over half of the legislative primaries in Pennsylvania there was a single entry.[11] However, competition for the state legislature as for other offices in the American system may take place either in the nominating process or in the general election or both. In states or districts where one party dominates, the primary election is the big contest. In states where the two parties are more nearly balanced candidates may face tough competition in both the primary and the general elections or only in the latter. The stage at which the contest takes place has important consequences for party organization and process, but from the psychological perspective, the important factor is whether or not there was competition for office that had to be faced and overcome.

Only six of the women on whom this study is based secured the nomination without a contest, and almost two-thirds say that it was necessary to overcome tough competition to get the nomination the first time they ran. This might be construed as evidence of the party's resistance to female candidates, but for the fact that even more of the male legislators in this sample also report facing such competition. (Two-thirds faced tough competition, another fourth had some competition for the nomination.)

Since the male legislators in the sample conform almost perfectly to the model of the ideal legislative candidate—successful, moderately young lawyers active in their towns and cities—and still encountered stiff competition, it may be that legislative office is becoming more desirable than it once was. Certainly state legislatures today raise and spend more money, deal with more problems, take actions affecting more people than ever before in history. Perhaps it is not as difficult to find candidates for the legislature as it was a few decades ago. Perhaps the office was always more desirable in most states than it was generally believed to be.[12] Perhaps the general upgrading of state legislatures in the last 20 years has resulted in heightened competition for office. Perhaps the most effective legislators tend to come from districts that feature competition for office. In any case, these data on males and females alike indicate that in the districts where these unusually effective men and women ran for office there was almost always more than one candidate for nomination who was able to command significant support.

The fact that so many of the women faced competition for the nomination is important for our general picture of women in public office. It constitutes conclusive evidence that these women did not "drift" into the legislature; nor were they simply "placed" there by supportive males. The point is worth emphasizing because of the widespread stereotype that women are "put" in legislatures by friends of their late husbands. Not one of these women was appointed to the legislature to serve the unfinished term of her husband. One was offered such an appointment and declined on grounds that her late legislator husband disapproved such appointments. This widow moved into the legislature only after she had won a hotly contested primary. The stereotype of the passive female political actor (which like most stereotypes may contain the proverbial grain of truth) is contradicted by the women who achieved the nomination because they sought and fought for it. This is not to say the initiative was wholly theirs. Some first conceived the idea themselves and took the initiative in approaching party leaders and/or friends; others placed themselves in situations where they were likely to be asked; only a few ran for office without significant personal initiative or effort. The first group can be appropriately called the Office Seekers, the second the Ready Recruits. The level of initiative and the organizational backgrounds of the candidates are variously related. Some Office Seekers and some Ready Recruits came up through the party ranks, others had backgrounds chiefly in nonpartisan community activities.

Office Seekers

The defining characteristic of Office Seekers is that *they* took the initiative in deciding to run for the legislature. They did not wait to be approached, they did not need to be invited or persuaded. They made the decision to run, and after making, it, set about winning the nomination. In the language of contemporary political science, they recruited themselves.

To speak of people recruiting themselves reminds us that the concept of political recruitment can be misleading. Recruitment calls to mind a process by which someone is selected and/or persuaded and/or drafted by someone else. This model, in which initiative lies with the recruitor, may be appropriate to political systems in which party leaders choose candidates, but is inadequate to describe what happens when the would-be candidate takes the initiative, wins a primary, and/or convention endorsement, and becomes the candidate. The direct primary makes it possible for a candidate to win a nomination without ever having been "recruited" by party leaders. So do some caucus and convention systems. Those who become candidates because they offer themselves in such procedures might be called "self-recruited."

About 40 percent of the women on whom this study is based made the decision to run for the legislature without being approached, or sounded out, or persuaded by anyone. Some made the decision to run on hearing that an incumbent had died or was about to retire; others simply decided they were better qualified than the incumbent and would try to unseat him. They either perceived an opportunity or they made one. Having made their decisions, they then informed and recruited others.

The decision to run constituted deviant behavior. Frequently she was the first woman in the district to run for the legislature; many decided to run in the face of openly expressed doubt about whether a woman should run, whether a woman could conceivably win. It is an understatement to say that their decisions were not always met with enthusiasm by party leaders. How did they make such decisions? By consulting themselves and their husbands. Why did they make such decisions? Because they were—to a woman—convinced they had a significant contribution to make to the policy process in their states, and because their husbands were at least willing and more frequently enthusiastic about the idea.

One legislator describes the process like this:

One spring day after one child had gone to the university and the other two had started high school, I was out in the backyard sitting on the bench with my husband when a son who was still at home brought the newspaper to us. It announced that Representative Mossback was finally retiring from the state legislature where he had represented the county for some twenty years. There was also some speculation about who would replace him. I put down the paper and said to my husband, "Now here, I would like to do this. I think I am qualified and I would like to do it." I was surprised to hear my own voice. I thought he would probably laugh. But he said, "Well go ahead and do it. I will pay your fee. I think you will do a better job than any man I know."

That was that. The decision was made. I didn't call anybody in the party or talk to anybody. I just went down the next morning and paid my fee to the local party chairman. He was so surprised his mouth fell open. I know I hadn't left his office before he was on the telephone telling everybody all over town that I had announced. Everybody was surprised and nobody knew what to do about it. Women just don't do that sort of thing where I come from. Least of all respectable, middle-aged ladies from good families. I know they said to each other, "Look here, just because we've asked her to help out, now she does this." They just didn't know what to do about it.

Unlike a general election where nominees can count on the support of the party organization, a primary race is a lonely affair. There is only one's self and whatever support one can muster from family, friends and associates. None of the Office Seekers was sponsored in her quest for the nomination by a pressure group or lobby on which she could count for money or for (wo)manpower. Most of the Office Seekers faced a contested primary. Several ran against incumbents. Most ran alone rather than as members of a slate. All who had primary contests faced male opponents. Few had substantial personal financial resources; their only resources for these contests were themselves—strong egos, strong motivation, and a local reputation for community service and leadership.

The act of taking initiative in seeking a party's nomination has special significance for women, since women are typically socialized not to take the initiative, especially in matters that involve self-assertion. Women who waited to be asked to run (the Ready Recruits) comment on the "feminine imperative" not to put oneself forward, not to demand, not to be aggressive in the pursuit of goals. The Office Seekers were not deterred by this imperative. Their motivation to seek office was stronger than their anxieties about being thought aggressive.

A second general point needs to be made concerning motivation. Not one of the Office Seekers stood to gain professional or occupational advantage from either running or serving. Their roles and personal situations precluded careerist motives of the sort that sometimes are said to lead young lawyers to offer themselves for office because—win or lose—they profit professionally from the activity. In seeking office these women reflected the same public spirited motivation observed among women political activists in California of whom a recent article said, ". . . for the woman leader it is more likely to be a 'labor of love,' one where a concern for the party, its candidates and its programs assures a relatively greater importance. If the male leader appears to be motivated by self-serving considerations, the female leader appears to be motivated by public-serving considerations."[13] Most of these women thought of the state legislature as a last step rather than a first.[14]

For Office Seekers, the commitment to public service had already been made; terms had already been served as officer in the League, the Business Women and Professional Clubs, in the PTAs, and all but two had already run for public office before they made the decision to run for the legislature.[15] For most, the race for the legislature was the first fairly high level political contest in which they would be involved as candidates, but it was viewed less as a beginning than as a continuation of a commitment to public service. The legislature would be a new phase—one made practical by changing family circumstances. They believed the legislature a useful arena in which to work on the state's problems and felt qualified by background and temperament to become legislators.

Sometimes the decision to seek legislative office was linked to a particular issue about which an already active woman felt strongly. One stated that she had "made up my mind I wanted to effectuate a change in my city charter and the only way I could was by going into the legislature and sponsoring legislation." Another decided to run because of the desire to keep schools open. But even when an issue was an important motive for running, the issue tended to be an incident in a process rather than the cause of a new pattern of behavior.

A minority of the Office Seekers had a strong sense of personal mission, as though politics were a "calling" to which they were morally obliged to dedicate themselves. The special zeal associated with such a sense of mission is frequently found in persons who have an overriding concern with a single issue or cause, and some of the Office Seekers describe their decision in just such terms. One such is a staunch conservative with a conviction that things were going from bad to worse in the U.S. and a belief that she personally had the duty to do what she could to "stop the drift and decay." Another, a "new politics" spokeswoman appalled at the Vietnam war, repelled by what she took to be the corruption and immorality of American public life, decided to run in the hope that she could "undo stupid things done in Washington."

The sense of personal mission was not always so closely related to specific ideological commitment. Sometimes it grew out of a more general sense of obligation to service through politics. This more general but equally intense sense of vocation was expressed in the following terms:

The way I feel about it sometimes is if I weren't in government I wonder how I could sleep at night.

I don't know exactly how I decided to run. I suspect I always knew that I would be involved in government. I really don't know why, I just knew eventually I would be.

After I had served on the constitutional convention I literally felt that I would never be the same. I had a higher degree of interest in government. We did such intensified study that after I had served there, I don't think a team of horses could have kept me out. I was that involved and that interested and I realized more than ever the need for qualified people.

After I decided to run I did go to one party leader and he said, "Well that is fine. I will be frank with you, if there should be a contest I think a man would have an advantage over you." and then I said, "Well, *nothing could* persuade me not to run. I know that I am needed there. And I never start anything I don't plan to come out the winner." I just knew I had to run."

The sense of mission overrode other pleasures and obligations and allowed these women to subordinate family and personal life to the drive for public office.

For most of the Office Seekers the decision to run entailed a willingness to face stiff competition first for the nomination and then in the general election. Though some think of themselves as people who seek to avoid conflict, none were deterred by the prospect of competition or conflict. Most of the Office Seekers had no concern about avoiding conflict. A few say that they relish it. "Boy," says one, "I love the competition and the conflict." "I am a very competitive person," asserts another. Such comments are rare, however, and it is not surprising that they should be, since from an early age girls are taught never to be competitive with males. A principal reason that the Office Seekers are able to contemplate a contest without feeling dismayed or threatened is their confidence in their ability to win. Their descriptions of the decision to seek office are peppered with such comments as:

I am the eternal optimist and I felt that I was going to win. I think the reason I did win was because eventually I was able to transmit this to other people.

I knew that I could win.

I had a very deep conviction that if I did run I would win . . . I knew that I would win if I worked diligently.

It never crossed my mind that we would be defeated even with the odds so heavily against us.

I never for a moment doubted that I was going to win it (the primary) . . . .

Only a few report ever having had doubts about the outcome. Was this self-confidence excessive, realistic, necessary? What is its relation to the decision to run? Obviously, it is easier to take on a conflict when one feels invulnerable. Denial of the possibility of losing (either negatively, by never thinking about it, or positively, by certainty of one's victory) diminishes the feeling of vulnerability and heightens a sense of strength and adequacy. This denial can be supplemented with a second psychological defense line that makes it possible to accept failure in advance of the fact:

> You can't let it be a big personal disappointment (if you lose). You have to excuse yourself as though other factors caused you to lose.

The sense of being qualified and prepared by previous service, the conviction that the work of the legislature was important and public problems were pressing gave most the confidence to announce; strong egos reinforced by past successes gave them the ability to face conflict with equanimity. And those who saw themselves as agents of a cause were armed against adversity by their sense of mission.

Ready Recruits

> I had always wanted to run for office .... But I suppose I was too kind of ... shy isn't the word, it is ridiculous, but I suppose that is the best description. I was too hesitant. I had too much of this feeling of, well you have to be asked. You mustn't push. You must take the back seat of the bus.
>
> I wanted to run for the legislature and over and over I expressed it mildly, but I never forced the issue, never got anywhere. Finally when an incumbent moved up ...

*　　*　　*

> The party never asked me to run, never even approached me, but I was approached by women's groups who asked me to consider it seriously and said they were depending on me. I said, 'Golly, you are asking too much. I'll take half a cut in salary. And I can't win.' So they kept coming back, and finally I decided I'd take a chance.

*　　*　　*

> I spent twenty years in the League of Women Voters and I was working on a major state project. I had served on my local finance board for two terms. I knew the community and for twenty years I had been involved in community activities—of the nonpolitical type. Then I was asked to run by some close friends who were very active in the Democratic Party, and then I decided to run.

The behavioral difference between Office Seekers and Ready Recruits is that the former took the initiative while the latter waited to be asked. But, as the above quotations indicate, almost anyone could do the asking. It was not necessarily an authoritative party group who made the suggestion; it could be friends, fellow club members, ideologically compatible associates, brothers, husbands—almost anyone would do. Waiting to be asked did not mean waiting for general agreement, for a free ride for the nomination. In fact, most of the Ready Recruits made the decision to run knowing there would be a contest for the nomination.

Why did they need to wait to be asked when most were clearly quite interested in running? Some waited because it never occurred to them to run until someone suggested it. But the ease with which they conceived themselves as running and serving, the quick appeal of the prospect, the speed with which they made decisions raise a further question. Why did a number of them never think of running for the legislature, when that is obviously the sort of thing they liked? To think about running, to conceive oneself as a legislator, requires a certain audacity. It is a very unconventional idea for a woman. And they are conventional women.

What of the others, those to whom it did occur? Why did they need to be asked?[16] The explanation probably lies deep in feminine socialization. It may be only that girls learn that to put oneself forward is aggressive, and that to be aggressive is to be unfeminine. Through years of waiting to be asked—to dance, to lunch, to go on a date, to marry, to make love—women learn to stand back and let others (principally males) take the initiative. Traditional socialization and roles habituate women to taking initiative only within quite restricted circumstances—circumstances determined by others. Women regularly take the initiative in planning children's birthday parties, PTA book fairs, Red Cross drives, menus. They make a wide range of consumer choices: what brand of detergent, what style of children's clothing, what color bedspread, what brand of TV, what to have for dinner, whether the children should have music lessons. And there are larger matters that in our society are generally left to female initiative.

Unemployed women have much greater freedom than men in planning the use of their time. They have more chance to take initiative in community affairs, church activities, and such. But, traditionally, the role of wife and mother involves a woman more in adapting than deciding: where she will live and on what budget are determined by her husband's career; how she will spend the early childrearing years is determined by the multiple needs and desires of her children.

Women do not have the habit of making long range plans for themselves. Few plan careers, or train for them; until recently, few planned families. Instead of initiating they respond, caring for children when they appear, getting a job when extra income is needed. Perhaps those women who "never thought" of running for the legislature, and those who thought of running but needed to be asked are especially good examples of culturally approved behavior. Some of them contributed a good deal to creating the situation in which they were asked, again playing the role of the girl friend who "sets up" a proposal, and the wife who manipulates the husband into doing what she prefers. It is interesting though that these legislators are not very favorably disposed to seeing women as the "power behind the throne" or as the manipulator who uses "feminine wiles."

Though they differ in regard to the important question of initiative, the Office Seekers and Ready Recruits share most other characteristics. There are no significant differences in their educations or social background. Their family lives are about the same; most in both groups seriously considered running only after their children were well along in school, and only if their husbands approved. Patterns of recruitment from within the party are reflected in experiences like the following:

I was asked by my party to run. I had not been particularly active but I decided that it was time for me to start being active and I was asked by my county chairman to run for the legislature. It was my first political office. I had never held any other party office but I had been very active in my community. To tell you the truth, it floored me when they suggested it. But I really, you know, immediately had the feeling that I might be able to make a contribution because that was why I wanted to go into political life. I didn't want to be a stamp licker or envelope stuffer. I wanted to be in the level that was making decisions and setting policies.

                                    *   *   *

Running for the legislature kind of crept up on me. I have been in politics ever since I was old enough to vote. I was a block worker. As soon as I was registered I offered my services to the party which was a little unusual in that day and age for a 21-year-old to become vocal and active. And I was received with open arms and people were always anxious for my help. I am a Republican. I came up through the ranks. You might say. I became very active in the Young Republicans and the Republican women about 1960 and my children were in school and up to that time I was pretty well tied to the house because of them and we did not have the income to support baby sitters and that type of thing, which has changed. I went from president of the local council to a member of the state board of directors of the state Republican organization and also county organization work.

In 1968 the incumbent legislator decided not to run. Our county chairman knew this and he approached me on whether or not I would be interested in running. He thought it was time women be recognized because the women have always been active in our county. Up to this time I had been active, but I said well as long as I was putting all this time in it I might as well be an effective voice rather than just on the sidelines, you might say, which is really what the Republican women are. The Young Republicans are a fine organization but they really have no clout. I had decided as I became more issue oriented working in legislative and congressional study groups, that the only way you have a say in what is done is to have the power to push that little button yes or no. And I had been preaching the fact that we ought to have more women active in government and the next thing I knew I was confronted with the situation. Well, here is the opportunity. What are you going to do about it?

I would have never considered it if I had thought I would have to go out and fight in the primary campaign because I would have never been able to win.

*   *   *

I decided to run for the legislature when I was chairman of the County Campaign Committee. I had been involved in organization politics a number of years. I was a committeewoman and I became minority chairman and ultimately the vice chairman and then I was chairman of a state party committee and traveled throughout the state to different counties and organizations. Then I dropped out and came back in on the campaign committee. It just happened that the young man who was in the seat that I now occupy had found himself unable to run again because of his business. He was a freshman and this always disappoints a party to put so much time and effort on a candidate and then have him run one term and quit. So I went then to the county meeting of the chairman and vice chairman and others to look over who we might run, and they said we think you might be able to win. We are not sure, but would you like to try, and I said sure. I said all right, I would be glad to do that. There was a big discussion about how a woman was going to affect the whole ticket because there never had been a woman running before but we all felt that the people would be realistic.

One difference between those "asked" to run by "the party" and those passed by some other individual or group is that the former might not face a contest for the nomination, the latter almost invariably did. The former were more likely to have been deeply involved in party organization, the latter somewhat more likely to have concentrated their activity on the Urban League, the Farm Bureau, the League of Women Voters, the PTA. But fundamentally, the pattern is the same: someone comes to her, proposes that she run for office and she accepts, readily convinced that she will be able to make a significant contribution by serving.

In addition to the question of initiative, there are other limited psychological differences between the Office Seekers and Ready Recruits, which are consistent with their different behaviors vis-à-vis the decision to run. Those who needed to be asked felt somewhat more vulnerable; as a group they had somewhat more concern about conflict and competition. Fewer felt "sure" they would win. More considered the possibility that they would lose and the idea did not appeal to them. They, too, are women who have a habit of success. "The first time you put yourself on the line, and you *are* putting yourself on the line, you have this ego involvement, and you know you simply can't lose, and all of a sudden the possibility is very real." They are not deficient in confidence; these women, too, have unusually high self–esteem and strong egos, but they seem not to be equipped with the psychological mechanisms needed to ward off and repress the reality of the risk and the possibility of defeat. Most of them *knew* they might be defeated. Perhaps this knowledge made their decision to run contingent on feeling they had supporters who could be counted on, perhaps the reassurance that someone wanted them in the legislature helped to arm them against the knowledge that some sizeable portion of the electorate would not want them there. They did not run for office in search of approval, but the encouragement of key persons was important to them.

The motivation of the Ready Recruits is not qualitatively different than that of the Office Seekers; a generalized commitment to public service and good government characterizes most. They are as likely as the Office Seekers to make devoted, serious legislators. They are as likely to campaign hard, work hard, and succeed at the job. Some of the women who hold positions of greatest responsibility waited to be asked. Neither are the Office Seekers more inner-directed and the Ready Recruits more other-directed. In running for office, both are pursuing goals long since internalized.

Waiting to be asked, in sum, does not signify passivity, lack of interest, or lack of commitment. It is an aspect of personal style from which it is possible to infer little about interest, commitment, or capacity to participate in conflict. There are stereotypes concerning the passive woman who becomes active as an act of obedience, or an act of interpersonal solidarity, who adopt the active mode out of passivity. These are not such women—not even those who ran for office at the urging of a close relative. Two first ran for office at the initiative of their husbands and both became active, enthusiastic participants whose political careers outstripped their husbands'. Another was recruited by her brother who had responsibility for filling a slate. She has since developed an extraordinary sense of dedication and vocation and today could not be deterred from a political career even by the brother who recruited her.

For some women and some men in politics, the need to be asked is important. Waiting for others to make an overture may entirely prevent some women from running; circumstances suggest that in some cases it might as easily not have happened. On the other hand, it may be easy to underestimate the initiative of the woman waiting to be asked. She may have rigged the situation and herself brought about the desired invitation. This is especially likely in those situations where the woman accepted with alacrity, and without misgivings.

Still, initiative is an important component of effectiveness and leadership and it is extremely unlikely that only one act—the decision to run—is affected by this type of reticence. It is an aspect of personal style that affects other interactions and possibly inhibits effectiveness. But interpersonal relations being what they are, it is possible that this quality of hesitation, waiting, is attractive to the men who hold power in political parties and in state houses. If so, this limit on aggressiveness may enhance a woman's opportunities as well as diminish them.

The fact that many of these active, energetic, political women waited to be asked means that hesitating at the threshhold of self-promotion does not necessarily indicate either passivity or ineffectiveness. Changing attitudes toward women may reduce the number who wait to be asked. The following comment suggests this may be the case:

I said, years ago, "I would like to run for the legislature." Everybody else wanted to run; men wanted to run for the legislature. My name wasn't even mentioned; it wasn't even brought up at the meeting of the screening of candidates for the party.

Why didn't they bring it up? Why didn't I just say, "Hey! I put in a bid to run for the legislature. I would like to be considered. Why not?" There I sat, and so I was passed over, and now, at my age, I am just running for my second term in the legislature. It is ridiculous, and it is my own fault, partly. Until we change our own attitudes about ourselves they won't change their attitudes about us. I'm not going to head for the back of the bus any longer. When I'm passed over for something I deserve, I'm going to say, like a man would say, "That's a hell of a way to treat me, after everything I have done for the party." That's something I have never felt to be in good taste, if you know what I mean—well, to hell with good taste.

The legislator who uttered those words is a handsome, well-born Republican of great charm. Her comments suggest that she is also fed up with waiting to be asked, but whether her statements reflect catharsis or resolve is difficult to determine. This patrician has been, if not radicalized, then at least mobilized. Still, lifetime habits of soft spoken acquiescence are not easily altered.

Lawyers

The differences between male and female career lines are frequently explained by reference to women's different (deficient?) career lines. The fact that women are generally *not* lawyers is frequently invoked to explain why so few run for state legislatures and for Congress. This makes it desirable to examine with special care the political experience and recruitment of the lawyers among this group of women. Does their experience differ significantly from that of the other women who are not lawyers? Do their political career lines more nearly resemble those of male lawyers, or of female non-lawyers? The presence of six lawyers in the sample gives us a chance to explore the consequences of profession, but the number of cases is sufficient only to provide clues.

There are suggestive differences and similarities between lawyers and non-lawyers. The lawyers are definitely younger than the median for non-lawyers; four of the six were under 40 when they first ran for the legislature, and the only legislator under 30 is a lawyer. Three have been continuously employed and have less experience in party and nonpartisan community activities. Two of these three have no children. The three who have not been continuously employed have fairly substantial party experience—one was precinct committeewoman for eight years and served as an alternate delegate to a national convention; another was county campaign chairman for six years; another had an extensive background of community activity.

All are relatively attractive, aggressive, competitive women. Four of the six took the initiative in the decision to run; two waited to be asked but readily accepted. Some feared losing, others never thought about it. All have strong achievement drives.

A woman who is a lawyer can win nomination and be elected to the legislature without the years of party or community service that characterizes most of women's careers. Presumably legal education can be substituted for apprenticeship in community affairs and vice versa. However, two caveats should be noted. First, if a lawyer chooses the traditional family role she is likely to enter the legislature only after the same prolonged volunteer experiences that characterize the non-lawyers. Second, the experience of one highly motivated young woman who was elected to the legislature before she had finished college indicates that it is not only lawyers who can bypass the routes by which most women gain legislative office. But, "if you are a woman and a lawyer," said one, "you have an instant credibility that most women do not have."

NOTES

1. Ohio Legislative Service Commission, *A Guidebook for Ohio Legislators* (Columbus, Ohio: 1970), p. 71.

2. Hyneman found that lawyers were easily the largest occupational category in thirteen lower chambers and twelve senates between 1925-1935. Charles S. Hyneman, "Who Makes Our Laws," in *Legislative Behavior: A Reader in Theory and Research*, ed. John C. Wahlke and Heinz Eulau (New York: Free Press, 1959), p. 255. Sorauf reported that only 20 of 106 Pennsylvania legislators were lawyers in 1959-1960. Frank J. Sorauf, *Party and Representation* (New York: Atherton, 1963), p. 72. Epstein reported that the number of lawyer legislators in Wisconsin had increased in the decade ending in 1957, but still constituted only about one-third of the legislature. Leon Epstein, *Politics in Wisconsin* (Madison: University of Wisconsin Press, 1958), p. 110. Malcolm E. Jewell and Samuel C. Patterson, *The Legislative Process in the United States*, 2nd ed. (New York: Random House, 1972), p. 75, report that lawyers constituted 40% of the Illinois legislature in the 20 years following 1935. They add, by way of explanation: "He [the lawyer] makes no great change when he

moves from representing clients in his private practice to representing constituents as a legislator."

3. The extent to which law *remains* a male profession is reflected in the 1970 census, which reports 315,715 male lawyers and 9,103 females; L.L.B.'s were awarded that year to 14,837 males and 978 females. *Statistical Abstract of the United States, 1972* (Washington, D.C.: U.S. Department of Commerce, Bureau of the Census).

4. Epstein, *Politics in Wisconsin*, pp. 105-106.

5. One former state president of the League of Women Voters saw the move in just such terms: "I wasn't sure that I could take the personal kind of bitterness or nastiness that goes with a political campaign, and I worried about whether or not I could lose, whether or not it would be just too personally devastating to lose."

6. Sidney Verba and Norman H. Nie, *Participation in America: Political Democracy and Social Equality* (New York: Harper & Row, 1972), p. 77.

7. Judith M. Bardwick and Elizabeth Douvan, "Ambivalence: The Socialization of Women," in *Readings on the Psychology of Women*, ed. Judith M. Bardwick (New York: Harper & Row, 1972), p. 56.

8. John Wahlke, Heinz Eulau, William Buchanan, and Leroy Ferguson, *The Legislative System: Explorations in Legislative Behavior* (New York: Wiley, 1962), p. 121.

9. Sorauf, *Party and Representation*, p. 73.

10. Epstein, *Politics in Wisconsin*, p. 90. Epstein notes (p. 117) that between 1925 and 1955 almost one-third of U.S. senators, congressmen, governors, and other state constitutional officers had served in their state legislatures.

11. Sorauf, *Party and Representation*, p. 84.

12. See, e.g., James D. Barber, *The Lawmakers: Recruitment and Adaptation to Legislative Life* (New Haven: Yale University Press, 1964), p. 28.

13. Constantine and Craike, "Women as Politicians: The Social Background, Personality and Political Careers of Female Party Leaders," *Journal of Social Issues* 28, no. 2 (1972): 235.

14. This may be characteristic of both women and men. An important study notes that "for most, the state legislature is likely to be a terminal point of their political career." Wahlke et al.; *Legislative System*, p. 121.

15. Leon Epstein notes the extent of competition for quite low level party office in Epstein, *Politics in Wisconsin*, p. 90.

16. For a discussion of the importance of being asked (a largely male sample) see Lewis Bowman and George R. Boynton, "Recruitment Patterns among Local Party Officials: A Model and Some Preliminary Findings in Selected Locales, *American Political Science Review*, September 1966; also Lester W. Milbrath, *Political Participation* (Chicago: Rand McNally, 1965), p. 101; and Barber, *The Lawmakers*, pp. 28-29. See also Ingunn Nordeval Means, "Women in Politics: The Norwegian Experience," *Canadian Journal of Political Science*, September 1972, pp. 381-382.

Chapter V

The Campaign

THE most dramatic part of the process of becoming a legislator is the campaign. Whether a primary or a general election, a race between two fairly evenly matched candidates, either of whom might win, is the most exciting stage in the recruitment process. Political scientists have paid relatively little attention to these contests except at the highest level. Local contests are in some ways most exciting because they are most apt to engage people who already know each other and because the candidates themselves dominate the process (unlike statewide and national races in which technique so frequently overshadows the human contestants.)[1]

Districts vary, candidates vary, resources vary; the campaigns of these women differ from district to district and year to year. Campaigning in western ranch country, a biracial inner city, and small town New England poses different problems, is conditioned by different traditions and different political cultures. But the basic interactions are apparently the same.

An election campaign is like a game in which the contestants are candidates, and the stakes are public office. Some of the rules are laws, some of the rules are customary, and some of the rules change with the identity of the contestants. As we shall see, some of the rules change if one of the contestants is a woman.

Campaigns are important for studying women in politics because campaigning requires so many types of behavior believed to be difficult, if not impossible, for women. To campaign it is necessary to put

oneself forward, to "blow one's own horn," to somehow demonstrate one's superiority and dominance. What can conventionally
well-behaved ladies do in such an arena? According to the conventional wisdom of a fading era they should not be there at all. But
they are there and they assert, contest, triumph. The problem is how.

How can a woman convince voters that she will be an effective
representative for them? That is the technical question with which
each of these women was confronted as they began their search for
legislative office. The precise answers depended, of course, on the
size and character of the district, the temperament and resources of
the individual candidate. Various strategies are available to a campaigner. In an urban area one can minimize personal contact such as
door-to-door campaigning. Whatever the strategy of communication,
there is also a choice of messages; it is possible to focus on personal
qualities, on party or group affiliation, or on issues. Then, there is
the strategy of self-presentation. How should a female candidate deal
with her femininity? She can emphasize it, stressing either moral or
physical "feminine" attributes; she can ignore it; she can apologize
for it or deny it. In this sample, there are various campaign styles.

The following accounts provide an overview of how these women
campaigned.

At the time that I made the decision to run (says a four-term legislator from a
small Midwestern city) neither I nor the party leaders thought I would have
an opponent in the primary. When a businessman who represented a slightly
different wing of the party filed against me, I realized I would have to win not
one but two contests. The prospect was not appealing, but it never occurred to
me to drop out and leave the nomination to him. After all, I had decided to run.
I had told other people I would run. And so I ran. It was a very tough primary.
My opponent was an unpleasant man who kept implying that it was a man's job.
I never answered him. I tried to run a positive campaign emphasizing my background and interests. Most of the party leaders were encouraging to me. But we
really have an open primary. So they didn't play any role in the primary
election.

I got so involved in the campaign that I really didn't have time to worry about
whether I would win. I had decided I would run the best campaign I knew how
and then if I didn't make it, well, then I would pick up some of the other
volunteer activities that I had engaged in.

I campaigned personally because although my name was well known there
were many people I had never met. Basically, I worked through the PTA, the
League, the church—through all those organizations I had been active in.

I know that I am best at face-to-face contact with people. Small group meetings were the most important part of my campaign. A friend would invite 20

people (mostly women) to get together at her house. It was through these small groups that I built up my hard core group of supporters and these were the people who then became my foot soldiers and volunteers to do the precinct work and the telephoning the last weekend before the election."

The coffee klatches also served as listening posts, where I could ask questions and listen to what was on the minds of lots of different kinds of people. I used them, too, in my campaign for reelection. I would explain my record to them, and they would ask me questions and I would listen. It works very well.

I generally had about six meetings a day, two in the morning, two in the afternoon and two at night—they would usually be some kind of breakfast, lunch or dinner kind of thing. I tried to develop one of these groups in each of the precincts in the district. There were 150 precincts so that makes a minimum of 150 of these coffee hours to start with, and you keep adding on extra ones. It is the hardest, most energetic kind of campaigning there is. Then, in the last weeks I added door-to-door campaigning. And, of course, I took advantage of every opportunity I had to speak to groups. There are always several large campaign rallies and, of course, my campaign manager scheduled me to speak at Rotary Clubs and so on. I also distributed cards with my picture and a brief biography and in the general election my name and picture appeared on a brochure put out by the party. In the course of the primary campaign I saw and spoke to thousands of potential voters.

I won the primary by a very large margin. The general election was easy by comparison. I got support from my party leaders. I was the one woman on the whole ballot.

I never thought about the special problems of a woman campaigning. Actually, I think women have some advantages campaigning in some areas. I think people are apt to trust you more. They are apt to think you more honest— that's the image there is—and in my state where corruption is a problem, that's very important. Voters also think a woman will be more conscientious than a man—that she will do her homework. They know a woman isn't running for office just because of personal ambition. I think you have to emphasize a feminine image. Voters don't want a woman to be a dainty little violet, they know you couldn't get the job done. So you have to reflect energy, stamina, force and motivation. I think some of the men of my generation resent an aggressive woman. So you have to guard against being overly aggressive. You have to be aggressive, but not show it too much. I guess it is the iron hand in the velvet glove that's needed.

A woman has some liabilities, too. There are men who never under any circumstances would vote for a woman. There are also men who are happy to vote for a woman and believe she has the assets I mentioned. Then there are several types of women voters, too. You've got your highly intelligent, highly motivated civic worker kind of women, like the League of Women Voters, AAUW, and these people, in general, they are all for you. They are delighted that you are running. They will give their life's blood for you. They identify with you and they are proud of you. They think, "There but for the Grace of God go I," and "More power to you." Then there's another set. There is the country club set who couldn't care less and they don't even bother to go to the polls for you. They are not antagonized but they are puzzled as to why you would want to do this odd thing. They feel maybe you have even lost a little social standing because you are running for office. Then there is the third kind. This is the woman who is apt to be jealous and actively resent the fact that you are running and is apt to be against you.

I like campaigning. I always thought I would. It is interesting. It's fun—meeting so many people, hearing about their problems and ideas, explaining your views to them. I enjoyed my second campaign, too. I never get personal or attack my opponent personally. I just ignore him. Altogether I spent only about $3,000 in both campaigns. One-third of it was personal money. A citizens committee collected the rest.

By the time this legislator was elected she was a seasoned campaigner. She had found a style of campaigning that suited her, one that she liked and thought she could win with. In subsequent campaigns she followed the same pattern, saying to friends in the party that it didn't make sense to abandon a winning formula. She has increased her margin of victory in each election.

Another, a seasoned legislator from a Southern state, describes her early campaigns this way:

I knew that the party leaders weren't exactly pleased when I told them I planned to run, but I didn't find out till later that one of them recruited an opponent to run against me in the primary. In my state, the primary is the one most important race.

Well there was quite a primary fight. One highly qualified man who had planned to run—though I didn't know it—declined to file against me. The fellow who did was a businessman who had run for office before and had been elected once. He had more political experience than I—no doubt about it. He also had the backing of the governor. I worked very hard. I spoke everywhere I had the chance. I did a lot of visiting with people, I talked to everyone, I tried to get the support of labor but in my first primary I didn't. I had some help from friends in the clubs I had worked in. The party officials were neutral. I know some of them respected me more than my opponent. There was a lot of resistance to a woman among the narrowminded and the uneducated. They still believed a man could do a better job. Some of them said to my face that just trying to get elected proved how silly I was. I knew there would be people who would say that sort of thing and it didn't bother me a bit.

My family had lived in the area for generations and had a good reputation. Everyone knew my name and that helped. But not enough. I was defeated the first time I ran. In my district, winning the primary is winning the election. Losing bothered me. I didn't like it at all. And I made up my mind that I would run again against the man who had beaten me—and when he came up for reelection two years later, I ran against him and beat him soundly. I defeated the man who defeated me. I outsmarted him. I have had no problem since then. I campaigned the whole time—the whole two years—without campaigning. And when I went into the election the second time I had labor and business and blacks and everybody. My opponent never realized that I had been working so hard. I never knew how badly I wanted to succeed, once I had decided to run. Frankly, I don't know where I got the determination and energy. I just knew this was something I had to do. Since I won and I was the incumbent, I got good support from the party. I think they respected me even though they know I'm sometimes independent. I won't vote for something I really think is wrong. My husband has been very helpful in my campaigns. He gives me money and advice, and works, too. I couldn't have done it if it weren't for his support. My children have been very proud of me. I think they all think I'm a more interesting person because I'm in the Legislature.

Some of my old friends think that I'm a nut wanting to run for office and serve in the legislature but that's not important. They always knew I was an independent kind of woman. A lot of my friends help in my campaigns. I like campaigning. I don't make a job of it. I just get around and talk to people all year round. And then in the last weeks before the election I make speeches. I think campaigns are a good opportunity for all of us—those running for office and those just voting—to think about the problems of our states and communities and discuss them. I think everybody profits from a campaign.

I honestly don't have a formula for success other than that I worked hard at it. I have gotten to know many, many people I never knew before I ran for office and I have worked hard at getting to know them. It took years to do that. I try always to be sincere. I try to neutralize any disadvantages I may have.

Clearly, this legislator was mobilized by defeat. When she speaks of campaigning so hard as something she "knew I had to do," she is describing a process which takes place in many politicians who "have" to win. With the determination comes the energy; the whole self is mobilized for the contest. This description of campaigning identifies the woman as a "political animal," with a major psychological investment in the political process.

A black legislator from an urban area also emphasized the hard work and drive necessary in a campaign.

If I had known how hard I'd have to campaign, I might well have decided not to run. My opponent, a white male lawyer with good connections, was well qualified in addition to being well financed. Everybody thought he would win. He put up a terrific fight. I respect him very much. There was very little difference in what we believed in.

Once I got started campaigning I loved it. I had a wonderful time. I had women's groups—AAUW and the League of Women Voters—that worked hard for me. I had youth. Seeing them get involved, working within the system, enjoying the success of winning, seeing the effect it had on them, was very inspiring. I think this makes it all worthwhile.

I worked very hard. I went everywhere. I visited shopping centers, I went door to door. I went to coffees in the mornings, two or three every day. I spoke wherever I could get an invitation. I learned a lot about making speeches.

My biggest problem was to convince people that I was a serious candidate. I think most people are a little amused by a woman running for office. A woman has a harder time getting established as a serious candidate. That is the biggest hurdle I had.

But I think a woman has some advantages, too. Sincerity shows through. I think women may be more humane in certain ways—though that may be just a hangup I have. It may not be so. Anyway I think a woman can appear more humane maybe because of the mother role. Other women think they have some-thing in common with you. And women constitute half the electorate.

A woman's biggest problem is raising money. That's because of not being taken as a serious candidate. Then people worry about whether, if you're elected, you'll carry a fair share of the load. I think the party is often afraid of this, afraid that they will have to carry your load and theirs too, and they don't like that and I can't blame them for not liking it. So a woman, like a black, has to work twice as hard to get across that "I'm here to do a job. I want to carry my share, I don't want you doing my job and in fact I will do some of yours if necessary."

The Requisites of Campaigning

As the foregoing accounts suggest, a successful campaign requires psychological, physical and social resources.

The social resources are most familiar; they include a local reputa-tion and many acquaintances. Commenting on legislative campaigns, Jewell and Patterson remark: "Most legislative districts are small enough (often less than 10,000 votes) for it to be practical for the candidate to reach many of the voters in person campaigning door to door, in the shopping centers and in small groups. Moreover, a legis-lative candidate who has been active in his community can build his support of a wide circle of friends and acquaintances. At this level, elections are often decided by the single criterion of which candidate has the largest circle of acquaintances."[2]

A legislative campaign may or may not require substantial financial resources because the amount spent on a campaign for state legis-lature varies greatly among districts and states. Several of the legisla-tors assert that they neither collected nor spent money, a condition made possible for them by reliance on personal campaigning and volunteer services, by local tradition, and by the activities of their party in printing sample ballots and doing a minimum of advertising.

Others spent thousands on media, printing and mailing costs. A few spent between one and ten thousand dollars of their own money. None seem to feel that women have special problems or disabilities in raising money *once they have established their seriousness and viability as candidates,* but this, as we have seen, may be especially hard for a woman.[3]

The physical resources needed for campaigning are energy and stamina. The psychological resources needed for successful campaigning are less frequently discussed but no less important. In the United States the psychological requirements for a successful campaign normally include a conviction that one is qualified, and a capacity for leadership, rational calculation, gregariousness, social initiative, flexibility, and a capacity for supplication, an ability to work hard and to engage in conflict. Not all candidates have all these qualities in the same degree, but the most successful have most of them.

The first requirement of a successful campaign is the ability to look at oneself and feel adequate to the task; this, in turn, requires self-confidence and self-esteem, two qualities which these women possess in quantity.

The initial step in preparing oneself for a campaign is to subjectively qualify oneself for office and disqualify one's opponent. Most (though not all) of these women felt themselves better qualified than their opponents. Frequently the two judgments were united in the original decision to run. They looked at their potential opponent and felt qualified by comparison. None saw themselves as less qualified than their opponent. Several volunteered that should such a situation arise they would resign as candidates.

I thought to myself as I listened to him speak that if that young fellow could run for the assembly I could, too.

If I can help this man run for office, why don't I run myself?

I always had confidence that if he could do it, I could do it. I was better prepared than he.

I never thought that I would be qualified to be in the legislature, then I found that the other people who were going to run were not even as well-qualified as I was.

One woman emphasized the crucial importance of feeling more well-qualified than her opponent this way:

I don't have the educational background or any of the attributes theoretically that make you wise enough to be a lawmaker. But then you look at the opposition and you know darn well that you are more qualified than they and this is the only premise that I have been able to run on. If someone opposed me whom I thought was far superior in knowledge and background experience than myself I would bow to their superior expertise. But I haven't had that. Now maybe this might be a form of conceit—feeling that you never had that situation.

A second psychological characteristic needed for successful campaigning is the ability to build an organization and attract helpers. With districts as large as state legislative districts, an individual candidate can hardly hope to do everything for herself. She needs invitations to speak; a team of loyal workers and a campaign manager who will help make the plans, the decisions, and schedules. Campaign workers are and must be mainly volunteers because financial resources are limited, and, in any case, many of the people whose help is needed cannot be hired. Therefore the ability to attract, inspire and retain volunteer workers is important. This aspect of campaigning came easily for most of these "organizational women," but it can create problems for people of certain temperaments as the following quotation suggests.

When you are used to controlling your own direction and suddenly you know that in order to accomplish your purpose you have many people speaking for you and about you and representing you. It is not an easy thing to do because sometimes you're being torn apart by other people. But that is a part of party politics.

Third, a campaign involves planning. Decisions have to be made about how, when and where to present oneself. If a candidate decides to rely chiefly on face-to-face contact—as most of these women decided to do—priorities have to be established about which people to meet, since it is impossible to talk personally with all the voters.

Fourth, since campaigning involves actually meeting the voters, there is a continuous need to advertise oneself, seek personal contacts, take initiatives in interpersonal situations. Flexibility and sensitivity are needed for communicating with voters of different kinds, for making a good impression, and winning support.

Every place you go is different. Some of them, you can tell when you go to the door, whether you're going to discuss the issues or merely say "Oh, does that bread smell good!" Or whether you're going to swap recipes or whether you're going to talk to the husband or the wife. Every district is different and every opponent is different and the secret of success is never to do the same things twice.

Fifth, a campaign requires asking others for support, explaining one's purposes, communicating a need for approval and votes. It makes one a supplicant. The capacity to ask for support with dignity, without diminishing oneself in one's own eyes or those of the voters also requires a strong ego.

> It is very difficult when you are campaigning because you're asking for favors and you are on a different footing with people than when you're just meeting people. You have to sell yourself when you're campaigning.

But you have to sell yourself without selling out.

At least two other psychological requirements for successful campaigning are required: a capacity for hard work and an ability to compete. Anyone who has been deeply involved in a political campaign knows that an enormous effort is needed—or is believed to be needed. The most time-consuming, tiring campaigning is face-to-face contact with voters. It is also very important in state legislative campaigns. Voters like to meet candidates, it lets them feel they have access; they like to feel needed; they like to take a look at the people who are soliciting their support. "The voters," commented Donald Matthews, "love those who seem to love them."[4] A legislator put it this way:

> It used to bother me because I thought that people would vote for you only because you had knocked on their door and identified yourself, not because you had discussed the issues with them. But I think it's really because you have taken the time. I know it matters because later people have said to me, "I was so impressed that you came around and knocked on my door."

But, she added:

> It doesn't always work out that way because we've got a perennial candidate in our district who has knocked on every single door in the country, and he doesn't get elected to anything.

Meeting people, then, is necessary but not enough. Many hours of grueling effort go into meeting the voters during a campaign. A campaign consists largely of what might be called purposive socializing—an endless round of meeting and talking to people for the purpose of enlisting their support. Such purposive socializing is tiring. It uses the self manipulatively, as an instrument. The more a candidate "likes" people, the easier she finds this endless round of socializing. At best, however, it is hard work. Most of the legislators make a point of how hard they worked in their campaigns. It seemed to many that victory is their just reward for effort; as though the effort itself gave the campaign a certain legitimacy. The following statement is typical:

> I campaigned very hard. I campaigned probably twice as hard as anyone else. I listened to everybody, read everything, did everything, worked. It is a tremendous amount of work and you can get very tired of it and I think when I get very tired of it I will quit. I did an enormous amount of coffees and a lot of going door to door. I like it but it's very hard work.

And there is competition. Success in a campaign means defeating an opponent. A campaign is by its very nature competitive (unless, of course, there is only one candidate). Objectively the decision to run in a contested election (and all these women have faced contests) constitutes a decision to compete, but an individual remains free to decide how to handle the contest. Even though one is involved in a contest it is not necessary *to think of oneself as* involved in a conflict. An opponent can be ignored both subjectively and objectively; it is possible to conceive one's campaigning as social and noncompetitive. The campaigner who declines to perceive herself as involved in a conflict will neither attack nor defend. She will simply proceed—meeting people, stating her own positions. So will the woman who knows very well that she is in a contest, but declines to present herself as a contender. Both temperament and strategy are involved in handling conflict in an election. The strategy of ignoring the opponent can be adopted because of purely rational calculation—an example was Richard Nixon's decision on the 1972 presidential campaign. On the other hand the decision to ignore an opponent can grow out of discomfort about engaging in conflict or aggressive behavior. Not infrequently such a decision is adopted for reasons of temperament and rationalized as strategy. A number of the women legislators in this study handle the campaign conflict by steadfastly refusing to attack or defend. They will not "engage in personalities."

He kept knocking me, and I never raised my voice against him. Never said one word against him, though I had many areas which I could have. He has a very bad reputation. He doesn't pay his bills. He has lost jobs because of his activities. Now I had all this information but I am too much of a lady and I am not going to reduce myself. I said to my husband, "If I have to do that then I am better off not being in the legislature because it's so against my principles and you know when you get involved with anything that dirty you can't come out without being smelly like that. You just can't do it."

I have a policy in my campaigning: no mud slinging.

I have never once spoken against an opponent. I never mention an opponent in any but the most gracious and charming way. I just emphasize my qualifications for the job.

I do not go to meetings and smear my opponent. I absolutely refuse to do it, I always have. Once in a very close race I knew a lot about a scandal my opponent had gotten involved in. I didn't use the material against him. I always said it was because I was too nice.

Others among these women do not shrink from what they describe as "forthright discussion of their opponent's weaknesses." Some political types need conflict the way fire needs air, it stimulates, mobilizes and justifies their efforts. There is, for example, a close relation between ideological style and conflict; ideology frequently mobilizes, stimulates and justifies an effort to defeat another. But these women tend to emphasize personal campaigning, personal qualifications and issue positions, and to deemphasize party and abstract ideology. Their choices are consistent with their strengths and with the relatively weak identification of local issues with partisan alignments. They are, of course, also consistent with the style of local politics in America. Political styles oriented to problem solving and interpersonal relations are associated with conflict avoidance.

In the questionnaire and the interviews many inquiries were made concerning feelings and thoughts about conflict in politics. The findings reveal an internally consistent picture of women who have few problems in handling conflict. They neither seek conflict nor are bothered by it. For the overwhelming majority conflict is not an important aspect of their political lives either positively or negatively. Very few have a high need for conflict; even fewer need to deny its reality.

Conflict is not an important or particularly difficult part of the

campaign for the women legislators. For most it is neither particularly welcomed or dreaded; the moral and social aspects of campaigning are enjoyed more than the contest. Enjoyment of conflict and
competition is neither socially encouraged nor admired in
America today. Women, particularly, are not expected to relish
competition. Cultural norms doubtless operate to minimize the
expression of satisfactions based on conflict. However, there is a
good deal of internal evidence in the interviews to support the finding that for most of these women the opportunity to vanquish an
opponent is not an important motive for engaging in political activity
nor are there important satisfactions derived from it. The same cultural norms that might minimize the expression of satisfaction in
conflict would also encourage the expression of distaste. Yet two-
thirds of the women did *not* identify competition and conflict as an
aspect of campaigning that they particularly disliked.

Talking to an elective politician or, still better, working in a
campaign, teaches or reminds one that campaigning in a democratic
system is not a gladiatorial contest. To be sure, there is competition
and an opponent and the goal is winning. But the chief instrument of
conflict is purposive socializing.

The campaign trail more nearly resembles an endless series of club
meetings than a duel. To defeat an opponent, one wins over voters.
Smiles, speeches, favors, explanations, congratulations, ingratiation,
deference, are the "weapons" with which a candidate "fights" her
opponent. An election is not, as is often said, a popularity contest; it
is a contest for who can best establish credibility, authority and
confidence in the minds of the most voters. In small districts, face-to-
face campaigning is the most effective means for establishing these
qualities. These activities involve the kinds of interpersonal sensitivity and skills which women are thought to be, and trained to be,
especially good at.

Probably the most important subjective requisite of effective
campaigning is the capacity to enjoy it. Since most campaigning for
legislative office involves personally meeting and dealing with people,
a distaste for campaigning will be perceived as disdain for the electorate. There is a good reason to believe that enjoyment of others in
a campaign cannot be dissimulated successfully. The emotional

dynamics of the relationship between candidate and electorate have been inadequately examined; it is understood, however, that a successful campaigner is mobilized by the effort and derives pleasure and satisfaction from it.

Running for office consists of extensive socializing at a superficial, purposive level. I do not believe that campaigning necessarily involves "interpersonal aggression," as Barber has suggested,[5] unless one defines all assertive, manipulative behavior as aggressive, but there is no question that it involves a style of behavior more frequently associated with male stereotypes than female ones. However, with very few exceptions, these women enjoyed campaigning.

> "I began a door-to-door campaign. The most fantastic experience I have ever had in my life. I thought win, lose or draw, this has to be a tremendous experience, spending an average of thirty to forty-five minutes with each family and covering more than 5,000 families."

In describing *how* they campaign, one after the other volunteered how much they liked it.

> "I love campaigning," said one legislator considering retirement, "that is the only thing I'm going to miss."
>
> "I love campaigning," volunteered another, "I really like talking to people about politics."
>
> "I like campaigning very much," said a woman recruited by her husband, "I am very stimulated by meeting people and listening to them. I really enjoy it. Almost everybody is nice in politics."
>
> "Coming into a group where I knew no one and presenting my credentials and talking to people and meeting people—this was what some of the others (on my slate) found difficult. I didn't. I love this. I did it easily. I enjoyed it. I found it exhilerating, not tiring. The whole process I found very exciting and very positive and I didn't particularly worry about anything," said one rather reluctant candidate of her first campaign.

Others said:

> "I like campaigning very much. I like people. I like meeting people. I like the opportunity to talk about government to people. I like running a personalized campaign. I don't think that I would like to run for Congress because you have to spread yourself so thin."
>
> "It's really a lot of fun to campaign. I don't mind it at all. In fact, I sort of like it."
>
> "It's a way of expressing myself, a way of channeling all the things that I wanted to say in a constructive way. I think campaigning is creative. It gives you an opportunity to listen to people and understand them."

"I enjoyed it. I had a wonderful time."

"I like campaigning. I campaign all year long, traveling over the state, making speeches, talking to people."

"I like campaigning because I like meeting people. I have no hangups about meeting people."

"I like it (campaigning) and I think that I'm good at it. I had a lot of practice campaigning for other people."

"I enjoy it all very much—meeting people, talking to them, listening to them. It's very worth while."

The picture is not monolithic. About one-fifth assert that they do not like campaigning. Two say flatly that they hate it. Significantly, both of these women dislike other aspects of politics; they are not likely to remain long in politics. The others who dislike campaigning explain it with reference to "shyness" or "reticence." Two assert that it takes too much time from their work in the legislature.

Why do most enjoy it thoroughly? Because it gives them a chance to meet people, they say, and these are very sociable women; because they feel they are helping to educate the voters, and they are interested in the quality of public life. Because they are politicians, they do not shrink from public attention. Campaigning gives them a chance to seek and receive attention—all in the service of a worthy cause. No wonder that it is a satisfying endeavor.

Then, too, they feel they have a contribution to make to public life. With considerable justification they feel themselves to be pure in motive, qualified by experience, and better equipped than their opponents to serve the district. Each of these is an important element in psychological preparation for campaigning. With remarkably few exceptions these women come to candidacy well prepared. This is the message they concentrate on communicating to voters: that they are well prepared for the job and confident that they can do it well.

One does not feel in talking to them that they enjoy campaigning *too much*. There is no evidence that they are dazzled and transfixed by being the center of attention. The absence of either shrinking or aggrandizing tendencies is another evidence that we are dealing here with extraordinarily confident, integrated and stable people.

The elements of campaigning discussed so far are common to male and female candidates. In addition to these, there remains for a woman campaigner the problem of how to handle her sexual identity, how to deal with the potential conflicts between the need to be assertive and take initiative, and the need to be a "lady." This is a problem that male candidates do not face; role requirements for an attractive male and an attractive candidate being very similar.

A woman is confronted with special requirements and problems: a special need to demonstrate her seriousness and qualifications; a special problem of establishing competence; a special need to be assertive without being aggressive; perhaps a special need to convince voters that service in the legislature will not entail neglecting her family. Women candidates and partisans may find these specific requirements objectionable and onerous, but they are real; they must be dealt with in the course of a successful campaign.

Does a woman running for office *necessarily* run as a woman? This is an important question whose answer seems to be yes—because sexual identity is an irreducible, ineffable part of the self. We are all either male or female. A woman running for office *is* a woman. Presumably what those legislators mean who say, "I never campaign as a woman," is that they do not emphasize female identifications, any more than male candidates emphasize male identifications. Few of the women in this study ran as an explicit representative of women's issues and women's problems. In describing their campaigns, few sound as though they had emphasized women's concerns in the way a black might articulate the group demands of blacks.

Only two of these legislators seem to have been active in groups directly and solely concerned with women's rights and women's status. Many, however, were deeply involved in traditional women's groups: groups of women joined together to accomplish some purpose not directly concerned with women's rights and status. There are many single sex groups in this society: Kiwanis, Rotary, Masons, Knights of Columbus, League of Women Voters, Eastern Star are a few examples. Sometimes these women's groups come to the aid of a candidate. One Southern legislator describes being both surprised and pleased when this developed during her campaign.

"I was dumbfounded that the groups with which I had no connection—I wasn't a member of Business and Professional Women; I wasn't a member of the Women's League, because I guess I have always been somewhat of a loner. But they

all organized. They organized a large luncheon for women; they organized meetings; they divided the telephone directory and made calls. When my opponent
came out saying 'elect a man to do a man's job' that made them furious. The
women were furious and that was the turning point in that election."

Here an overt attack on a woman as a woman backfired and mobilized opposition. Other candidates found in the course of their
campaigns that women might turn out to be their most loyal
supporters or their most determined detractors.

Few tried to make femininity an asset in a campaign probably
because it is very difficult to do so. Several said that they believed
emphasizing their femininity to be the best strategy for a woman
running for office. They spoke, however, of style. A woman, they
thought, should act like a lady and not emulate male politicians. No
one proposed emphasizing women's issues or welding women into a
power base—as Jews, Italians, Irish, Chinese often serve as a power
base for their candidates of kind.

It is clear that in their quest for nomination and election many
encountered resistance and problems because they were women. In
some places, party leaders manfully resisted the nomination of a
woman. The grounds were always that a woman would run less well
than a man. Other would-be female legislators encountered an insulting incredulity. Some were explicitly attacked as women by campaign opponents—"It takes a man to do a man's job."

Many of the women in this study perceived women to be at some
disadvantage in politics. Only one-fifth think women have as much
chance as men to become leaders. Slightly over half believe that men
in party organizations try to keep women out of leadership positions,
and an equal number agree that many voters will not vote for women
candidates. But the slurs and problems they encountered were not
ultimately disabling. They won. The attitudes expressed by so many
of the women about the role of sex identity in recruitment and
campaigning are as interesting as the facts themselves. Their comments reveal the same fascinating gap between perception and reaction as in descriptions of legislative experience. They perceive
themselves as somewhat discriminated against—as women, and they
deny that it *really* matters much. Between the perception and the
response something intervenes that prevents feeling what might be

considered "normal" resentment. This gap between provocation and response is fascinating and perhaps important.

There have been subtle changes in recent years affecting how femininity should be dealt with in a campaign. In the past women more frequently felt compelled to persuade voters that they could be as rational as men. Three of the women mentioned that formerly they used to say that, "I can work like a horse and think like a man," but that "I wouldn't be caught dead saying that now." Several assert that, "I don't see myself as running as a female candidate at all." "I never campaign as a woman or as a black, I just try to be myself." Still, like the woman who made the above remark, they know "too much aggressiveness is not acceptable in a woman."

Others felt that it was desirable to emphasize their femininity. "You cannot be a woman who is trying to be a man. You've got to be yourself and if you are a woman, you have to stay a woman and be proud of being a woman." One highly successful and ambitious woman said, "I work overtime at being feminine in every way in actions and in manner of speech."

Some choose campaign "gimmicks" that emphasize their femininity. One distributed thimbles; two others passed out cards with good recipes on one side and their qualifications on the other. One claimed to have a new slogan that emphasized both her sex and age: "Get off your fanny and vote for granny." Mostly they didn't think too much about it. Comfortable in their sexual identity, they simply moved forward without much self-consciousness.

Almost all are convinced that women have assets as well as liabilities in campaigns. People are nicer to you, they think. People trust them more. People are more ready to believe they are honest and unselfish, and more understanding than a man is likely to be. Opponents sometimes try to use sex against them. Two men in the interviews ran on the slogan "Elect a man to do a man's job." But men opposing women were unlikely to attack frontally, the way they might attack another man because, "Even the most hardened bigot, remembering his mother, will react unfavorably to a man when he is ungracious to a woman." The rarity of women candidates can also be an asset. It distinguishes the woman from other candidates and helps her make an impression. Being a woman is not an unmitigated liability though few doubted that it posed special problems. The problems are thought to be especially acute for young women. "If you look too young and you are a woman then they think you have babies at home and that you should be home taking care of the babies."

One woman in her early thirties with two young children provides a vivid description of these problems.

> The biggest threat for a woman is posed by other women, especially women in my own age group. They would say, "She has a handsome husband and a beautiful home, three nice children, and she practices law. What more does she want?" They feel that if they say it is all right for her to be in politics—which they view as a glamorous job—it somehow lessens their own role as homemaker. Also they think they couldn't fit it into their lives—which include playing bridge and making bread and going to the store and all that sort of thing, therefore, they think if she finds time for politics it must be her children are neglected. This was very frustrating. . . .
>
> Well I sat back and I thought, "Well, now, you're going to have to sell yourself to these women, so first of all how do you do it?" Well, first I tell them the story of my life. Then you have to convince them why you are doing this. Not because you think it's a glamorous job, but because everyone has a responsibility to government and you feel that. Which I believe to be true. Then in some way you have to convince them that you are not deserting your family.
>
> I did not sense this attitude from older women. Older women were always quick to come up and say, "I think this is good that you are running for office." Now I realize that they had reached a stage in their lives when they are no longer competitive for or with anyone and they knew something was missing but they didn't know what it was.
>
> So I go to women of my own age group and say, "I want you to think about something very carefully. Now you are antagonistic to me but if I came to you and said, 'Let me be your school teacher, or let me be your nurse,' you would think that is fine. And there are a good many of you that have spent more time than I have out of the home. But the reason you are resenting it isn't really because of my children, it is because you think that the job is glamorous and it is jealousy and it is a threat to you and it shouldn't be that way. Being a school teacher takes just as much dedication and probably more time because your time is structured. Well, as a politician I have more freedom to run my life and still be the places I have to be." And usually it works.

The older women with children who are grown or nearly grown do not face this problem, but the situation of the younger woman is very important to the future influence of women in politics, since if women are to get to the top, they must start early.

One respondent suggested that black women were exempt from many of the problems of acceptability that plague white females. Their long tradition of working outside the home, of shouldering economic burdens, and of frequently assuming the responsibility for the family, reduce the sense of social shock felt when they offer to perform one more role that traditional dominant culture defines as male. This may relieve the black woman of part of the special problems confronted by other women seeking public office. It seems unlikely, though, that it relieves them entirely of the need to "deal" with their sex as a factor in a campaign.

On Winning and Losing

Obviously the women in this study eventually won a seat in the legislature. But, as we have seen, not all won the first time they ran. About one-fourth have at some time lost a legislative election. Two lost their initial elections, two lost when they tried to move to the Senate, several lost a race after winning, then ran again. Losing holds no terror for them. The same high self-esteem which gives them a generalized expectation of success armors them against failure. Frequently, it is reinforced by "avoidance" defenses which block out awareness-threatening interpretations of events.

All these women are achievement oriented, and some are explicitly competitive; none like to lose, but they are not terrified by the prospect nor destroyed by the experience. The ability to lose is a key characteristic of politicians as is the capacity to bear conflict. The capacity to lose without being psychologically destroyed or crippled requires, above all, *a high opinion of the self which is not basically vulnerable to the response of voters.*

This does not necessarily imply self-esteem invulnerable to the opinion of others, only that the fundamental evaluation of the self is not at stake in all interpersonal relations. The attitudes of husband, children, or others related by ties of intimacy may be very important—even crucial—to the self-confidence of these women. But the reactions of constituents are not threatening to their self-esteem. The capacity to have positive, pleasant relations with others without a large (and therefore dangerous) psychological investment is a fundamental requisite for participation in democratic politics. More than a strong ego is involved. The capacity for "purposive socializing" also requires the ability to withhold a portion of the self, to limit empathy, subordinate interactions to goals while sensitively responding to the cues of others. There are, of course, psychological characteristics associated with "manipulative" and with "functional" human relationships. They are the psychological bases of the infamous "public" personalities of politicians. It is doubtful that without these ego-defenses any political actor could or would run for office except by accident. Offensive as they are to the philosophers of existential encounter, these traits exist in all functioning adults (a life of total vulnerability to others being quite simply unbearable and unlivable). They are found in higher degree in successful politicians. They enable the politician to seek the approval (votes) of multiple others at a bearable level of risk.

Responses to the questionnaire indicate self–consciousness about the ability to risk losing and failure. Almost three-fourths say they do not get very upset when they fail at something they try. Four-fifths deny that it is difficult for them to overcome disappointment.[6] Most indicate that they have ready interpretations of loss which define it as irrelevant to basic self-estimates.

Losing is bearable but winning is better. The women in this study enjoy winning, but they do not enjoy it too much. Two of them probably get intrinsic pleasure from conflict. The remainder participate in the competition that campaigns entail as means to ends other than winning. After a hard, often grueling campaign, victory seems to most just reward for hard work.

There is no evidence either that winning per se enhances self–esteem, it seems to be interpreted as proof of skill and industry, not of loveableness.

NOTES

1. For a study of congressional campaigning, see David A. Leuthold, *Electioneering in a Democracy* (New York: Wiley, 1968). See also Lewis A. Froman, Jr., "A Realistic Approach to Campaign Strategies and Tactics," in *The Electoral Process*, ed. M. Kent Jennings and L. Harmon Ziegler (Englewood Cliffs, N. J.: Prentice Hall, 1966). On campaigning for the state legislature, see John W. Kingdon, *Candidates for Office: Beliefs and Strategies* (New York: Random House, 1958).

2. Malcolm E. Jewell and Samuel C. Patterson, *The Legislative Process in the United States*, 2nd ed. (New York: Random House, 1972), p. 133.

3. Jewell and Patterson's comments on the wide variation in campaign costs indicate that

the variations among the amounts expended by the women in this sample are normal for legislative campaigns. Ibid., p. 134.

4. Donald R. Matthews, *U.S. Senators and Their World* (Chapel Hill: University of North Carolina Press, 1960), p. 69.

5. James David Barber, *The Lawmakers: Recruitment and Adaptation to Legislative Life* (New Haven: Yale University Press, 1965), p. 55.

6. I am not speaking of the ability to risk and bear up under defeat as a moral quality but as a psychological one. The diverse elements in an election bear to some extent the personal factor. Party, issues, timing also influence the outcome and prevent an election from being a clear-cut referendum on an individual. Still, everyone understands that voters choose between people, too.

Chapter VI

Women in a Man's World

"WHAT'S a nice lady like you doing in a place like this?" Not a few students of state governments have said that the political culture of the state house resembles that of a locker room. Their point is not merely that legislators are overwhelmingly male. Men's Sunday School classes are also male, but they do not—normally—share the *macho* culture of the locker room, the smoker, the barracks. Apparently state legislatures do. Describing the Pennsylvania legislature, Sorauf asserts, "Legislative chambers in the states often bear the signs of the male club, and a woman legislator may be viewed as an intruder into smoking room company."[1] Epstein confirms the same in Wisconsin. "There is an atmosphere of the male club about a legislative body which is discouraging and difficult for women to appreciate (and to be appreciated in)."[2] Among the folkways of state legislatures none appears to be more widely shared than the tradition of the *masculine* legislature.

Perceptions of reality are a function of expectations as well as events. The failure of a group of men to invite a woman to go out on the town, for example, may be (1) ignored entirely, (2) interpreted as a mark of respect, or (3) interpreted as rejection. The evening itself may be perceived as either (1) relevant to legislative business, or (2) irrelevant. Demands on the self also influence perception, interpretation, and description. A demand that one be "positive" in thinking about events and people (and a number of these women make this demand on themselves) can lead to ignoring and/or redefining, and/or forgetting or denying "negative" events and feelings provoked by them. The expectations and demands an individual brings to a situation greatly influence the accuracy with which events are perceived and the direction in which they are distorted.

These remarks constitute a preface to the discussion of women's

106

view of how they are perceived and treated by men in the legislatures. No claim is made that the women in this sample accurately
and fully described "how it is" for a woman in the legislature. But
attitudes and beliefs are an important part of the reality of interpersonal relations. How women feel that men feel about them affects
their relations with others in legislative halls.

This chapter is devoted to exploring and describing how women
who managed to get the voters' endorsement win a place for
themselves in this man's world.

Crashing the Gates

A woman entering a men's club is confronted by a myriad of subtle
and not so subtle patterns of speech and behavior that underline her
status as that of interloper. "Off color" stories and rapid apologies,
invocations that ask divine blessings only on the "men assembled
here," the men only lounges define a woman as "outsider." "They
never even had toilet facilities for women" reports one woman who
was first elected in 1955 to the legislature of a northern, urban state.

In a salutary effort to correct the accumulated errors of previous
formal, legal analyses, recent work on legislatures has stressed
informal aspects of legislative behavior. The convention has developed of likening a legislature to a club. The analogy is useful to illuminate formerly neglected aspects of legislatures. However, it is important, too, to know where the resemblance stops.

A legislature differs from a private club in some key respects. There
is no membership committee that examines, accepts, and rejects ap-
plicants for membership. That crucial function is performed by the
many nonmembers who comprise the electorate. Not only can a
legislature *not* control its membership; it also cannot define its functions—these are set down in constitutions. For the performance of
these functions, legislators are responsible to their constituents.
There are no life memberships granted in these "clubs." Perhaps the
most important difference between a legislature and a private club is
that legislature is—or clearly should be—a working body, not a social
group.

A legislature is the patterned interactions of persons chosen by popular vote to perform some rather specific and limited functions: mainly, to make and revise authoritative rules for the state. The relatively clear, limited purposes for which legislators meet give their interactions a goal oriented, functional cast. The rule making function does not itself preclude feminine participation, though in most cultures there is a formal (legal) or informal presumption that males are best qualified for authoritative roles. But, in the U.S., women are qualified to participate in the functions of the legislature in principle and in law. Students of institutional behavior know, though, that whatever their missions, institutions develop lives of their own— bodies of procedure, norms and corporate interests. And students of human behavior know that people bring to goal-oriented tasks personal needs, wants, styles, preferences. Institutional and idiosyncratic factors always shape and color goal-oriented interactions.

To be an effective legislator it is never enough to be elected. Each legislator must win a place and a name for herself, establish her credibility and her authority. The women interviewed in this study are in substantial agreement about how this can be done. There is somewhat less agreement about the emotional and symbolic environment in which it must be done. Specifically, there is more agreement about how to make one's way than about the degree of male prejudice encountered in the effort.

Not all report that they were treated as "strange creatures," or "delicate flowers," or just ignored. A few, especially black women and white conservatives, feel that they were "welcomed" and "assisted" beyond the call of duty. Many, however, say that their initial welcome was wary and less than warm, not exactly unfriendly, but not friendly either. Memories of the first months in the legislature include a good many symbolic rebuffs.

Symbolic Putdowns

My very first day, the Speaker introduced me to the House, referring to me as "the sweetheart of the chamber." Apparently, there had been a woman in the House previously who just loved to be called the Sweetheart of the Senate. I got the Speaker off to one side and I said, "Now look here, I do not ever want to hear that again," And I never have. or:

When I first arrived I got very disturbed because three days in a row the chaplain of the House referred only to men in his prayer, and there were four women present. So finally after the third day this happened, I went into the hall after he got done and I had got to the point where I couldn't take it any more and I went out and I told him, "pardon me Reverend, but there are four women in this assembly and I would advise you not to leave us out again."

In entering the legislature women are defying conventional expectations; they are role deviants and so should expect to be met with reluctance and disbelief. And they are.

The socially conservative women on whom this study is based describe again and again symbolic putdowns with which they are greeted. These fall into several categories:

1. *Excluding:* Some linguistic conventions define women as outside the group. Every reference to the "men of the house," to the legislator as "he," excludes women. So do "male" jokes and "male" profanity from which the women are carefully guarded.

2. *Killing with kindness:* "In the beginning I was submitted to the most subtle form of put down. It is over-chivalrous, over-protected, over-courteous, and you're sort of bowed to and scraped to when you first come in. You are given first choice of a seat, then other members get seats in the order of seniority. You're treated like a very bright child." Elaborate courtesy, exaggerated courtesy, public flirtation all may be used as or felt to be devices for excluding women from equal and professional status. The "Sweetheart" or "darling of the house" is *not* an equal participant.

3. *Emphasizing Differences:* Women can also be excluded from full membership in the society of legislators by being perceived as having interests so limited and/or specialized that they are—by nature—excluded from much of the business and discussion of the house.

4. *Putting Women in Their Place:* Another way of putting women down is through explicitly insulting, rejecting remarks, such as: "I can't stand smart women, they scare me"; "You should be in the kitchen not the Senate."

These interviews with women who are *not* hostile to males leave little doubt about the existence of a pervasive initial reluctance in many legislators to take women seriously and accept them as colleagues. This initial reluctance is impersonal, conventional, and especially strong among older legislators.

Does it matter? What difference does it make if the chaplain blesses only the men, if a legislator announces on the floor of the house, "I like women to be cuddly and kissable and smell good"? (The legislator reporting this remark said that she replied "Well that is just the way I feel about men.")

Doubtless, women with weaker egos, with more need for affection and approval from their environment, would be sufficiently hurt by such treatment that their effectiveness would suffer. Women with greater demands for inclusion and greater vulnerability would doubtless be enraged, and rage would impair their effectiveness. But, already accustomed to winning friends, influencing people, overcoming obstacles, most of these women regard the doubts and even the slights of their male colleagues as one more problem to be dealt with—not as a threat to themselves or their effectiveness. Nearly half believe that a woman has as much chance as a man to become an influential legislator, and most of the others think that even though most women are bypassed a few outstanding women can achieve influence. Only one thinks it nearly impossible for a woman to become influential.

Because they have strong egos and are not seeking love from their colleagues, because they have lived their lives among men like those in the legislature and do not hate them, most of these legislators shrug off verbal slights and exclusions and get on with the job of winning the respect and credibility of their male colleagues.

Learning the Ropes

There is no sex based difference in reports about how to "make it" in a legislature. The comments of these women make it abundantly clear that they see the task very much as previous studies report it is seen by males. It is necessary to get acquainted with fellow legislators, to learn who's who among them; to develop friendships and alliances, to gain acceptance and respect. It is necessary to learn the rules of the game in the legislature—the process and procedures. It is essential, too, to become acquainted with the resources available to legislators. One legislator put it this way:

If one is to be a good and effective legislator when she first arrives in the legislature, she must listen, work, study, learn. She must find out where the power structures are; where the effective people operate. Who the effective people are—not only in the legislature but among the auxiliary resources because there are many clerks, lobbyists, researchers and others who can help you tremendously and are really quite a source of power. The first term you can't hope to be effective, but you can prepare yourself to be effective.

Another described the initial task this way:

Getting to know other legislators, number one, you learn how friendly you ought to be with them. You learn their habits and their attitudes and what their interests are and how you want to approach them if you want them to help you support a bill and how touchy they are.

And then you've just got to learn about the legislative process. I was fortunate in having a friend—a man—who helped me over the first few weeks. I am sure he kept me from stumbling.

I moved cautiously . . . I didn't just go busting in.

I believe I have won the confidence of most people in the House—that I am respected.

The experience of the freshman legislator is in some respects like that of a freshman congressman. She is expected not to be too "forward," not to speak too often or too insistently. If she is wise and wants to get ahead she will show her respect for those with experience.

Strong party organization and observance of party discipline can simplify these tasks for new individual legislators, but few state houses have the strong organizations and habits of party discipline that enable an individual legislator to rely on the party to point the way, clear a path, make room. Party leadership and party ties play a role, but the individual remains to an important degree on her own.

It is probably easier to make one's way in a state legislature than in the Congress. The high turnover of legislators affects patterns of interpersonal relations, the flexibility of the structures, and the task of winning acceptance. The rate of turnover in most states assures a degree of flux in interpersonal alliances not characteristic of bodies whose membership is more stable. With each election, a good number of newcomers present themselves at the state house. Because there are many newcomers, they are not isolated. Because turnover is high, a variety of assignments stand vacant. Because the average tenure of state legislatures is low, there is more chance to make a place for oneself in a relatively short time. And in addition to high turnover and short tenure, short sessions, low pay, and the generally non-professional character of most legislatures narrow the gap between newcomers and others—most of whom are amateur lawmakers.[3]

The situation of a woman entering a state legislature is difficult, but not as difficult as it might be; not as difficult as the situation of a woman entering the Congress. Many of the problems she will face are the same as those faced by a man entering the legislature: he, too, needs to master rules, learn his way around, make alliances. Her task is, or is generally believed to be, somewhat more complicated and somewhat more difficult.

Several women feel they got a good deal of help from their male colleagues in their first session—help well beyond the requirements of civility. A black woman commented:

> It may be that it takes women longer to be accepted, and that a woman can never get quite as chummy with her colleagues. Still, they all welcomed me. They made me feel needed.
>
> I had no instance of discourtesy or anything that was unpleasant and I had instances of helpful support from some people who hadn't known me and had no reason to be helpful except they were.

Functioning Effectively

"Well, first, you don't have to be loved to be effective. Anyway, once they learn that you're serious and work hard, there's no problem," said one doughty distaff legislator when asked how a woman can become an effective legislator.

Sex is an ascriptive characteristic—like hair color, body build, family name; and a legislature is a task oriented institution. In a modern legislature, we are told, it is performance that counts.

What is effective performance? More specifically, what constitutes effective performance in the view of these women legislators? What do they believe to be the requirements for success? Are there special rules for women? Do they have an outsider's perspective on the life of the legislature? Is there a "feminine" perception of a legislature? Do they see the "rules of the game" as male legislators see them? Are these "male" rules, devised by and for men, and uncomfortable for women? These are interesting questions never yet explored. The following pages are devoted to discussing the feminine view of legislative norms.

Legislative norms state collective expectations about the appropriate behavior of legislators in the conduct of their jobs. They define obligations and prohibitions; conformity to them is normally a precondition to effective functioning. Largely unwritten, these norms prescribe how members shall—and shall not—treat one another, how they shall—and shall not—behave on the floor and in committees.

Patterns of behavior become institutionalized because they facilitate the accomplishment of purposes. Legislative norms serve multiple purposes: they facilitate and smooth interpersonal relations; they communicate (and regulate) the identity of formal and informal hierarchies and the standards of etiquette appropriate to them; they diffuse conflict. They state demands and prescriptions. Many subsequent studies have confirmed Wahlke, Eulau, Buchanan and Ferguson's comment, "Understanding of rules of the game is sufficiently important that the individual legislator's possession of it will affect the part he plays in the legislative process."[4]

Since norms are largely the product of habit and experience, they deal with collective, recurring events. Because women legislators have been few, it is to be expected that few norms will explicitly concern relations between male and female legislators. And such turns out to be the case. In these tradition conscious bodies there exist few guidelines and little precedent to guide the wary. Should a man stand when a female colleague enters the committee room? Most women give a firm no to this conventional courtesy. Should a woman pay her own check when out to dinner with a male colleague? Most women think so. Should female legislators permit male committee chairmen to excuse them from such indelicate tasks as visiting a sewage disposal plant? Female legislators say never. Should a woman permit the men to open doors for her? (Of course.) To buy her a drink? (Occasionally.) To hold her coat? (Don't be silly.)

What kind of restraints, if any, are needed to stave off gossip and safeguard a reputation? Should a married woman legislator be escorted by a married male? Should a woman join her colleagues at a night club? Under what circumstances? May she drink with them? Should she insist that they demonstrate respect by "guarding" their language? One woman precipitated discussion as well as laughter when she stated her guiding rule. "Never enter a room with a bed in it." Others, pointing to their age and long standing marriages, disagreed. Age, they say, eases the problems of male/female association because men are more "comfortable" with women of middle age. However, most believe that common sense and normal discretion are adequate guides to conduct. It was emphasized, however, that "feminine" wiles are out. Tears, batting eyelashes, feigned helplessness are intrinsically out of place in a legislature, they think. Furthermore, they don't work. "Behavior," Eulau has told us, "including legislative behavior, is meaningful socially only when it occurs in the performance of appropriate roles." [5] There are no "feminine" roles in a contemporary legislature, and stereotypical "feminine" behavior is neither meaningful nor effective. Each woman works out for herself a formula for dealing with males as equals in these task-centered institutions and as long as her practices do not violate conventional sensibilities, her personal preferences will probably be honored.

One of the sex specific problems faced by women in entering the legislature is to communicate her expectations and demands. Since the legislators have little or no experience in dealing with women as working colleagues, they are frequently uncertain in their behavior, and transfer to the legislative arena habits of social and verbal deference. The result is "elaborate politeness" described by many. It is up to the woman to make clear the inappropriateness of such behavior. There is wide agreement that women must accept no special treatment and ask no special favors. One woman who has established a reputation for leadership describes the first step in developing easy relations with her colleagues.

I'll never forget the day I walked into the party caucus in the Senate, all those men stood up and I said, sit down. I asked for a point of personal privilege. I said I don't want any special privileges. I'll take my lumps with each of you, but by the same token I want my share and I don't necessarily want it out of the middle, I just want what's coming to me, and they have been just great. I haven't had any problem at all.

The more important rules of conduct described by these women as governing personal relations among legislators turn out to be those already familiar from previous studies of legislative behavior. They prescribe friendliness, consideration, integrity, and modesty and are, we are told, the same for women as for men. Each has a specific meaning and function in the legislative process.[6]

Friendliness

"Always be friendly," said one legislator, commenting on the requirements for acceptance and success. "Friendly" relations should be maintained within a committee, a delegation, a party caucus, and it is expected that they will transcend party lines and ideological divisions.

Friendliness in the legislature does not imply *friendship*. To the contrary, legislative friendliness is normally relatively impersonal. It implies neither intimacy, nor personal vulnerability, nor exchange of confidences. It entails no strong personal commitment. But it is more than ritual courtesy. Friendliness entails a basically warm and positive attitude toward fellow legislators. It includes respect, courtesy, tact, empathy and cooperation. The friendly relations that characterize legislators is similar to the friendly interpersonal relations that help bind party and campaign organizations. Indeed political activity in the U.S. is characterized at all levels by a kind of ubiquitous purposive friendliness lacking in societies with less mobility and more formal, vertical relations. This type of generalized non-intimate friendliness is highly functional for organizations. It stimulates cooperation, limits personal competitiveness and combativeness, depersonalizes disagreements and generally expedites the work of the legislature. It serves the same function as the careful decorum observed on the floor of the Congress or the British Parliament.

Friendliness usually includes participating in some social activities outside the legislature. But how much? The importance of after-hours socializing to the work of the legislative bodies is rather heavily emphasized, especially in journalistic and anecdotal accounts. One of the disabilities believed to be suffered by women legislators is exclusion from these extracurricular activities. Information on the legislators' attitudes toward and participation in such activities was sought in the interviews: the resultant picture of the social lives of female legislators is best described as mixed. A few women *never* socialize with their colleagues as a matter of principle. For them, after-hours socializing is associated with liquor, lobbies and deals—all disapproved. "I don't smoke and I don't drink and I go home to my husband," commented one upright legislator. "Why would I want to spend my time fooling around in bars with lobbyists when I can be at home with my family?" said another.

Views such as these come as something of a surprise from women who have made their way into "men's" roles. They remind us how varied are the personal styles of public figures, and how recently the private virtue and public acceptibility of women (and to a somewhat lesser extent of men) was associated with Temperance Leagues and King Alcohol with public corruption.

Others among the women—and they are much more numerous—participate to some extent in the social life of the legislature. This social life is obviously varied—and includes quasi-official occasions when a whole committee has dinner together, lobbyists receptions, private dinners and cocktail parties, and evenings "out on the town." Nothing in these interviews suggests that state legislators' social lives approximate popular images of revelry. For one who takes his legislative job seriously, life in the legislative session is clearly *not* an endless round of parties and entertainment. Still most of the women interviewed in this project believe there is a good deal of informal getting-together after hours, that the business of the legislature is discussed in these informal social groups, and that it is useful to participate. "It is," said one woman, "when people relax and say what they mean. You get to know them better; you can establish relations of trust more easily." Several others refer to such participation as "indispensable" to gaining influence in the legislature.

Not surprisingly, it is the social life of the legislature that most closely resembles the male club.[7] Because it is oriented to relaxation and enjoyment rather than to work, socializing provides greater scope for sex specific behavior. "In the beginning I was only rarely invited to go along with some of them after we finished for the day. So during the first session I went to the functions that everyone attended but not besides. Since then I'm almost always invited." Still a good many women are invited to go along with groups of males after hours. Several comment that if they go—"It is important to know when to say no—not to go along if they're going out for an evening 'with the boys.' " Personal restraint and lack of an invitation limit the social activities of most. A very few appear to have themselves become "one of the boys" and feel no constraints. The extent of participation varies with circumstances, as well as personal preference and social acceptability. Women (and men) who live in the capital city or commute to the legislature spend less time getting together for fun. Those who live in the capital during the session spend more. In several states two or more of the women in the legislature share apartments near the capitol, and entertain fellow legislators on a regular basis.

The relationship between socializing and legislative effectiveness is ambiguous. The evidence suggests that, though helpful, participation in the social life of the legislature is not essential to establishing a position of power in the body. One of the most influential of the legislators in this study doesn't drink, doesn't smoke, and doesn't fraternize. Others among the most influential engage in limited after-hours social life. The latter point out that the limits on their participation are self-imposed. "I am welcome, I am free to join them if I want to. The speaker pro tem has a very nice suite and after every session a whole group goes in there and has drinks. But I don't drink. I mean I may have *a* drink, but that is about it. They sit there and drink until eight-thirty or nine o'clock, I am hungry and I want to go on out to dinner. But I do go in on occasion because I know you get a lot of information because the men do talk more freely there. And when I do go in, I am perfectly welcome." Two of the most influential women say that they participate fully in the after-hours social life and regard it as indispensable. "You get as much done off the floor as you do on it," said one, adding "I try not to let the night go by that I don't go to see somebody or talk to somebody on the telephone."

However, there is near complete consensus that it is *not* necessary to be "one of the boys" in order to be effective and influential in the work of the legislature. Eulau's conclusion about the role of after-hours activities expresses fairly the views of nearly all these women. "To sum up, we may say that the political roles of a legislator, as a member of a party, an officer of the chamber, or chairman of a committee, are more compelling than his social role as a friend, a good fellow, and a dinner companion." [8]

Like friendliness generally, socializing involves more comradeship than intimacy. It is a style of personal relations thought to be more characteristic of males than females; and probably more attractive to them. Few of the women in this study sound as though they very much enjoy the social activities surrounding legislative life. Neither are they repelled by it. A good many—though not all—have developed close relations with one or more female colleagues. These relationships are more personal, more intimate, more in the famous "feminine" style of friendliness.

Consideration and Integrity

Consideration and integrity too are aspects of interpersonal relations directly relevant to effective legislative performance. Consideration involves taking account of others in the planning and conduct of legislative behavior. It means checking with fellow committee members, clearing plans with leadership and other interested parties. It means consulting with all those who have an interest in a bill or a proceeding, and, where appropriate, coordinating efforts. It means giving advance notice and scheduling discussions at times when all those concerned can participate. And it is more. To be considerate a legislator must be ready to oblige the reasonable requests of his colleagues, to be sensitive to their legitimate needs, not to make unreasonable demands of them. Habitual consideration across party lines and ideological divisions softens disagreements on policy and helps to prevent partisan differences from developing into schisms. Important, too, are its softening effects on interpersonal irritations and animosities, the potential for which is present in every group, perhaps especially in political arenas where private purposes and public goals clash daily.

Personal integrity also has crucial legislative functions. To "do business" with each other, legislators must be able to count on the good faith and responsibility of their colleagues. Keeping one's word is important, but integrity, in its legislative context, involves more: declining to exploit one's colleagues, refusing to take unfair advantage or mislead, are part of integrity. They are crucial to the limited trust which members of a committee, for example, must have in one another to work effectively together.

Consideration does not require "dealing" with fellow legislators—trading votes on bills of special interest to each party. But neither does integrity forbid it. It does require that deals must be "square" deals in which both parties are fully and accurately informed and it requires, too, that, once made, deals be honored.

Women in this study have differing attitudes about "dealing." Some denounce vote trading as a species of irresponsibility. Others say they practice it only with reluctance and in situations of extreme need. "I have trouble wheeling and dealing and trading votes. It bothers my conscience." Many, however, see it as one more way of aggregating and compromising interests.

"Dealing" with integrity requires the same reliable honesty and accuracy needed for other legislative relationships.

Effective functioning does not require that a legislator accept as final the analysis of a colleague. But a committee in which *no* member could trust the "facts" reported by any other member is a committee which could never perform its function. Accuracy, decency, honesty, fairness, responsibility are all aspects of the "integrity" which members of the legislature require of one another—male or female.

Modesty

The informal rules which prescribe acceptable behavior for legislators serve, among other purposes, to limit idiosyncrasy, tame competition and conflict and to police tendencies to self–aggrandizement. The latter, believed to be especially strong among politicians, is discouraged by powerful if unwritten prohibitions against various forms of exhibitionism. Speaking too frequently or too long is apparently frowned on in all state houses. Though the public often perceives talking as the chief business of the legislature, members know otherwise. Learning *not* to talk—in committee and, especially, on the floor—is one of the chief lessons awaiting the freshman legislator. She who speaks only when she has specific knowledge of a subject under discussion will be listened to and respected. Not so her more garrulous colleague.

Modesty also forbids noisily or inappropriately claiming credit; "grandstanding" or pretending to expertise which is not in fact possessed. The legislator must learn to listen as well as to talk, respond as well as initiate. Modesty is not to be confused with submissiveness or acquiescence or weakness. It does not forbid a member from demonstrating mastery of a subject, providing this is done discretely, nor from demonstrating political strength ("muscle") in an acceptable manner.

Freshmen legislators are confronted by especially high requirements for modesty. The freshman is expected to listen, observe, work and learn. She will seek help and advice from those with more experience and speak even less than others.

One third-term legislator describes learning this rule the hard way.

I introduced too much legislation for a freshman. I introduced bills on welfare reform and consumer protection and civil rights and women. I had them ready to go at swearing-in time and I was just waiting to go into the bill room, and that really turned everybody off. They were all my bills. I had no co-introducers and they all felt that I was really pushing too hard, trying to do all this without consultation. Then I learned, I have to do it with them. I have to bring them along. I cannot just ramrod things through. I know now that I can't get an individual bill passed. I have to sell a whole committee. I learned that passing a bill is going to be their thing and not my thing.

Modesty is also believed to be especially important for women. Aggressiveness and exhibitionism are unacceptable in both women and men but in women they are judged with special harshness. Several of the most influential women refer to their practice of not claiming credit for all the bills they in fact work out and introduce. "I care not," said one, "who, in the house, gets credit for the passage of legislation in which I am interested," and added, "I feel that as a woman I don't have to be out on the front line. Credit can go to others. What matters is getting the legislation through." Before, however, concluding that this woman hides her light under a basket, it is well to note that enough credit seeps through to have made her a power of first rank in her legislature.

The instituationalized norms of interpersonal behavior characteristic of American legislatures do not pose special difficulties for women. At least not to these women of large experience. They see nothing particularly "masculine" about the ritualized courtesy, friendliness, modesty and careful consideration with which legislators are expected to treat one another as they go about their work. Nor do the approved patterns of feeling among legislators create special problems for these women. Ultimately it is probably not possible to treat one's colleagues in the prescribed fashion without respecting them. These women do respect their colleagues. Many had a good opinion of legislators before they were elected and have not been disappointed. Others who came to the state house with a lower regard for its inhabitants describe their surprise and growing respect in learning that sincerity, hard work, and a genuine regard for the public good are so widely shared. It is no surprise that those with the strongest ideological bent have the lowest opinion of the other legislators, and that a high opinion of one's colleagues generally coexists with a high opinion of one's constituents—and vice versa.

There is massive evidence in these interviews that women can establish good working relations in legislatures providing that they are willing to live by the rules. Since most of these rules are similar to those that these women have already internalized in years of civic and party activity, conforming comes naturally.

They perceive interpersonal relations as a dimension of the job. Since good relations with colleagues facilitate the job performance, maintaining them is part of doing the job. It is not the equivalent of seeking affection. Only four women in this study seem oriented chiefly to being "liked" and approved; the remainder, while not indifferent to their fellow legislators have a fundamentally instrumental orientation to interpersonal relations. For them, being respected is more important than being liked.

That virtually all believe they have succeeded in establishing the desired relations with colleagues is one more measure of their self-confident approach to life.[9] From the data available in this study it is impossible to know whether these women see themselves as others see them. However, how they see themselves as viewed by others is itself an interesting measure of their perception of the social world and is suggestive of their orientation to it. It is also a powerful indicator of their feelings of efficacy.

The following comments describe their perception of how they are perceived in their legislatures. The comments prove that (with only four exceptions) these women are convinced that they have established good working relations with their peers. Some think they are respected chiefly for political reasons, that is, for the harm they might do; others chiefly for their moral strength and/or personal qualities; most, however, are convinced they are respected for their effectiveness. Together these comments constitute impressive evidence (1) of the transference to the legislative sphere of generalized attitudes of self-esteem and efficacy, and (2) of the fact that these women see their environments as fundamentally friendly.

Emphasis on Political Strength

"I know that I am respected and influential."

"I think they like me but also fear me. They know I am very positive and can be obnoxious."

"They know they must take account of me because I will cause trouble if they don't."

Emphasis on Moral Strength

"I believe they respect me because they know I am genuinely interested in public service."

"People know where I stand, and that I stand on principle. They respect me for it."

"I know I have a reputation of being honest and a fighter for what's right."

"They fear my sense of conviction."

Emphasis on Expertise

"They respect me because I always have the facts."

"They know when I stand up to talk, I know whereof I speak and they like me for it."

"I am accepted as having great competence in my field."

"Everyone knows that I am very knowledgeable in committees."

"All of us know we are quite competent in our own fields . . . others know I am, too."

"They had to be educated to the fact that I am as competent in that field as they. Now they know that."

Emphasis on Personal Qualities
"I have very good rapport with other legislators."
"I know I relate well to people and they like me."
"I know I am trusted and respected."
"I am thought to be sensible and hard worker."

Emphasis on Being Likeable
"I know that I am well liked."
"People like me in spite of themselves."
"The others like me because they like to have me come along."
"I know the other members of my committees like me, and that's very important."

Emphasis on General Effectiveness
"I am one of the more effective members and people know that."
"I get tremendous support."
"Everyone respects me because I get things done."
"They know that I work hard and have an impact."
"I think they rate me very high as a legislator."
"Everyone knows that I am effective in getting things done."
"They know I get my bills through."

Not Well Regarded
"Others take advantage of my work because they don't think I will fight it."
"I think there's still a lot of hostility on the part of the uneducated and the bigots."
"Some people who support the vested interests just can't stand me."
"I can't accomplish much in that legislature because they're so shortsighted."

In summary we can say that with very few exceptions, these women not only feel that it is possible to win professional acceptance and cooperation of their male colleagues, they are convinced that they have done so. They do *not* feel caught in the double bind described by numerous contemporary feminists. They would not agree, for example, that "Women at work, women trying to make careers for themselves in fields where they have to mix with men, are conspicuously caught in the 'damned if you do and damned if you don't' vise created by this attitude."[10] Neither have "learned to play the game" described by that author as involving "Quiet acceptance, withdrawal from competition, and behind the scenes fuming."[11] To the contrary, they believe, and many of them demonstrate, that a reasonable, persistent, hardworking woman can develop good working relationships with male colleagues in the heavily "masculine" institution of a state legislature. Perhaps they have few problems with interpersonal relations because these are not their primary concern. This is a hypothesis to which we shall return later.

One special strain on these good relations relates to women's rights. Half a dozen legislators volunteered comments that becoming active on a "woman's" issue such as the Equal Rights Amendment introduced a strain into their otherwise excellent relations with male colleagues.

> In my first two terms I tended to introduce things, based on my experience, on education, and county government, and on the environment. I got really very generous and gracious help from fellow legislators in getting them passed. But last year I became a member of the status of women committee and joined in sponsoring bills trying to remove some of the discrimination women encounter in various areas—especially employment. I detected a clear change in attitude of men whom I considered good friends whenever one of these sex discrimination bills came up. It was almost as if I were a dentist probing a nerve. It is a sensitive area. And then the Equal Rights Amendment came up. I am still bruised from that experience, It's terrible—you introduce a perfectly good bill dealing with perfectly clear-cut kinds of discrimination and some don't even treat it seriously. It was treated with ridicule, off-color jokes, sarcastic remarks and rather lewd humor. Most of the opponents did not address themselves to the merits at all but just kept up a machine-gun fire of hostility directed at me and the other woman legislator personally.
>
> It was very difficult—psychologically. I don't think men have the same limits on what is permissible and they are not as likely to be ridiculed.

Another, a leader in her legislature, notes the same phenomenon:

> I got persuaded to carry the Equal Rights Amendment. I don't know how much of my credit I used up on that one. The men really didn't want it. They don't understand what it does and doesn't do, and they are afraid that it is going to do something that it shouldn't do. And then, they think "What is the matter with you women anyway, you've got everything you want and what more do you want? You've got our names, you've got our bank accounts, you've got our lives. What more can you possibly want out of life? What is it that you're after?" I know how they feel. But while I was carrying a divorce bill I became aware of the problems of divorced women—entering the job market, not being paid as much as men, getting credit established. I have some empathy with those problems. But, it irritated the men that I carried the bill. They don't really like a woman to go for women's rights. . . .

Job Performance

Where, when, how long a legislature shall meet are prescribed by law and constitution; how it will organize to accomplish its business is set down in written regulations and precedent. How and where an individual legislator fits into the work is determined in part by law, rules, and precedent; in part by her personality and performance. The formula for success—which in a legislature means influence—varies only marginally among states. Considering the diverse political traditions, populations and problems of various states, the prescriptions for gaining and wielding influence are remarkably similar. There is no disagreement about its basic ingredients: good committee assignments, hard work, good interpersonal relations and seniority—but not necessarily in that order. Membership in the majority party helps, as does an influential position in the party caucus, especially in those states where legislative parties are strong.

Committee Assignments

It is clear that important work is done in committees in most legislatures, that some committees are more central than others to that work, that some committees are "duds" where what is said and done matters little to anyone.[12] Committee assignments influence the areas of legislative policy on which a legislator will concentrate, and the limits of her influence. They also influence with whom she will become well acquainted and under what circumstances. In brief, even in states where party caucuses dominate committees, initial committee assignments matter, so do subsequent changes.

A desirable committee assignment is one which a legislator wants because it puts her in a position to influence the outcome of greatest interest to her. Her interest may be in maximizing influence on the proceedings of the whole legislature, or it may be focused on some specific policy area—education, welfare, prisons, taxes. In either case, a "good" committee assignment may be either to a "key" committee such as ways and means, appropriations, rules, or to a committee that deals with a subject of great interest.

There is a widespread belief that women receive undesirable committee assignments. According to this view, the male leaders of party and legislature—and the leaders *are* male—discriminate against women in making committee and subcommittee assignments, systematically excluding them from the powerful committees, and shunting them, regardless of their interests and preferences, onto the "poor" committees desired by no one because they influence nothing or, at best, to those committees whose subject matter is presumed (by these same males) to be especially suited to women.

These beliefs were treated as hypotheses and a systematic effort was made to investigate women's initial and subsequent committee assignments. The questionnaires and interviews revealed a very high degree of consensus on these matters.

First, as regards initial assignments and *most* subsequent assignments, there is no discrimination against women. The high turnover of legislators creates many vacancies on committees, limits the role of seniority in committee assignments and makes it possible to accommodate the preferences of members, new and old.[13] Because preferences are solicited at the beginning of each session and are generally honored, there is little "sex stereotyping." Women assigned to education, public health, child welfare, and other "women's" subjects, are usually there because they have requested the assignment.[14]

One result of these practices is a very high degree of satisfaction with committee assignments. Four-fifths say they are very satisfied with their committee assignments. Only two are dissatisfied.

Satisfaction does not equal power. It is entirely possible for one legislator to be satisfied with committee assignments at which the more ambitious would chafe. The high level of satisfaction reflected above may only reflect a low level of ambition. But it does establish the fact that male prejudice has not prevented these women from being where they want to be. And we have the assurances of most that they encountered no special, sex specific obstacles in getting there. It is, we are told, sometimes necessary to engage in ingratiation and manipulation to get into desired committees—if those committees are desired by many. Good political sense, a little flattery, and an understanding of the system is useful and sometimes necessary to move where one wants to move. One legislator of long experience divulges a "trade secret" to explain how she manages to get the assignments she wants, session after session.

I realized after a while that the Speakers re-name the committees whenever it is convenient. You can put two or three together and create new committees, or you can just change the names. In fact, there is a great deal of flexibility. Since I understood how it worked, I have never asked for education or health or what-ever, as most people do. I analyze who is running for Speaker and I look at his supporters and I'll see that Mr. Smith and Mr. Jones, two capable legislators, are his key supporters. So I will ask to be on their committees because I know they will get two key committees. Then there is another advantage because those two chairmen know that you requested them and so they are friendly to you to begin with. You rarely know exactly what the main legislative issues will be in advance of the session, so if you choose the chairman, and you say "I would like very much to serve on so and so's committee because I have always admired his work and I know he would be nice to serve with." So you are in right away and when he appoints subcommittees, you get to be chairman of one of the sub-committees. It makes sense, doesn't it?

This description of the politics of committee assignments may seem repellent because of its frank manipulation. But there is nothing sex specific about either the account or the process.

The few women who—after extended experience in their legis-latures—determined to make their way into the inner citadels of power encountered different obstacles. These citadels of power are few; and few legislators gain entrance to them. Their name and formal status varies from state to state. It may be the rules com-mittee, the legislative council, ways and means, the speaker's cabinet, the executive committee of the party caucus. But whatever it is called, there is in every legislature some group of movers and shakers whose decisions have unique influence on what happens and does not happen.

The problem of making one's way into one of these key groups reminds us that it takes influence to get influence. Seniority, in-fluence in one's party and committees, and acceptability to the lead-ership are requirements for membership. Sexual bias apparently slips in via the last named. *The men who control access to the inner citadels of legislative power resist the inclusion of women.* Not all, but most of the women who have achieved high positions in their legislatures have a story to tell about the obstacles they overcame.

One legislator describes her efforts to be appointed to the powerful Rules Committee.

I was the first woman to serve on Rules. I had served six terms and that was the only time I ever put up any type of fight to defend my position. My county was the second largest in the state and I had the seniority and they were going to put a man on from my county who was newly elected. I knew it was strictly on the basis of sex that this decision was being made, and I knew it wouldn't be right for me not to defend my position. So I did defend it. I demanded to be put on Rules and I was. As soon as I made the demand, they caved in. After that I served as Chairman of a powerful committee each year. But if I hadn't made the fight on Rules, I never would have reached that point because they would say, "Well, we can hold her back. It won't matter." So I think there are times when you have to stand up and fight.

Another legislator's experience was of the same order:

I had to fight for my rights to get the appointment to the (powerful two-house committee), and it was really quite a battle. They were actually trying to under-mine the rules and violate the requirements of good politics in order to put a man on. He was not qualified, under the rules, and I was. I had to bring out the rules and regulations and demand my rights from the Speaker in order to get that appointment. Once I really went after it, there wasn't any problem. But I was frankly surprised that they would go so far to keep a woman off that body. It's curious, because once I was appointed, there was no problem. Now, I'm interested in becoming the Chairman (of that group). I have already got commit-ments from a majority of the men to support me for vice-chairman. I think I can make it.

Another reported that in her state:

Women who were entitled by seniority to be part of the leadership were never invited to leadership meetings perhaps because they had never pressed to be included. So, we women in the two houses of the legislature got together and pressed the point that there were women excluded from the leadership who were, *under the rules of the house,* entitled to be included. Once we made the demand, the leaders acknowledged that we were correct, and from that point forward, the two women were always invited to meetings of the leadership.

These experiences, and others like them, illustrate the problems that confront women not on their arrival, but as they attempt to move out of the ranks into leadership roles. It is as though bound-aries of male exclusiveness have been constricted. Where once a "Men Only" sign marked the entire legislature out of bounds for women, today the line has been redrawn around the centers of legislative power. But it is only a line that women are dared to step over, not a battlefront which is defended at all costs. In the above instances, male prejudice was strong enough that leaders were prepared to evade or disregard normal rules of procedure in order to avoid ap-pointing a woman. But the same leaders, once challenged, quickly gave way. Once admitted into the inner citadel, the women confronted no further problems, though they might in moving up yet another rung of the ladder. The effort to freeze women out of leadership ranks (a subject to which I shall return later in this chapter) obviously continues, but it is only half-hearted and only partially successful.

Performance in Committees

The requirements for winning influence in a committee are the same for women as for men. Punctuality, regular attendance, flexibility, a willingness to hear all sides of a question, mastery of the subject matter, are expected of women and men alike; but a woman seeking to be influential should work a little harder, be a little more punctual, have a little better attendance record, and know a good deal more if she hopes to overcome the doubts of her colleagues and win their approval.

To win a position of authority on the committees in which she sits, a woman may find it necessary "to go the extra mile." But none among these respondents doubts that it can be done. "There is always respect for diligence, helpfulness, and knowledge," they say again and again. And prove it with stories about how one legislator or another disarmed her detractors and converted the skeptical by her mastery of the details of complex legislation. Knowledge, they seem to be saying, is power. At least it is the key credibility and authority in committee and on the floor. On being appointed to the Education Committee, one said, "My first act was to enroll in the university to study public school finance." Others describe working late throughout the session studying legislation, preparing for hearings. To the extent that women face special problems in legislatures they can and frequently do overcome them with information. "You prove yourself by knowing the facts and figures. They learn they can come to you and find out about a subject. You become an authority and you are respected." Like the Lawmaker of Barber's study, these women "know from . . . past accomplishments that satisfaction can be won with diligence and intelligence."[15]

Should a woman become committee chairman (nine of these legislators were chairmen), she is expected to conduct herself like other (male) chairmen: to be fair and judicious, to honor commitments, to be considerate of members, and to get the work done. It is surely significant that not one of the committee chairmen in this study reports difficulties in managing these relatively authoritative roles. Behavior is so structured that male members apparently find no insurmountable problems in working "under" a female chairman. One woman with long experience as chairman of important committees summed up the rules for running a committee effectively:

> As chairman, it is most important to be very fair, to allow both sides to present their thinking and their issues, to allow sufficient notice for the hearing and notify all parties so that they can have someone there to represent them, to allow full discussion and then let the committee itself make the decision. I have found that my committee members turn out for meetings if they are given sufficient notice. Notify them, give them complete agendas of all the votes and keep them well informed; make sure that you provide the same full information to all parties; then conduct the meeting in an orderly manner. Then you have no problems.

Being Influential

Speaking to these women and reading their interviews makes it clear that they work very hard at being good legislators—at getting along well with their colleagues and, especially, at informing themselves about legislation. What they do not learn through informal, after-hours socializing, they compensate by earnest application and study. They think that they have succeeded in becoming effective legislators and I do not doubt it. They do not doubt that women face special problems in making a place for themselves in these arenas devoted to the accumulation and exercise of power, nor that, with tact, perserverance and hard work, these problems are overcome. None believes that the special problems faced by a woman handicaps her in effectively representing her constituents.

Almost all give themselves high marks as legislators, and back up these ratings with persuasive testimony to their effectiveness. Two-fifths describe themselves as "one of the most influential members" of their committees; the remainder say they are fairly influential; none counts herself among the least influential. As regards the legislature as a whole, four-fifths see themselves as fairly influential and the remainder as among the most influential. None is a speaker or a majority leader and few believe that it would be possible for a woman to achieve these topmost leadership positions. Students of state legislatures have identified various characteristics which are deemed desirable and/or necessary in a Speaker. Position on controversial and salient issues, regionalism, group support, knowledge of the process, personal friendships, party regularity and position, are usually identified as the determinants of eligibility. It is curious and very significant that, to my knowledge, no one has named an even more important requisite: maleness.[16] However, let there be no mistake or ambiguity about it, there are powerful women in the sample on which this study is based—women whose decisions and opinions affect broad areas of public policy, women who have gathered together "fragments of power"[17] and know how to wield it. In these cases, the interpersonal skill, knowledge, drive and hard work have been reinforced by seniority—the product is power. The formula is simple:

> You gain influence, first, by being a person that the committee chairman, the Speaker, and the party leader is willing to work with and listen to; and second, by demonstrating that, on the major items of legislation before the house, you have the facts.

The structure of power which most describe is less like a pyramid than a castle with multiple towers and turrets, one of which may be somewhat higher than the rest.[18] There are, they say, multiple foci of power; and multiple limits on power. Not only does the power of committees vary among legislatures, each committee has its own structure of influence, and it may or may not be integrated into a more comprehensive power structure. The power of a speaker or majority leader may be limited by the expertise of a committee chairman. On the other hand, if that chairman is a close ally of the speaker or majority leader, his (the chairman's) power enhances rather than competes with the speaker's position. The women confirm the interdependence of leader and follower. Jewell and Patterson commented, "There are wide differences in the strength of sanctions available to leaders but leaders seldom have the power to influence significantly the member's chances for renomination and reelection. For this reason, legislative leaders must rely on persuasion, tact and bargaining; their success often depends on their ability to sense the mood of the legislature. The legislative leader

seldom gives orders to anyone."[19] A female legislator from a border
state put it this way, "I have a very good relation with the Speaker. I
need his cooperation and I know it, but he needs mine, and he knows
it, too."

"Making It" in the Legislature: A Concluding Comment

So far in this chapter I have attempted to abstract the interpersonal
and social dimensions of the legislator's job from their complex context. The reason for this effort is that interpersonal relations are
believed to be the source of unique and debilitating problems for
women in state legislatures; such discrimination against women as
exists being grounded, not in the laws of the land nor in the rules of
parliamentary procedure, but in the attitudes of male legislators who
guard the gateways to power. It seems useful to pull together and
summarize here information on how women perceive and react to
male reactions to the women among them.
    Though these women differ markedly in education, skill, interest,
geographical and other background characteristics, and though they
differ greatly in amount of legislative experience, legislative role and
influence, the manner in which they perceive and respond to the
special problems of being a woman in a male arena is remarkably and
significantly similar. The striking similarity of perception and response is very suggestive and significant. By emphasizing similarity of
response, I do not intend to suggest the absence of variations and
exceptions. These, however, are few, so few that we are warranted in
speaking of a female style of psychological adaptation to the social
world of the legislature.
    These women show a high degree of awareness of male attitudes
toward women in the legislature. Very few doubt that a woman
stimulates a special response in her male colleagues. The few who
initially denied that women were confronted by somewhat special,
sex specific problems generally got around to describing some such
problem before the end of the interview and amending their original
statement. More specifically, most of the legislators perceive that to
"make it" in the legislature, a woman will probably have to work

harder and be "nicer" than a male—at least in the beginning until she has demonstrated her seriousness and ability. In addition, almost all perceive that there are sex specific limits on how high a woman can rise in the legislative hierarchy; certainly no woman could be speaker or majority leader. These demands—"to walk the extra mile," to inform oneself especially well, to be especially sensitive to one's colleagues—are accepted as "givens" in the environment.

But the impact of these special demands and limits is muted by the response. The demands are minimized: "People say that they test women in the House. Sure they do. They also test every man that's elected." Furthermore, the women legislators perceive and feel male doubts more as a challenge than a rebuff. They do not feel hurt or diminished, nurse grudges or plot revenge. They do not get angry and suffer the incapacitating effects of rage, guilt and anxiety. They do not withdraw, abandon their goals or limit their efforts for achievement. Nor do they *ever* use male resistance to excuse themselves for failures to achieve a desired goal. Instead, they react with the same determination, persistence and hard work with which they have confronted other challenges in other arenas.

That is to say, in their reactions to the problems of being women in a men's world, these women show remarkably little involvement with self. Because their basic self-esteem is secure, they are not vulnerable to slights from initially skeptical male colleagues. Had they not already faced such slights in their campaigns for nomination and election—and from persons closer to them? And because they are not vulnerable and do not feel threatened, neither do they react defensively. They respond to slights with neither aggressiveness, submission nor withdrawal, but with the same persistent effort and purposeful friendliness that has helped them achieve goals in other collective enterprises.

Why should it be otherwise? The goal of most, after all, is not to establish relations of friendship or affection, but to play an effective role in the legislative process. This preoccupation with the job creates a "functional" rather than a "personal" orientation in interpersonal relations. I do not mean to suggest, thereby, that these women dehumanize their male colleagues, only that most do not seek approval for its own sake, and that they do not attempt to recreate in the legislative chamber the intimate personal relations for which women are believed to have a special penchant. Maintaining an "impersonal" though positive attitude toward their colleagues apparently poses no problems for these women who are already practiced in purposive socializing. The presumed need of females to personalize situations is nearly absent in their accounts of legislative life.

Altogether the legislative norms governing interpersonal contact pose few problems for them. They do not see the informal rules of behavior as "masculine," nor make special demands that the rules be altered to meet "feminine" requirements. Instead, they adapt to the conventional requirements of legislative behavior "asking no quarter, giving none."

The strategy they choose for making their way in the legislature emphasizes work and the development of expertise. This choice is, of course, consistent with the earlier lives of these achievement-oriented women. It is also consistent with their positions in legislatures. By relying on expertise rather than friends and the buddy system to achieve influence, they minimize their disabilities and choose a competitive terrain on which their male colleagues have no special advantage.

In assessing their situation and prospects, these women show great realism which serves not only to orient them in their environment, but also assists them in making a way into the influence structures of these male preserves.

A significant finding concerning interpersonal relations is that the perceptions of these women are very much like those of male legislators who have been the subject of numerous earlier studies. There is no evidence in the interviews that they bring into the legislature distinctive orientation to interpersonal relations. These interviews provide massive evidence that women in a legislative context *can* be fair, judicious, thick-skinned and good humored, that they can adapt to and operate in an environment of impersonal friendliness. Their descriptions of "making it" in the legislature demonstrate that they do not wear sexual blinders. The social world that they describe is that described in Wahlke, Eulau, *et al.*, Sorauf, Epstein, Patterson, Barber, Keefe, Jewell, Ogul and other students of legislative behavior whose evidence was based chiefly on males. There is no evidence here of a sex specific perception of social reality.

NOTES

1. Frank J. Sorauf, *Party and Representation* (New York: Atherton, 1963), p. 67.
2. Leon Epstein, *Politics in Wisconsin* (Madison: University of Wisconsin Press, 1958), p. 105.
3. Keefe and Ogul point out that "a persistent condition of the American state legislature is a high rate of turnover among members . . . there is widespread agreement that legislative turnover is excessive in many states and that greater membership stability would contribute to strengthening the institution." William J. Keefe and Morris S. Ogul, *The American Legislative Process: Congress and the States*, 2nd ed. (Englewood Cliffs, N.J.: Prentice Hall, 1968), p. 135. See pp. 135-141 for further discussion of high turnover and low salaries. Further discussion of low pay, high turnover, short sessions, inadequate staff, and so on, may be found in Donald G. Herzberg and Alan Rosenthal, *Strengthening the States: Essays on Legislative Reform* (Garden City, N.Y.: Doubleday, 1971), especially pt. 1, "The Scope of Legislative Reform"; publications of The Citizens Conference on State Legislatures (4722 Broadway, Kansas City, Missouri, 64112)—for example, "Report on Salaries, Expenses in 50 State Legislatures as 1973 Sessions Begin," Research Memorandum no. 16 (December 1972) and other Research Memoranda. Of course, the standard textbooks like Keefe and Ogul and Malcolm E. Jewell and Samuel C. Patterson, *The Legislative Process in the United States*, 2nd ed. (New York: Random House, 1972), provide detailed data.
4. John C. Wahlke, Heinz Eulau, William Buchanan, and Leroy C. Ferguson, *The Legislative System: Explorations in Legislative Behavior* (New York: Wiley, 1962), p. 168.
5. Ibid., p. 243
6. These norms of interpersonal conduct have been described in many studies of legislative bodies. The most influential discussions are probably Donald R. Matthews, *U.S. Senators and Their World* (Chapel Hill: University of North Carolina Press, 1960), pp. 92-117; Wahlke et al., *Legislative System*, pp. 141-169; Keefe and Ogul, *American Legislative Process*, pp. 149-154. The same "rules of acceptable behavior" have been recently reported as binding in the Kansas legislature. See Marvin Harder and Carolyn Rampey, *The Kansas Legislature* (Lawrence: University of Kansas Press, 1972), p. 5; and in Wisconsin, see Ronald D. Hedlund and Wilder Crane, Jr., *The Job of the Wisconsin Legislator* (Washington, D.C.: American Political Science Assn., 1971), pp. 41-52. See Wayne R. Swanson, with Allan H. Rouse, *Lawmaking in Connecticut: The General Assembly* (Washington, D.C.: American Political Science Assn., 1972), pp. 10-12.
7. The extent to which barriers to full participation in informal socializing hamper professional development has been stressed by many students of women. See, e.g., Jessie Bernard, *Women and the Public Interest* (Chicago: Aldine · Atherton, 1971), pp. 111-113; idem, *Academic Women* (University Park: Pennsylvania State University Press, 1964), pp. 302-303; Rita James Simon et. al., "The Woman Ph.D.: A Recent Profile," *Social Problems* 15 (Fall 1967): 221-236. On barriers to women in Congress see Frieda L. Gehlen, "Women in Congress," *Trans-Action*, October 1968, pp. 37-39.
8. Wahlke et al., *Legislative System*, p. 235.
9. Their evaluations are similar to those reported in Patricia Goren Bach's study of "Women in Public Life in Wisconsin," Alverne Research Center on Women, unpublished manuscript, p. 17.
10. Kirsten Amundsen, *The Silenced Majority: Women and American Democracy* (Englewood Cliffs, N.J.: Prentice Hall, 1971), p. 4.
11. Ibid.
12. It is also clear that the role of committees varies from state to state. Wise emphasizes the subordination of committees in Pennsylvania to the party caucuses. Sidney Wise, *The Legislative Process in Pennsylvania* (Washington, D.C.: American Political Science Ass., 1971), pp. 39-41. Contrast this with a parallel study of California which describes each committee as a "little 'fiefdom' controlling a more or less important slice of public policy."

Joel M. Fisher, Charles M. Price, and Charles G. Bell, *The Legislative Process in California* (Washington, D.C.: American Political Science Assn., 1973), p. 63.

13. A recent study of the Wisconsin legislature comments: "A new member would be well advised to give particular attention to his initial committee assignment, for his preferences will be honored if the appointing officers find it impossible." Hedlund and Crane, *The Job of the Wisconsin Legislator*, p. 7. The same point is made concerning California in Fisher, Price, and Bell, *The Legislative Process in California*, pp. 54-55. All agree that freshmen have little or no chance of being appointed to key committees.

14. For a good general discussion of committee assignments in state legislatures, see Jewell and Patterson, *Legislative Process*, p. 226.

15. James D. Barber, *The Lawmakers: Recruitment and Adaptation to Legislative Life* (New Haven: Yale University Press, 1965), p. 206.

16. For a discussion of requisites for leadership, see, *inter alia*, Charles W. Wiggins, *The Iowa Lawmaker* (Washington, D.C.: American Political Science Assn., 1970), pp. 2-3.

17. The phrase is David Truman's. See David Truman, *The Congressional Party* (New York: Wiley, 1959), pp. 104-105.

18. Similar power structures were reported in Wayne L. Francis, "Influence and Interaction in a State Legislative Body," in *Empirical Studies of Indiana Politics*, ed James B. Kessler (Bloomington: University of Indiana Press, 1970), p. 49.

19. Jewell and Patterson, *Legislative Process*, pp. 161-162.

Chapter VII

Legislative Perspectives and Roles

MANY of the questions and much of the debate about women in politics turn on whether there are cognitive differences between women and men *which are relevant to their political behavior.* The assumption that women think differently than men was made by both advocates and opponents of women's suffrage. The former argued that votes for women would elevate American public life, end war, alcoholism, child labor, while the latter were sure that women's special mental and emotional makeup rendered them unfit for public life. The questions and the debate recur with each new step toward women's full participation in power. The drive for greater female participation in the national political conventions of 1972 featured not only an appeal to equity but a prediction that the presence of more women would produce more moral decisions. Some women's groups are not shy about claiming that because of their more developed moral sensibilities women in office will behave differently and *better* than (many? most? all?) their male predecessors.

Is it true? Do women perceive public life differently than men? Do they have different political interests? Are they likely to favor different solutions? M. Kent Jennings and Norman Thomas report that their study of delegates to national conventions reveals that "members of the Michigan elites do not differ substantially by sex in their perceptions of the political process, the nature of their political party, and the party's role in the political process."[1] But it was a very small sample.

Social science theory suggests the likelihood of politically relevant differences between the sexes. Women's socialization, roles and life experiences are very different than men's. A large body of social theory, especially that dealing with the sociology of knowledge, postulates the existences of a relationship between position in society and perspectives. Class, age, ethnic and racial identity, geographical location are presumed to affect perceptions and perspectives because they affect experience. The experience of being poor or jobless is thought to affect one's perspective on many aspects of social reality. Should the experience of running a household, bearing and caring for children have any less effect?

Sex differences precede birth, and the social process of sexual differentiation begins not long after. Sex role differences are perceived by children long before they start school.[2] Studies of political socialization have documented early sex differences in perception of candidates' styles of political conceptualization, levels of interest and information and political efficacy.[3]

Girls, more than boys, tend to personalize the political system, to see government more in terms of authority figures and less in terms of institutions. Further, girls are more likely than boys to attribute responsiveness and benevolence to authoritative figures.[4] These findings are consistent with the widely held belief that girls (and women) have greater affiliation needs than boys (and men), and they are oriented more to the concrete and the personal and less concerned with the abstract, general and remote. Whether differences between male and female perception and conceptualization are rooted in physiology or experience, it would be surprising if distinctive socialization and distinctive adult experiences did not influence perceptions of and orientation to politics.[5]

There are good grounds for believing that women bring to the political arena special preoccupations, assumptions, approaches, and that their political behavior is different from that of males. But is it true? Whether such differences exist is an empirical question on which the evidence is mixed and incomplete.

Polling data on masses give a mixed answer. Since personality is often said to have greater salience for women than issues,[6] it is reasonable to suppose that sex-based differences would be reflected in the reaction to presidential candidates. But, in presidential elections the difference between women's and men's candidate preferences has not been greater than five percent since 1952, with one exception. Six percent more men than women supported Stevenson in 1956, while six percent more women than men supported Eisenhower. In 1972, the difference was only one percent. One percent more women supported McGovern; one percent more men supported Nixon.[7] In 1960 the difference was only two percent; in 1964, two percent; in 1968, four percent more women supported Humphrey, while four percent more men supported Wallace.

Women cannot be readily described as either more liberal or more conservative than men in presidential elections. American presidential voting habits tend to confirm Duverger's conclusion that, "Upon the whole, women vote much as men do. Their entry into the electoral arena has not fundamentally altered the strength of the parties."[8] Duverger does demonstrate, however, the somewhat more conservative character of women's voting habits.[9]

Issues provide a different measure of political orientations. The table below shows that recently differences between women and men have been greatest where the use of force is involved—war, bombing,

Issue Orientations, 1972, The Sex Gap

ISSUE	EXTENT OF DIFFERENCE
Approve bombing North Vietnam	−18*
Approve greater equality/opportunity for women	−11
For stricter wage/price control	− 9
For stricter firearm controls	+ 8
For reducing penalties for marijuana use	− 8
For improved opportunity for blacks and other minorities	− 6
For spending more to control pollution	− 6
For tough sentences for lawbreakers	− 5
For national health insurance	− 3
For reduced defense spending	− 1
For amnesty for draft evaders	+ 1

Source: *The Gallup Opinion Index,* Sept. 1972, Oct. 1972
*A minus indicates that fewer women than men took the position, a plus indicates more women than men.

guns, punishment. There is also frequently less female support for programs aimed at equality and welfare. At the level of mass opinion, women do not turn out to be reliably or generally more "tender-hearted" than men; only more opposed to the use of coercion as an instrument of social policy. This generalized aversion to coercion is not necessarily associated with greater support for the underdog, identification with the outcast, or generosity. We may note, too, that, as the "weaker" sex, girls have ample opportunity to develop a distaste for "brute force" (at which they are always at a disadvantage) as a means of resolving problems.

But masses and elites do not differ only in numbers and the orientation of an elite cannot be reliably inferred from the orientation of masses. It may be that the unusual women who run for political office differ in more ways from the unusual men who seek office.

Chapter II suggested that the men and women surveyed in this study have much in common: deep roots in the community, a history of joining and participating, conventional roles and life styles and strong egos. But they differ in some important respects: the men have years of professional experience, frequently preceded by still more years of professional training. Those who are lawyers have practice in adversary proceedings, in representing various interests, in seeing the world from diverse perspectives. Salesmen, contractors and other businessmen have the experience of identifying with interests, of making profits and providing services. Women whose principle roles are those of homemaker and mother have a different experience. Their roles, grounded in affection, emphasize nurturing, empathizing, sustaining. As wives and mothers, women experience the economy directly as consumers and indirectly through their husbands' jobs. Traditional roles train women to be experts in empathy and feeling, in the concrete, the personal, the practical, while men in conventional roles most closely associated with politics develop expertise in dealing with concepts, things, impersonal relations.

It seems likely that each sex brings to the legislature the special sensitivities, skills and perspectives associated with their other roles, and should this be the case, there are likely to be significant differences in legislative interests, perceptions, goals and procedures.

Yet, analysis presented in the last chapter reveals that the women in this study describe the social world of the legislature in the same manner that that world has been described in studies based chiefly on males. Description of interpersonal relations and legislative norms revealed no sex specific biases in the perception of social realties.

Perhaps politics attracts only those women who most closely resemble men, and/or perhaps role has less impact on political perspectives than is frequently supposed. Should either of these latter possibilities be true, differences between male and female perceptions and responses will prove trivial and inconsequential.

This chapter will explore the perceptions and role behavior of the women in this study with a view to finding tentative answers to the following questions:

Do women conceive politics differently than comparable men?
Do they have distinctive political goals?
Do they have distinctive legislative interests?
Do they have distinctive role orientations?
Is there a "women's" approach to problems of public policy?

The Political World: Expectations

Is politics basically the institutionalization of the struggle of each against all? Is it the arena for realizing human potential? For the development of leaders and followers? Is government an instrument for solving problems, for doing good, for self-realization, for compromising differences, for regulating conflict and keeping the peace?

How a person conceives politics and government tells us a great deal about her basic character and experience. Because it is a large and complex human activity the political sphere is like a projective test: its diversity, scope and complexity invite personal interpretation and displacement. Selective attention, selective response, diverse personal experiences with the agencies and processes of government all make for individual perceptions and responses to the political arena. People with extensive political experience have more sharply defined, more highly differentiated, more elaborately rational and sophisticated conceptions of government. But they do not necessarily share the same views of the political universe. In any political system the processes of selection and recruitment screen out those with highly deviant perceptions of politics (except for a few experts in dissimulation who may slip through). But in any large, heterogenous state there is a range of "acceptable" perceptions recognized as realistic.

Conceptions of politics vary, but they vary within limits set by the political culture of the time and place. Conceptions may vary with class background, generation, occupation, region, and perhaps, by sex. No one knows much about the extent to which the political culture of the woman differs from that of the man. Women are said to be more submissive, less assertive; does that trait affect their orientations to political authority? Women are believed to be more peaceful, less combative; does that affect their perception of political conflict? Born into different regions, classes, circumstances, the women in this sample grew up in different political subcultures; there is no special reason to believe that their conceptions of the political world are similar just because they are women. Nonetheless there are striking similarities in their conceptions and orientations to politics.

In his book on *American Federalism*, Daniel Elazar[10] argues that American political culture includes two quite divergent conceptions of the political order, each of which is widely disseminated in overlapping constituencies throughout the country. One is the famous "marketplace" theory of politics which postulates a polity comprising self-interested, competing individuals; politics is the arena of competition; government both the prize and the regulator. According to this view a political party is an alliance or an aggregation of individual interests; party competition is concerned above all with the control of offices; and a party's goal is to remain in power; politics is an arena in which conflicts of interest are compromised; the "problems" with which government deals are problems of who gets what, when and how; politicians are professionals, specialized in the representation of interests, expecting to benefit their personal interests in the process. Compromise is the key political skill, and "broker" the key political role. The marketplace conception of politics describes the interest-based politics that have dominated the American scene since the Civil War. This conception of government should thrive in the state houses of America—institutions frequently described as the playgrounds and happy hunting grounds of "the interests." A study of the Pennsylvania legislature reveals that a large majority of legislators in that state embraces this conception of government.[11] Since the legislative role of "broker" is closely related to the "marketplace" conception of politics, the existence of large numbers with this role orientation in the nation's State Houses also constitutes evidence that the "marketplace" conception is widespread.

The other conception of politics deeply rooted in American political culture is what Elazar calls the "moralist" conception which "rests on the fundamental conception that politics exists primarily as a means for coming to grips with the issues and conerns of civil society, it also embraces the notion that politics is ideally a matter of concern for every citizen, not just those who are professionally committed to participate in the political affairs of his commonwealth."[12] In the moralist conception, political parties are associations of persons united in the pursuit of a common vision of the public good; politics is a means of communicating to others one's serious purposes, and politicians are most frequently persons moved by a sense of a public duty and readiness to serve. One would expect to find this conception represented in state legislatures; state governments deal annually with problems that affect directly, concretely in crucial ways the security and quality of life of the millions who live in their boundaries.[13]

The women in this study are overwhelmingly inclined to the latter—the moralist—conception of politics. As they see it, conflict is not an important dimension of politics; politics is not a jungle in which each is pitted against all. Nor is it a zero sum game where one person's advantage is another's disadvantage. In fact, there is almost nothing of the "game" model of politics with its teams, alliances, strategies, victories and losses. Almost completely missing, too, is that tamer "marketplace" or "pluralist" version of conflict-based politics in which government serves as broker among competing and conflicting interests.[14]

None of these women thinks of government as principally concerned with compromising or policing. All describe government in terms of solving problems and achieving progress. All—including the most "liberal" and "conservative"—are prepared to use government to solve social problems and to enhance the well being of individual citizens. They expect that government will take deliberate action to solve problems. They display a tendency to conceive problems as technical rather than as political or moral, and to conceive their solutions more as a matter of fact-gathering and consultation than of moral or partisan struggle.

Government, for most, is one instrument among others through which good citizens can seek to improve the quality of life. Their conception of government is the public service conception; it is consistent with civic work, with shared purposes, with common needs rather than individual goals. The pursuit of the public good is its central purpose. This pursuit is neither a great crusade nor a ceaseless struggle, but a sustained effort to correct specific ills, solve specific problems, enhance well-being in some specific ways. The purposes of government, then, are the continuing improvement of the community, through limited, incremental gains rather than wholesale destruction and rebuilding.

Within this broad framework of agreement, there are differences among these women. Some favor a more activist role for government; others are convinced that government should act only where there is broad consensus. The following exchange is typical of many divergent views about what government can and should do.

> The one thing you can say is that, bad as our legislatures are in the nation, they are, as a rule, representative bodies, and you cannot really look down on the quality of legislatures without at the same time looking down on the people —because they are, by and large, representative of the people, in my opinion. You don't agree? The legislature will not change and reflect different attitudes and roles until we get society to change.

> I want to rebut that. I think it works both ways. I also think that society will not change until the legislature changes because legislatures. . .are part of the cause of a mounting frustration on the part of society. . .politicians are not giving to the people the leadership that the people actually deserve and want . . .

Obviously the second speaker in this dialogue conceives her goals and her job differently than the first legislator, but both believe government can serve the interest of the community.

Neither interpersonal nor partisan conflict is important in the conception of politics revealed in these interviews. There is little talk of the struggle for personal preferment, of contests and factions, of ambition pitted against ambition. Ideological conflict is also muted. On a liberal/conservative scale somewhat more of these legislators describe themselves as liberal than conservative, but the role of comprehensive ideological orientations is low, except for fewer than six legislators.[15]

De-emphasis on conflict does not imply a Rousseauistic conception of human nature. As these women see it, cooperation is not so much offered as earned—by reciprocity, consideration and good performance. In descriptions of needing to "work" for the nomination, "earn" respect, and "win" consideration for preferment in the legislature, there is no assumption of spontaneous benevolence and sympathy. People (including men) are perceived as neither implacably hostile nor reliably benevolent, but as moderately self-interested, as capable of being won over and brought around. The moralist conception of government requires only that governors be capable of public spirit and broad concerns, not that they be free of self-interest.

One corollary of the general de-emphasis on the role of conflict in government is a low level of explicit concern with partisanship and partisan conflict.[16] Democratic political parties are vehicles of competition. Whether public office itself is conceived as the prize to be won or sought as a means to implementation of program, party is an instrument of the contest, the chief mechanism of government by adversary proceeding. Parties "oppose" one another in elections; they "oppose" one another in legislatures. A party is held together (especially in the two-party system) by its opposition to a postulated "other" party. Such instruments of conflict are not central to the moralist conception of government. The facts that legislative parties are weak in many states, that much of the work of most legislatures is carried out by consent make it easier to ignore and de-emphasize party. For whatever reason there are few references to interparty or intraparty disagreements, to the mechanisms of party unity and discipline.

It is not that they are hostile to party or conceive themselves as mavericks. There are no proponents of nonpartisan politics, and few who are hostile to party. Most simply do not relate party to their purposes and activities because they conceive these are directed toward a nonpartisan conception of the public good, and government as the instrument of its achievement.

The very low emphasis on party in these interviews is interesting because of the importance of party in the lives of the legislators and in the political system. Most of these legislators have a life-long, inherited identification with a political party and a long history of party activity. They run for the legislature as candidates of a party, they serve in legislatures organized by party, and most report they usually vote a straight ticket. Most generally go along with their own party leadership; there are few mavericks among them. My point is not that they do not *act* like loyal party agents—most clearly do—but that party has little importance in the way they conceptualize politics and describe their purposes in it.

There is no evidence that the de-emphasis on party is a specifically feminine orientation. In their study of four states, Wahlke, Eulau, Buchanan and Ferguson found that few legislators in California and Tennessee rated interparty conflict as important in the affairs of their legislatures (though almost all those from New Jersey did so). [17] Keefe and Ogul remind us, too, that in state legislatures, "Legislation having a major impact upon conditions of private and public life within the state—involving schools, governmental organization, constitutional reform, state services, and other areas—is often shaped and adopted in actions in which the parties either are in general agreement or have taken no stands." [18] Since these tend to be the areas of greatest interest to these legislators, this fact may alone account for the low emphasis on party.

Is the de-emphasis on conflict distinctively feminine? There are some theoretical grounds for thinking so, but the little empirical evidence suggests otherwise. By participating in contests for election and, frequently, for nomination as well, the ability of these women to bear conflict was demonstrated. Still, their "consensus, public service" conception of government is especially consistent with their backgrounds and experience of the traditional woman.

The tendency to conceive government in terms of the public good rather than as a battleground also makes for a positive orientation to authority. This, in turn, is reinforced by good experiences with political leaders. Overwhelmingly, these women have a high opinion of the people who staff the government. Most identify with them and believe in their basic good will and good intentions. Generally they think well of legislative leaders who are described as "fair," "just," "one of the fairest men in the world." It should be emphasized, though, that this broadly supportive attitude does not imply submissiveness, a readiness to acquiesce in unfair treatment, nor unwillingness to organize and oppose the leadership for good cause.

Personal and Political Goals

Political orientations hang together. Conceptions of human nature and politics—of what politics is and what it can accomplish—are related to the personal and public goals of politicians. They influence importantly what kinds of people, seeking what ends, enter politics. The "marketplace" conception of government emphasizes competition, compromise, and self-interest and economic interests. Its assumption that people will attempt to use public power to accomplish private purposes permits—even encourages—the frank statement of personal ambitions. Conversely, a public service view of government which conceives politics as an instrument for achieving the public good is most compatible with goals emphasizing collective purposes, the duties and obligations of citizenship. The goals of these women legislators are part of a total orientation to politics and life.

People—all people—bring to politics, to all other activities, private goals. These private goals are, by definition, self-regarding. Private goals concern the "intense predispositions"[19] of the individual; they reflect fundamental value preferences and basic needs. Individuals express these "intense predispositions" in many different areas of their lives. The person predominantly oriented to power, for example, will express that preoccupation in relations with her family and friends by habitually domineering or manipulative behavior, by withdrawing or otherwise refusing participation in situations which it is impossible to control, by emphasizing power relationships in her perceptions and descriptions of events. Similarly a person principally concerned with search for approval will bring that need into all the arenas in which she enters. Those whose days are dominated by the restless search for approval seek it from children, friends, relatives, and even such casual associates as the grocer and milkman. Those oriented to knowledge will seek learning opportunities and in the most various of situations. They will be oriented to learning about whatever can be learned—about recipes, or organizations, or politics, or whatever. She who is especially concerned with wealth and income will seek out situations which offer the opportunity to make money; she will tend to see people in terms of wealth, will tend to believe money is what makes the world go round.

Most people have multiple values; they love their families, value the good opinions of others, want to make a good living, seek to understand their world, desire to control the circumstances of their lives; still, the intensity of involvement with values tends to be uneven. Value priorities are revealed in cumulative actions, perceptions, priorities; they may or may not be fully conscious. The businessman who, in the absence of objective economic pressure, spends virtually all his waking hours in his business, to the neglect of his family, the clubwoman who feels the pressure of community needs more intensely than those of her husband and children, the man or woman who year in and year out never "had the time" to read books, may or may not be fully aware of the value priorities that lie behind their allocations of time. Not infrequently, people resist acknowledging their preoccupation with some value or values especially wherever these preoccupations do not coincide with dominant cultural norms. The value priorities or "intense predispositions" which dominate one's life lead one to choose one course of action rather than another, to see events in one way rather than another.

Obviously value predispositions are not the only determinant of behavior; situational factors such as the opportunities available are also important, as are other personal characteristics. But value predispositions are a very important determinant of political (and other) behavior and of an individual's goals. Goals are here defined as the conscious ends toward which action is directed. Private goals are self-regarding; they concern what's "in it" for the individual. A private goal may be the desire to enhance one's wealth, to become famous, or to have a good conscience. Public goals relate to public purposes.

Some important questions about politicians concern the relation between their private and public goals. Are the private goals inclusive or exclusive? Are they compatible with the public goals and with the public good? The woman who seeks public office because of the opportunity it offers for private enrichment has exclusive private goals not consistent with the public good. The woman who runs for office because she needs something "to occupy her time," and the young lawyer who runs for the legislature to advertise her name and benefit her practice have exclusive goals which are nonetheless not fundamentally incompatible with public purposes. The politician who possesses an open, inclusive ego may have personal goals which embrace large groups, even a whole community; where identifications are extensive, "self" interest comprehends the interests of many others.

The private goals of these women are diverse. A few, like Barber's "Spectators" were people with time on their hands and a high need for approval. Others, about a fifth of them, looked toward developing a political career and saw the legislature as a step in that direction. More were attracted by the desire to influence public events and were propelled by the determination to do so. None was attracted by financial gain or the desire to enhance a nonpolitical career. Most, however, had internalized much earlier a demand on themselves to contribute to the welfare of the community, and came to politics via the same orientation to public service that had inspired their earlier community service. As Robert Lane commented in a recent book, "The need for self-esteem may lead to political participation through satisfying the superego of the individual who sees participation as a duty."[20] When the need to serve the public good has been internalized as a demand on the self, private goals and public good coincide, and the community benefits. A highly developed sense of citizenship and personal responsibility for collective well-being is found in many regular participants in community affairs.

Public goals enjoy more prestige than private ones. They are thought to be higher, nobler, more moral and are more frequently and frankly articulated. Self-regarding goals are frequently thought

to be more "basic" or "real" than public goals. There is no empirical
justification for regarding private goals as more "real" than public
ones; nor is there any justification to regard economic or power goals
as more "real" than those concerned with rectitude. Close study of
the data of history and anthropology reveals that man (and woman)
is social and moral as well as selfish and self-seeking, that people
accumulate identifications and virtues as well as power and money.

Most of the women in this study are moved by a serious, persistent
commitment to community service. Contributing to the public welfare by participation in public life is a continuing demand they make
on themselves. Some of them have broad, general service goals
oriented to a continuing concern with the quality of public life.
Following are some characteristic statements of broad goals oriented
to the political system itself.

> What I would most like is to help restore confidence in government.

> My motivating drive is to be in a position to help strenghten the republic form
> of government.

> I am in politics because I think a lot of changes are needed in the institutions
> of government and I would like to help bring them about.

> To make government more responsive to people is to strengthen government
> and help people—both at the same time. That's why I'm in the legislature.

Another put it this way:

> I think it is very important, if you are in politics, to accumulate power. I
> would like to be in a position of power, not for its own sake, but because of
> what you can accomplish. I know it is often said that power corrupts and that
> absolute power corrupts absolutely, but power, properly used, is a magnificent
> thing. It really is. And if you really believe that this activity is worthwhile, and if
> you believe in the system as I do, then the way that you can really make that
> system work is to be in a position of power. Then you use power to solve
> problems and to strengthen the system.
> I am very fearful, frankly, that if we continue, as we have in many areas, to
> hack away at it from so many different sources, that we are going to weaken this
> republican system of government beyond repair. So I want to be in a position of
> power, so I can affect that."

Many, indeed most, of the women, have fairly specific public goals
oriented to a foreseeable but not too distant future, oriented to the
state rather than the nation or the world. Their commitment is to
public service, the orientation is to quality of life, the goal is to use

available resources to bring about relatively concrete improvements in the life of the state. Most are issue oriented. But their issue orientation is not ideological, nor is it associated with a single issue which can be dealt with once and for all. Their issue orientation is to local and state problems which may or may not be associated with a partisan struggle or a "larger" ideological orientation. Their political goals are for the most part problem-solving goals:

To see a problem and to resolve it in a way that the people of the state want it is the most exciting thing about politics. My goal is to help solve these problems.

Overhauling the state's educational system is my principal goal. It is very inadequate and could be made better. If it were, the whole population of the state would profit.

What I like to accomplish is the passage of legislation that takes on a problem and solves it. This is what makes all the time spent and the work done worthwhile.

I think the only proper goal of a legislator is to contribute to finding solutions for the problems that plague her state—every state has such problems.

My aim is to bring into the halls of the state government the needs of the people of the cities. There are so many problems in the cities—health, housing, welfare—and I want to help to achieve a really open society.

There are many issues I want to do something about—the property tax, automobile safety, hunting and fishing laws—there are many things that need attention.

Getting more people into the system, participating, is what I would most like to do. We need more old people, more young people, more old maids because certainly our legislative process in America means representation of all the people—even the screwballs.

My main goal is—and this sounds pretty idealistic—to help make the world a better place to live in. Not necessarily by doing big things but by helping particular people of my state with their problems, using legislative office to help solve their problems.

In scope and style the substantive goals held by these women tend to be pragmatic and incremental. Rooted in existing grievances and possibilities, their goals look toward limited rather than final solutions, and are held together by a commitment to improving the quality of life in the state rather than by a comprehensive ideology.

Is there anything specifically feminine about the problem-solving goals these women bring to the legislature? We cannot say. Women are said to be more concerned with the concrete than the abstract, and indeed, the goals of these women are derived less from abstract ideologies than from experience. Abstract ideologies have a small importance in their political lives. Their goals are neither remote, universal, nor apocalyptic. But the same is probably true for men. A person oriented exclusively or even primarily to the "big" questions of national and international politics is not likely to seek state legislative office, nor to remain there long. (In this sample those few women with overriding interest in the "big" questions are very interested in moving out of the legislature into higher political office.) There is no evidence to support the view that the orientations of men who run for the state legislature are to more abstract and distant ends, or less "parochial." Neither is there evidence to prove (or disprove) that women have more inclusive identifications than men, or a higher sense of public duty. Barber found women especially numerous in the "spectator" and the "lawmaker" categories; Robert Lane comments that, "Women's relatively high sense of citizen duty suggests that their increasing participation is prompted more by the role as moral leaders than by the concern with parties or issues." But their findings are only suggestive. Because of traditional sex roles women are less likely to bring "careerist" goals to public office, indeed, many have no career interests beyond the legislature.

Legislative Interests

The answer to the question of whether women legislators have special "women's interests" would seem to be a qualified yes. Education and health are believed to express women's special interest in "humane" policy areas, and the women in this study show special interest in these areas. Collectively, however, they are also interested in all other major areas of public policy.

The substantive area in which these women have greatest interest *is* education, with health not far behind. Substantive interests are reflected in committee assignments and in discussion of legislative interests. Interest in education and health seems to be a special interest of women as women. It derives from their pre-legislative experience as wives and mothers with a special concern for nurturing families, caring for and educating children, helping young people grow into responsible adults. One women explained the relevance of her housewife's and mother's role to her legislative career this way:

Before I went to the legislature I had no career, and I hadn't been schooled in subjects relevant to state government. So I tried to find legislative areas in which to concern myself in which I had some interest and experience. Certainly children was one area and health. And, of course, as a housewife I had an interest in consumer protection and housing. So I tried to concentrate on these areas. I introduced the first consent laws, for instance, giving a twelve-year-old or older the right to consent for treatment in VD and pregnancy. And I sponsored a program for unwed mothers and a very strong comprehensive child abuse law. Those are things that I have been interested in that I felt I could relate to; or maybe give some of my personal experience to—nothing that I had gone to school to learn, just interests developed through day-to-day living as a housewife and mother.

Another, sensitive to sexual stereotyping, commented:

I know some people feel the men like to pigeonhole women by putting them on education, but I wanted to be there. During my years in the PTA and on the School Board I got interested in many aspects of educational policy. I knew a lot about it, I thought I could make a contribution there, and I have. Furthermore, education is the largest single item in our state budget. You could hardly call it unimportant.

Education, health, childcare, youth development, are by no means the only interests of these women even of those who have a special concern for these subjects. There is wide interest in financial affairs, state and local government, the environment, and a variety of other policy areas.[22] The following table states the distribution of committee membership. Because the formal names of committees vary greatly among the states, I have used categories which describe the substantive concerns of these committees rather than their names. Formal committee names may or may not reflect substantive concerns.

Legislative Interests of Women Interviewed

COMMITTEE MEMBERSHIPS	NUMBER OF WOMEN SERVING
Education (including higher education)	25
Health (including mental health and public health)	17
Appropriations (including budget, fiscal policy)	15
Local government	11
Environment	9
Taxation	8
Judiciary	8
Legislative (apportionment and elections)	8
Commerce and Labor	6
Constitutional revision	4
Banks and banking	4
Agriculture	3
State government	3

Role Orientations

"Role orientations are a legislator's own expectations of the kind of behavior they ought to exhibit in the performance of their duties. They may be considered as providing the promises in terms of which legislators make decisions."[23] They are role conceptions rather than role demands.[24] Role orientations derive from ideas about what government is and ought to do, what legislatures are and ought to do, from interpretations of the expectations of others (what constituents, party leaders, other legislators expect), from self-conception and from personal goals. Role orientations can be quite specific. What should (can) a person with my experience, goals, skills, resources and limitations do in their first, second and third terms as legislator?

Since Wahlke, Eulau, Buchanan and Ferguson pioneered the investigation of role orientations of legislators in four states, there has been substantial research into the distribution of role orientations in the state houses of the nation. So that the role orientations of these women can be easily compared with those of legislators already studied, I shall classify them in the standard categories derived from the four-state study. That several of these categories are not useful in discriminating among these women legislators is itself a finding of some significance.

There are, for example, few "brokers" in this sample, a fact consistent with the de-emphasis on conflict and compromise. There are no "ritualists," women concerned more with procedure and routine than with the content of bills.

"Inventors" are plentiful. The "inventor" role has an obvious and close association with policy interests and with the idea that government is an agency for achievement of the public good. And just as most women in this sample conceive government as a means to achieve the public good, most conceive their roles as a search for new solutions to problems and new paths to progress. "The inventor," says Eulau, "is interested in solving the current problems of his state—public welfare, education, highway construction, the rehabilitation of the mentally ill, and so on."[25] The "inventor" is much like Barber's "lawmaker," deeply engrossed in the substance of the state's problems and the effort to devise legislative solutions. Two-thirds of the women in this study are inventors. The pragmatic, problem-solving goals described earlier in this chapter are "inventor" goals, and their descriptions of the job—of what they do, how they feel—describe the inventor role orientation.

Interesting questions have been raised concerning legislative inventors. No one doubts their usefulness. Students of American legislative behavior admire legislative creativity, and find the concern with substantive questions admirable. Eulau's attitude is characteristic when he says, ". . . a legislature's effective performance will depend on the presence of members whose orientation to their legislative role is in terms of social inventiveness. These, it seems, are the legislators who, by virtue of a broad view of the lawmaking task, can give meaning to the whole legislative business." But he also raises a question entertained by others, "Is the inventor orientation wholly outdated and unrealistic in view of contemporary requirements for expertise and executive power in policy making?"[26] In his article on "State Legislative Politics," Thomas Dye argues the affirmative: "The fact that few of the legislators interviewed even claimed to approach their task in a creative manner is evidence that legislators themselves recognize that the function of policy enaction has shifted from the legislatures to the governor, executive agencies and interest groups. The true inventors in the legislature are probably frustrated men since seldom does the legislature do anything but respond to the inventiveness of the governor or civil servants or active pressure groups."[27]

How many legislators conceive their role as "inventor" is not known; but it is by far the most widespread substantive role orientation among these women. It should be kept in mind that most of these women made a long range commitment to the legislature; furthermore, they were chosen for the study because they are effective legislators. They are therefore in no sense typical of either all legislators or all women in legislatures. It is perhaps not surprising, then, that so many see the job as one of creative policy making.

Are women legislators more likely than men to adopt the "inventor" role? Certainly, background and experience make them less likely to become "brokers." Perhaps experience in community service predisposes them to become "inventors," a role more consistent with their problem-solving conceptions of politics. Presumably women with occupational backgrounds and a political history more similar to that of men would not be especially prone to the "inventor" role.

Turning now to representation, note that Kent Jennings and Norman Thomas report "a sharp cleavage" between men and women in their perception of whether a delegate should "use his best individual judgment" or should rely on party leadership and public opinion, with men far more likely to emphasize the former and women the latter.[28] This study does not exactly contradict their findings but it suggests that perhaps the question should be reviewed. About one-third of these women describe their roles chiefly in terms of representation of the district. "The main thing that I have done is develop the ability to get things done for the people back home. It may not be passing a law. It may be helping them accomplish something vis-à-vis an executive agency. I led a protest to the highway department and got a route changed over the vigorous protests of the traffic engineers." Another quarter are "tribunes" who see themselves as representing "higher" causes and are quite unconcerned about the preferences of their districts, except as these may prevent their reelection. Approximately one-half see no conflict between representing the majority of their district and following their own conscience.[29]

To most of these women, the dichotomy between their district's opinion and their personal opinion is unreal. It is, after all, derived from a model that postulates conflict between a gross, short-sighted, self-interested majority and a wise, far-seeing public spirited representative. The model assumes that the majority and the representative will have different values or at least significant differences in perspective. Such differences are probably not the rule in democracies, especially at the lower levels of government. Most of the women in this study share the dominant values of Americans today; they differ from most citizens only in the amount of time they are prepared to devote to implementing these values and the energy they spend seeking ways to do so. Interviewing them reminds us that the conflict between the majority and the conscience of the representative is not written in the stars, but occurs only occassionally, and then chiefly in times of crisis and rapid change.

Denying that there were issues about which a majority of her district thought one way and she another, one legislator put it this way:

> The first job of a legislator is to represent her constituents. You are there because they chose you and trusted you. It's interesting, everyone who runs for office does a lot of talking about listening and never gets around to doing it. I sincerely believe that a legislator has a moral duty and a political responsibility to reflect the interests and the opinions of the people in her district.
>
> But that's not as simple as it sounds. I quickly came to see that the legislature deals with many problems about which my constituents have no opinions, some of which do not pertain to the district at all. And there are some times when I feel the people in my district would have different opinions than they do, if only they knew more about the subject. Being a legislator is tough because you have to balance different considerations. Sometimes they conflict. You have to represent your constituents, and be prepared to explain your behavior to them and answer for it, you have to keep in mind the whole state, and you have to look ahead all the time—because you have a kind of responsibility for the future. Anyway, a representative's first duty is to her district, but that is no problem to me. You have to remember that there are sensible people in my district and I am a lot like them. I don't mean to say there aren't people with cockeyed ideas and selfish interests in my district, but there aren't too many of them, and they sort of balance each other off.[30]

Structural roles concern where a woman wants to serve in the legislature. Does she desire a leadership position in the party? in the house? Does she see committee work as the center of the legislative process? Does she desire to attain a committee chairmanship? to establish herself as an expert? to be everyones' friend? or a special friend of the leadership? or an eternal "outsider" who functions—or attempts to function—as the conscience of the House?

Do the structural goals of women differ from those of male legislators? Do different women seek different structural roles? Are fewer women interested in establishing themselves as leaders? as subject matter experts? as committee chairmen? Unfortunately these questions, too, cannot be answered definitively or comprehensively on the basis of available data on either men or women.

Few legislators of either sex desire to become legislative leaders and no one becomes a leader by accident. Most of the women in this study are too committed to other aspects of their lives to throw themselves into legislative politics with the intensity required for leadership. To develop influence, not just on specific policy outcomes of specific committees but on the organization and operation of the whole legislature, requires an extraordinary commitment of time, energy and attention. It is leaders who are most nearly the "complete politicians" for whom politics and the business of government is the consuming passion. It is the leaders, too, who must become experts in the accumulation and exercise of influence. Democratic leadership skills are subtle and sometimes mysterious. Influence in a legislature precedes nomination to a formal leadership role rather than follows it. It grows out of expertise in the process and substance of legislation and especially out of interpersonal relationships. Democratic leaders display the consideration, reciprocity, friendliness that characterize successful legislators and, in addition, they are authoritative. Leaders gain influence in part because they are believed to be influential people—people skilled in affecting the desired behavior of others. About one-third of the women in this study clearly desire to be leaders; half a dozen of these have achieved positions from which their influence is felt on the whole legislature, not just on a substructure.

More of these women in this study have goals that relate to specific policy areas. For those oriented to policy making in specific areas, the committee is the heart of the legislative process. Becoming the committee chairman or becoming a knowledgeable and authoritative source of information are operational goals. Most of the subject matter specialists are potential chairmen. Because expertise can be attained by personal effort and exercised independently of seniority and the buddy system, it is a realistic goal for women without long service in the legislature. There are also personal and social factors which would seem to enhance the attractiveness of this role for women legislators. Some of these have already been alluded to. First, the expert's role is self-selected, and therefore independent of the legislative power structure and the friendship network. Second, success is available through hard work and persistence, both of which are habitual to most of the women in this study. Third, the development of subject matter expertise is a natural and logical course for persons with a "problem-solving" orientation to politics. Fourth, it is a role from which it is possible to achieve a limited area of influence on legislative policy without long tenure or broad alliances, and many of these women are interested in having an impact on policy sooner rather than later. For all these reasons, the role of subject matter expert is especially compatible for women of the type described in this study. Judging from the studies of role distribution in legislatures (since legislators are overwhelmingly male, we can read these general studies as describing male role orientations—give or take a percentage point or two), one would conclude that *these* women were more likely to become subject matter experts than were most males. But we have no way of estimating whether the same would be true for men of comparable tenure in the legislature.

Responses and Approaches: A Female View

Are women in the legislature more practical than men? more moral? more dedicated and hard working? Differences in attitude and performance were explored in group sessions with these women. One way, probably the best way, to approach this subject is to reproduce a discussion that actually took place.[31]

Some of these remarks may sound like female chauvinism to some readers and, undoubtedly, male comments on the legislative behavior of the two sexes would be quite different.

I believe that men more than women are wedded to the administration chart, where everything is bureaucratized. If we have $250,000 to spend for hemophilia patients, for example, women are much more apt to say to the superintendent of the hospital, "Certify that that patient has hemophilia and that the family needs help financially," and simply pay the hospital. The men will be much more apt to say, "We need a hemophilia bureau. We need a chief. He has to have assistants, of course. They will all have to have Blue Cross and other fringe benefits, and secretaries, and they are going to have to have field workers." It is an entirely different approach.

I think men are more dreamers, in a sense; large schemes appeal to them. I think it is not an accident that you can hardly get something passed unless there is going to be some tremendous expenditure involved in it. . .I think the psychological and practical appeal to them (men) is less than the organizational and the administrative. If women had been given all that money we wouldn't be on the moon; but I do think we would have been recycling garbage all over the country. Women are more concerned with the guts of living, I think. . . .I think our goals are simpler and more practical and our methods are more idealistic.

*   *   *

I notice that the few women we have. . .(in my house) are not beholden to special lobbying interests. I say this with great pride. They will represent citizen's groups, the League of Women Voters, a citizen's group that has banded together for a particular ecological purpose, the citizen's group that is truly concerned with the safety of children walking to and from school—that type of thing. But they are not paid by the lobbying interests. . . .

They operate on a more idealistic basis. . . .Maybe I am being idealistic about them. But among all the women I work with, none of them are taking money; none of them are taking bribes. . . .

*   *   *

Special interests do not seek out women as they do men.

*   *   *

That's right; because they feel it is a waste of time.

*   *   *

I feel women are definitely much more issue oriented; much more idealistically motivated than men. . . .I think it's a distinct disadvantage in the sense that we tend not to be as power-oriented. . .so that we are considered. . .to be not practical—which is, of course, not always true. . . .And the other disadvantage we have is that we tend not to organize power groups within the assembly in back of our particular programs and come in with a block of votes. We are not as ruthless as men in this regard. This is a handicap.

We tend to be very conscientious in our committee attendance. By and large, we tend to do a great deal of homework and therefore we overcome the handicap of lack of power by being prepared on the issues.

*   *   *

I would like to voice agreement also. We work harder than our male counterparts. We tend to have the humanistic approach, the human priorities. We cut across red tape and have no qualms about it. We could be innovators.

*   *   *

I thought it was sort of assumed in our legislature that women would be the sentimental ones, and would crack up and cry about a lot of things. Unfortunately, that has not been the case. The men are usually the ones who become very much upset. I have seen them actually cry. I have not in my experience in the legislature seen a woman cry over a thing. We are pretty hard-nosed over issues. Our committee made a visit to a State School for the Retarded, and I was amazed at seeing our gentlemen legislators actually touched by this to the point where they became emotionally upset and I thought they were not too rational in their approach to the matters affecting the school after that.

* * *

I led the fight for a liberalized abortion bill. The most dispassionate, carefully measured debate was between a Catholic woman and myself. She was the chief opponent, I was the chief proponent. We always led off the debate. Then came the men afterwards, with the tears, beating of the breast, tearing of the hair.

* * *

My experience is that there is much more posturing among the men than there is among the women. . .and furthermore I think they are often less rational.

* * *

Being a woman makes it easier to get close to people, first; and second, being women we have a better basic understanding of human needs and wants.

* * *

There are many men who have the characteristics we have been discussing generally and who are honest and direct. The lobbyists don't contact them. There are many who are hard working and there are some who wheel and deal. There are very few women who wheel and deal; that is true. But there are some. . .some men have more "female" characteristics than most women do. . .and some women have more male characteristics than some men.

* * *

I have seen a grown man cry about social welfare legislation. He mopped his tears and blew his nose and was crying pretty hard. I had to take him out! He happened to be my leader at the time. He just plain broke up.

I have also seen a woman cry and did the same thing for her. I don't think we are all that different. I believe we have a tendency to think of ourselves as different. We even think of ourselves as better and superior—and we really are not. We are superior to some—and we are inferior to others. We don't care any more about certain things, and we are all tied up with special interests. But we think of our special interests not as special interests but as matters of general interest because they are our interest. I don't think women are any different from men in the legislature. Some of us are good, and some of us are not.

* * *

I take exception to that. I don't think the country would be in the same situation it is now if women were in leadership roles, as they should be, if legislatures reflected the population, the 50 percent. I don't think we would be in the Vietnam war. I don't think women are inclined in this manner. I do not agree.

* * *

That is what they said. My mother was an ardent suffragette. . . . They believed that with the vote in the hands of women, the world would be different. But the terrible truth is that it is not. . . .At the stage we are now we are different. But once we really get power, if we sit behind that smoke-filled room door where the real decisions are hammered out, where we sit as speaker, as governor, are we going to be so very different? I am afraid we are not, because the truth of the matter is that we are all human beings first. . . .It is only because now we come to government the way the Founding Fathers did, full of hope, full of drive, with our lives, our fortunes, and our sacred honor. . .well that is the way that women are now in politics. . . .The tavern owners and the motor dealers and the oil people do not approach us because they know this is in our minds and hearts.

But wait till we start handling things. Wait until someone offers us $100,000 to do something or other. Are we going to be so very different? I doubt it.

*   *   *

Yes. Are we saying that because women get involved in fewer conflicts of interest, that women have a higher standard of ethics than men and will accept these kinds of favors? Or is it because we are in the minority? Most of us, too, are independent, because we have husbands to support us and we don't have to depend entirely on our jobs in the legislature for our livelihood, and men do; and everybody knows that legislators are not being overpaid. . . .

*   *   *

Since I disagreed with all of you on that first round on the difference between men and women legislators, and said there really wasn't any, except in numbers and selection, let me say now that I do think that there is one fundamental difference between a male legislator and a female legislator and that deals with lobbyists. The men are much more subject to flattery; and (I think) this is the way a male lobbyist operates right from the beginning when they get a freshman in. They use flattery, the personal approach; "You are great!" and "No one quite like you has come down before!" They flatter the males into friendship with them. Women cannot be approached that way, because they have all known that form of approach since they were thirteen—and we don't sell out because somebody buys us a meal.

But where do you get a man who comes to the legislature at the age of forty who has been wined and dined by anybody? He has always had to do the paying. Then he gets to the legislature and he is given the full treatment.

*   *   *

I don't think you can say men are more susceptible to flattery. I don't think you can make generalizations like that.

There were other discussion groups in which similar conversations took place. Women were said to be more realistic, more moral, more humane, more grandiose, less corruptible, less pompous, less sentimental, and women were said to be like men. But it was also asserted with feeling that *if* women were less easily or less frequently corrupted, then the reason lay less in their superior virtue than in their freedom from economic responsibility.

A few legislators were firm in the conviction that identifiable and predictable differences in behavior exist between the sexes. This view, that there are ineffable, inevitable differences in male and female perspectives, is an interesting, potentially dangerous, argument for women attempting to move into "men's" roles.[32] However, in the legislative context it can also serve as the basis of a demand for increased representation of female perspectives. If women have distinctive views, approaches, interests, then no man can represent them adequately. A group specific epistemology can be applied to any group. The following comment from a black legislator illustrates the possibilities for its extension:

She (a white legislator) cannot think like a black. She just cannot. She can sympathize with me but she cannot empathize. You cannot put yourself in my place. By the same token, that man cannot think like a woman, much as he might desire to do so.

The questionnaires included inquiries about differences between male and female legislators. *All* of these women affirm that women in politics can be just as logical and rational as men. But a majority seem committed to the belief that there are significant differences in the political behavior of the two sexes. Eighty percent feel the country would be better off if there were more women in public office; about the same number reject the notion that men are better suited to politics than women. Approximately 60 percent find women "more idealistic" than men in their political attitudes; and 87 percent deny that their sex is more "hard-nosed." One does not find male legislators acquiescing in all their views. Fewer than half of the men think that more women in government would improve the life of the nation. Somewhat more think men better suited than women for the political life. The following table reflects the answers of the women and men legislators, plus a representative national sample of males and females.

This juxtaposition of attitudes reveals that these women legislators think better of women in politics than do other women, or males in or out of the legislature. It also reminds us that, in their views about women's temperament and roles, these women legislators are deviant. Their views do not merely reflect the "feminine" perspective on women and politics because they have different views than most

Sex, Temperament and Politics

	WOMEN (%) LEGIS-LATORS	WOMEN (%) NATION-ALLY	MEN (%) LEGIS-LATORS	MEN (%) NATION-ALLY
The country would be better off if women had more to say about politics (agree)	80	56	49	51
Most men are better suited emotionally for politics than most women (agree)	17	63	45	63
Women in public office can be just as logical and rational as men (agree)	100	74	90	71
Women in politics will usually be more idealistic than a man (agree)	61	46	41	40
Women in politics are usually more hard-nosed and aggressive than men (agree)	9	31	24	29

The national figures are taken from *The 1972 Virginia Slims American Women's Poll: A Study Conducted by Louis Harris and Associates*, pp. 15, 29, 30.

women. In fact, as the table makes clear, the views of most women agree with those of most men about women's political potential. As compared to public opinion, the attitudes of the women in this sample could be more accurately characterized as more feminist than as feminine.

It would be a mistake to infer from these views that these women are necessarily leaders, followers, or fellow travelers of the women's liberation movement. Very few of these legislators are or have been active in the Women's National Political Caucus, NOW, or any other of the organizations associated with the movement. Their reactions reflect the social conservatism which has already been emphasized, and also illuminate some of the problems involved in welding women, particularly women who seek to win elections, into an effective political bloc.

Approximately 60% of the legislators expressed opposition to the women's liberation movement and many criticisms were leveled against the women's liberation movement. These criticisms reflect statements by successful women about the movement. The views most frequently encountered are summarized below:

Women's liberation has an inaccurate conception of women's situation and problems. Specifically, few of the legislators believe that women are "an exploited group," that women are "most unfairly treated";[33] this view is, however, either the premise or the conclusion of most women's protest literature. Few of these legislators believe that they are deprived, denied freedom and self-fulfillment; exploited by men and society. Overwhelmingly they see such views as exaggerated, if not simply absurd.

Women's liberation is hostile to marriage and the family. The legislators feel that in its zeal to "liberate" women from traditional roles it denigrates those roles of wife and mother, advocates irresponsibility in child rearing, attempts to persuade women that their fulfillment lies in a spurious "freedom" from interpersonal responsibilities.

Women's liberation is extremist in its criticisms and its proposals. In the eyes of many, women's liberation is a branch of radical politics—and so is regarded with the same distaste as they regard the counter culture, the "new" politics, student riots, dropouts and flag burners. The belief that women's liberation is anti-system, an impression created by its most radical spokeswomen, does not enhance its attraction for women with a generally good opinion of the society and government.

Women's liberation is partisan and sectarian. Even such "moderate" wings of the women's movement as the Women's Political Caucus and NOW are widely regarded as partisans of the most liberal wing of the Democratic party. More conservative Democrats described the Women's Caucus as pro-McGovern, while many Republican women simply described it as "Democratic." Some accuse women's liberation spokeswomen of "using" women to strengthen a particular position to sectarian politics. They point out that it may be as much in the interest of women to strengthen the family as to legalize abortion or provide a national day care program; to provide for a strong national defense as to bring "peace now."

These women of conservative values, dress, speech and life style generally do not admire the "liberated" vocabularies, ideas and manners of some of the "stars" of the women's liberation movement. To the contrary, they find much that is offensive "to common decency" in the public behavior and reputations of these women.

Women's liberation makes it harder for women to be elected to office. This view, voiced by many, reproaches women's lib for complicating, by their extremism and irresponsibility, the problem of women seeking public office. There is, they say, a kind of guilt by association at work, with all women seeking to do traditional "men's jobs" lumped together as "extremist nuts and bra burners." Precisely such criticisms of the movement were encountered by some of the legislators during their campaigns.

Legislators favorable to women's liberation fall into two categories: those who find women's liberation too strident and "far out," but believe it to be fundamentally useful to the cause of broader opportunities and equal rights for women, and those who explicitly support and identify with the movement. Approximately one-fifth of the legislators fell into each of these categories.

"It is," said one woman, "like getting the attention of the donkey by hitting him over the head. Some of their (women's liberation) positions are extreme, and they certainly aren't very lady-like. But having somebody out there shouting about women's rights makes everyone more aware of the problem, and, in the long run, helps all women."

The women who identify with the women's movement do not see the movement as extreme or crude. They explain its poor image as being a result of distorted coverage by the media which, in the effort to create news, emphasize or even create sensational incidents. "No spokeswoman for the women's movement ever burned a bra," one commented. "That's just sensational journalism." To supporters it seems clear that women will achieve political and social equality only through the kind of organized, concerted effort that has produced results for other deprived groups. The vote was won this way; equal rights will be won this way; political power will be exercised by women only after they unite to claim it. The supporters are not bothered by the movement's alleged extremism or sectarianism; they share the positions in question.

Disagreements about the women's movement within this group of legislators illuminate the problem of uniting women in a single, political action group. Beyond agreement on some few, very basic beliefs about women's rights and women's place, these women see issues as Republicans and Democrats, liberals and conservatives, easterners or westerners. They did not at all agree with the proposition advanced by various speakers at the conference that *as women* they should support a particular child care bill, or health program, or welfare scheme. To most these seemed "political" questions, to be resolved by political philosophy and the local context rather than by sex.

The Equal Rights Amendment was perceived by almost all these legislators as a true "women's issue." With only three exceptions they supported ERA; most had been active in its behalf in their legislatures. Conservatives as well as liberals believe that it is needed to eliminate large accumulations of discriminatory legislation, and to guarantee equality under the law. Several women commented on how surprised they had been to discover the number of discriminatory laws on the books in their states. "In carrying a no-fault divorce bill," said one middle-aged Republican, "I became aware of how many legal disadvantages—employment and credit—a woman is confronted by. Then I became convinced of the need for ERA, and carried it in my legislature." The same woman had grave doubts about many of the so-called "women's issues"—day care centers, welfare provisions, and strongly resented the suggestion of another participant that "if only women knew their own interests they would all support George McGovern." "That," she said, "is for the birds. It's an effort by a sectarian political group to use women's problems to swell their ranks. But ERA is a real 'woman's issue.' "

NOTES

1. M. Kent Jennings and Norman Thomas, "Men and Women in Party Elites: Social Roles and Political Resources," *Midwest Journal of Political Science* 12, no. 4 (November 1968): 484.

2. See, for example, J. Kagan, Barbara Hasken, and Sara Walsen, "The Child's Symbolic Conceptualization of Parents," *Child Development* 32 (1961): 625-636.

3. See especially Herbert Hyman, *Political Socialization* (New York: Free Press, 1959); Fred Greenstein, *Children and Politics* (New Haven: Yale University Press, 1965); David Easton and Jack Dennis, *Children in the Political System: Origins of Political Legitimacy* (New York: McGraw-Hill, 1969); Robert D. Hess and Judith V. Torney, *The Development of Political Attitudes in Children* (Garden City, N.Y.: Doubleday [Anchor], 1968); and D. B. Lynn, "Sex Role and Parental Identification," *Child Development* 33 (1962): 555-564.

4. Hess and Torney, *Development of Political Attitudes* pp. 203-208.

5. There is suggestive evidence that cognitive styles can be altered by socialization, and specifically that a problem-solving, masculine approach can be cultivated in girls. See Eleanor Maccoby, "Sex Differences in Intellectual Functioning," in *The Development of Sex Differences*, ed. Eleanor Maccoby (Stanford: Stanford University Press, 1966), p. 51.

6. See, *inter alia*, Maurice Duverger, *The Political Role of Women* (Paris: UNESCO, 1955), pp. 70-71, and Robert E. Lane, *Political Life* (New Haven: Yale University Press, 1958), p. 138.

7. *The Gallup Opinion Index* Report No. 90 (December 1972): 10. Further details are available in *The Gallup Poll: Public Opinion, 1935-1971* (New York: Random House, 1972).

8. Duverger, *Political Role of Women*, p. 72.

9. *Ibid.*, pp. 50-67, passim. But his final conclusion (p. 72) is that "woman's vote brings about no great change in the situation existing before the grant of women's suffrage."

10. Daniel J. Elazar, *American Federalism: A View from the States* (New York: Crowell, 1966), pp. 85-86. A suggestive essay on the political culture of a state is Edgar Litt, *The Political Cultures of Massachusetts* (Cambridge: MIT Press, 1965). See also Edwin Andrus Gere, ed., *The Massachusetts General Court: Processes and Prospects* (Washington, D.C.: American Political Science Assn., 1972).

11. R. Michael Stevens, Occupation: "Legislator": An Exploration of Political Culture in the Pennsylvania General Assembly, mimeographed (Philadelphia: Center for the Study of Federalism, Temple University, January 1971).

12. Elazar, *American Federalism*, p. 91.

13. For a recent statement on the importance of state governments, see Ira Sharkansky, *The Maligned States: Policy Accomplishments, Problems and Opportunities* (New York: McGraw-Hill, 1972).

14. Hess and Torney report that girls more often than boys emphasize consensus rather than conflict in describing politics. Hess and Torney, *Development of Political Attitudes*, p. 218.

15. On this scale 11 percent classify themselves as very liberal, 36 percent as somewhat liberal, 31 percent as moderate, 17 percent as somewhat conservative, 6 percent as very conservative, and none as either radical or reactionary.

16. This is consistent with the Hess and Torney finding that "Political parties are more salient for boys than for girls" (Hess and Torney, *Development of Political Attitudes*, p. 217), and that "...males are more politically active and partisan-aligned" (ibid, p. 220). However, *The American Voter* authors report finding no differences in extent or intensity of party identification in men and women. Angus Campbell, Philip E. Converse, Warren E. Miller, and Donald E. Stokes, *The American Voter* (New York: Wiley, 1960), p. 489.

17. John C. Wahlke, Heinz Eulau, William Buchanan, and Leroy C. Ferguson, *The Legislative System: Explorations in Legislative Behavior* (New York: Wiley, 1962), p. 353. Also Dye suggests that partisanship in state legislatures is often low, especially legislatures dominated by one party. Thomas Dye, "State Legislative Politics," in *Politics in the American States: A Comparative Analysis*, ed. Herbert Jacob and Kenneth N. Vines (Boston: Little, Brown, 1965), pp. 184-188. A recent study of the Kansas legislature reports that party is an important though perhaps diminishing influence on legislative voting. Marvin Harder and Carolyn Rampey, *The Kansas Legislature* (Lawrence: University of Kansas Press, 1972), p. 145. In Wisconsin, the role of party in the legislature has become increasingly important. See Ronald D. Hedlund and Wilder Crane, Jr., *The Job of the Wisconsin Legislator* (Washington, D.C.: American Political Science Assn., 1971), p. 11. Sidney Wise emphasizes the role of party in the Pennsylvania legislature in *The Legislative Process in Pennsylvania* (Washington, D.C.: American Political Science Assn., 1971). So does Darrel V. McGraw, Jr., *The Role of the Lawmaker in West Virginia* (Huntington: University of West Virginia Press, 1970), pp. 84-87. See also Sheldon Goldman, *Roll Call Behavior in the Massachusetts House of Representatives* (Amherst: Bureau of Government Research, University of Massachusetts, 1968).

18. William J. Keefe and Morris S. Ogul, *The American Legislative Process: Congress and*

the States, 2nd ed. (Englewood Cliffs, N.J.: Prentice Hall, 1968), p. 66.

19. The phrase is, of course, Lasswell's, as is the following conception of value maximization. See, *inter alia,* Harold D. Lasswell and Abraham Kaplan, *Power and Society: A Framework for Political Inquiry* (New Haven: Yale University Press, 1950). See also Harold D. Lasswell, "A Note on 'Types' of Political Personality: Nuclear, Co-relational, Developmental," *Journal of Social Issues* 24 (July 1968): 81-91.

20. Lane, *Political Man, op. cit.,* p. 131.

21. Lane, *Political Life* (The Free Press, 1959), p. 161.

22. The principal legislative interests of women in Werner's study of 1963-1964 women legislators were, in the following order: social welfare (including family life), governmental processes and operations, education, urban life, and health. Emmy E. Werner "Women in the State Legislatures,'" *Western Political Quarterly* 19, no. 1 (March 1966): 46.

23. Wahlke et al., *Legislative System,* p. 246.

24. The distinction between role conception (a psychological datum) and role demands (a social datum) is important for behavioral analysis of institutions. See Daniel J. Levinson, "Role, Personality and Social Structure in the Organizational Setting," *Journal of Abnormal and Social Psychology* 58 (1959): 170-188.

25. Wahlke et al., *Legislative System,* p. 255.

26. Ibid., p. 256.

27. In Jacob and Vines, eds., *Politics in the United States,* p. 183.

28. Jennings and Thomas, "Men and Women in Party Elites," p. 487.

29. Sorauf also reports informants who said conflicts were rare and quotes one who says: "A man usually agrees with his district, since he's one of them and typical of them." Frank J. Sorauf, *Party and Representation* (New York: Atherton, 1963), p. 124. Note also that Portnoy's "legislator" is able to harmonize broad policy and constituent representative roles. Barry M. Portnoy, "Membership in the Club: Denizens of the Massachusetts House of Representatives," *Harvard Journal on Legislation,* (January 1969), pp. 199-235.

30. The discussion of representation by these women illustrates the problems of representation so effectively dealt with by Hanna F. Pitkin, *The Concept of Representation* (Berkeley and Los Angeles: University of California Press, 1967). For further discussion of representation see J. Roland Pennock and John W. Chapman, eds., *Representation* (New York: Atherton, 1968), particularly chaps. 1-9, pp. 3-127.

31. Only the extraneous comments have been removed.

32. For an interesting discussion of such "social epistemologies" see Robert Merton, "Insiders and Outsiders," *American Journal of Sociology* 78, no. 1 (July 1972): 9-47. Merton argues that social epistemologies deny both individuality and a shared culture.

33. The quotes are from Kirsten Amundsen, *The Silenced Majority: Women and American Democracy* (Englewood Cliffs, N.J.: Prentice Hall, 1971), p. 6. She is one of many spokeswomen for the movement who see women as "an exploited group" and "most unfairly treated."

Chapter VIII

Four Legislative Styles:
A Typology

SO far in this study, data have been presented on the backgrounds, recruitment, patterns of adaptation, and orientations of fifty women legislators. The time has come to see how personality, experience and legislative behavior fit together to produce different types of political women. Some personal characteristics are shared by all, or almost all, whether male or female, who build careers in elective office. These include broad identifications, a sense of personal efficacy, a habit of participation, and an ego strong enough to risk defeat. But as the preceding chapters demonstrate, there are also significant differences in background, personality, goals, and style. This chapter delineates four nuclear types of political actors represented among the women in this study, and describes the interaction of personality and institutional practice.

Personality and Role

That personality has effects on legislative behavior can hardly be doubted, but it is frequently ignored in favor of concentration on impersonal factors. The literature on legislative roles and role orientations is useful in explaining how complex, hydra-headed legislative

170

bodies accomplish their functions, but it rarely attempts to explain role distributions. Even studies of behavioral orientation which focus on the individual legislator rarely take account of personality factors involved in role choice and role performance—perhaps because legislative behavior is highly institutionalized. The impact of individual personality on the legislative process is muted by the elaborate system of roles which channel activity, of norms which prescribe standards of conduct, and of incentives which reward acceptable behavior with friendship, shared confidences, increased influence, and punish unacceptable behavior with various exclusions. But the impact of personality is only muted.

There remains an opportunity for the expression of individual character and personality; first, because there is a wide choice of roles available to a legislator; second, because these roles can be combined in various ways; and third, because the elaboration of roles still leaves room for large variations in personal political style. It is these—role choice, combination, and personal style—which define a legislator. The legislator is a *person* performing certain *roles* in a certain *way*. The legisla*ture* is composed of legisla*tors*. The legislative function can be analytically conceived as comprising roles; but a legislature consists of people in roles. Legislators not only react to the stabilized (institutionalized) expectations of others, they also bring their own expectations and demands to the interactions. Political behavior results from the two interacting. It is commonly understood that legislators are not interchangeable parts; they are not faceless ciphers whose behavior results automatically from role expectations. It is common knowledge that the man makes the office as well as the office the man. Dwight Eisenhower and Harry Truman filled the office of president very differently. The role of Senate Majority Leader is not the same when filled by Lyndon Johnson and Mike Mansfield.

By focusing on persons in political roles we can trace the interrelations of personality and role. These interrelations are multiple, complex, often subtle; but they yield to close analysis of case materials. Using the Lasswell framework for analysis,[1] it is possible to identify four "nuclear" types which link intense personal predisposition and political role. For each of these types intense personal predispositions are expressed in personal and political goals, in inter-personal style, in the self-system, role choice and management. I call these four types leaders, moralizers, personalizers, and problem solvers.

Value Preferences

Value preferences are manifested in perceptions and descriptions of reality, in preoccupations, in ambitions, in choices about how to invest time and energies. All value preferences are relative in the sense that one value is preferred as compared to others which might have been pursued. Almost everyone has multiple values; certainly, no one is likely to be elected to office in competitive elections who is or is believed to be fanatically intent on pursuing a single value. Indeed, in a campaign, democratic politicians typically take pains to present themselves as persons who love their wives, children and parents, who have achieved a respectable degree of economic and occupational success, who have an adequate understanding of the world and a good moral character, and who desire power only to maximize the well-being of the community. However, most people develop value preferences as they grow up and at any given time in their lives prefer one kind of reward to others.

Four distinctive patterns of value predispositions are found among these women. There are those with a) a preoccupation with power, b) a preoccupation with rectitude, c) a preoccupation with gaining approval and affection, and d) a multi-value orientation which gives nearly equal weight to affection, rectitude and power. The latter are easily the most numerous in this sample, although all are here represented.

Political Goals

In the previous chapter it was pointed out that political goals vary as to scope, specificity, concreteness, and substance. Each of these dimensions is related both to personality predisposition and to role choice. Abstract, remote, universal moral goals are associated with the ideological style in politics and are characteristic of the specialist in rectitude who attempts to serve as "conscience" of the house. Conversely a woman preoccupied with interpersonal relations, one who seeks and needs approval from others, is more likely to have vague and undifferentiated political goals because in fact she has little interest in the concrete substance of politics or public policy. A democratic politician deeply and effectively involved in the pursuit of power is most likely to have goals that are general, but concrete and realizable.

Self-system

Personality constitutes the internal context of political events. This context influences perspectives and interpretations of political life and molds personal responses. A growing body of literature demonstrates the impact of guilt, anxiety, hostility, self-esteem and other components of the personality on political beliefs attitudes and activities.[2] Characteristic patterns of self–management, characteristic attitudes toward the self and others are reflected in feelings of personal competence and political efficacy, political goals, ideological styles, role choices and performance.

The relationship between self-system and political behavior are important but not simple. Demands on the self may facilitate or inhibit performance; anxiety may stimulate or incapacitate; hostility may produce either aggressive or submissive behavior; achievement needs may stimulate or inhibit goal achievement. The whole range of such effects are, however, relevant to political performance and constitute the most important single determinant of political style.

Interpersonal Style

In the course of growing up and growing older, a person develops characteristic ways of being with others, of presenting herself and responding; she develops characteristic needs and goals vis-à-vis others. One person comes to look for approval, another for dominance, a third may be preoccupied with establishing superiority. The styles are as various as people are various. Interpersonal needs and goals are anchored in basic personality and rarely change much during adult life, though the expression of them may vary with changing contexts. Along with needs and goals, people develop characteristic modes of behavior for achieving these goals. Will crying achieve what a temper tantrum may not? Is ingratiation the shortest route from need to fulfillment? Temperament and experience combine in habitual styles of treating others. Description by our legislators of relations with colleagues in and out of the legislature reveals several distinctive patterns of interpersonal strategy and style, each of which is related to predispositions and to legislative role.

Personality and Role: A Typology

POLITICAL TYPE	VALUE PREFERENCE	GOAL	INTERPERSONAL STYLE
Leader	Power	Impact on total process	Electric
Personalizer	Affection	Acceptance and approval	Ingratiation
Moralizer	Rectitude	Increased righteousness of political process and output	Ideological affirmation
Problem-Solver	Multi-value (affection/ rectitude/power)	Community service	Purposive socializing

Four Political Styles Introduced

I. The Leader

The leader has special concern with authority and influence. She is interested in the whole business of the state but gravitates to the key committees and central policy problems—whatever those may be. Her energies are mobilized by the search for preeminence and influence and she works tirelessly in their pursuit. Her principal satisfactions are derived from their achievement.

The leader carries in her head a sophisticated map of the influence structure and a plan for arriving at the desired place in the structure. Her goal in interpersonal relations is to win and maintain support and influence. Her interpersonal strategy is eclectic because it must be to establish influence vis-à-vis many others. Since leadership depends on the responses of others, the interpersonal skills of the "leader" must be highly developed, permitting her to interact with subtlety, sensitivity and flexibility, and "warmth."

There are six women in this study who can clearly be categorized as "leaders."

II. The Moralizer

The moralizer is distinguished by the priority of her involvement with questions of right and wrong, good and bad and her tendency to emphasize the moral dimension. Her focus of attention is large moral/ideological issues. Her concern with concrete policy areas is derivative from their relation to broader ideological categories. For her, legislative activity is a phase in the struggle against evil. Her energies are mobilized by abstract ideological goals and moral imperatives, and her relations with others are dominated by moral categories. Because of nearly complete confidence in her standards and priorities she tends to an inflexibility in interpersonal relations. Because the moralizer makes her own moral system her criteria for giving or withholding support, she is always something of a maverick and an agitator in her legislative behavior. Because her basic source of concern is outside the legislature, her attention is not likely to be fully engaged by state legislative problems. There are four such women in this sample.

III. The Personalizer

The personalizer is preoccupied with interpersonal relations, more specifically with the search for approval and affection. Involved in an endless search for reassuring responses, the personalizer sees herself as object. Her focus of attention is always other people. "Impersonal" matters of public policy are perceived in terms of personal positions and alignments. "Impersonal" processes, such as committee hearings, are perceived in terms of the attitudes of committee members. Since politics is an interpersonal process in which people interact continuously with one another, in which interpersonal sensitivity is a requisite of success, all effective participants take account of interpersonal responses. The personalizer is distinguished from others by the *priority* she gives to the emotional responses of others. Her goal is to win approval; her principal political satisfactions derive from approval. Her interpersonal style is conciliatory and ingratiating. There are four such women in this sample.

The personalizer is a great deal like Barber's Spectator,[3] but she is distinguished from the Spectator by a greater commitment to politics as an arena in which satisfactions are sought. A distinguishing characteristic of the Spectator was her unwillingness to run for reelection, as though preoccupation with interpersonal relations were incompatible with long range political participation, but the personalizers in this sample demonstrate that, just as power can be sought in the family or the church, the search for approval can be carried on in the legislature.

Personalizers are not attracted to any specific legislative problems. Seeing themselves as objects, being preoccupied with the responses of others limits their initiative. Concern with approval makes them meticulous in conforming to the perceived expectations of others and can lead them to work hard for a committee, party or constituents. However, persistent anxieties about themselves prevent "personalizers" from seeking or assuming leadership roles.

IV. The Problem Solver

The problem solver is a truly multivalue personality whose commitments to family and policy-oriented public service coexist peacefully. She is oriented to affection, rectitude, and power; but affection is sought in the family not the legislature. Rectitude in the form of an internalized demand on the self to serve the community leads her into politics, but does not cause her to conceive politics as a battleground in a continuing struggle between good and evil. To the contrary, the problem solver sees government as an instrument for serving the community. Her legislative goal is the passage of legislation in specific, though not necessarily narrow, policy areas. Her focus of attention is the substance of legislation. Her interpersonal style is what I have termed "purposive socializing." She is fundamentally friendly, open, reasonably empathetic in her relations with others, but her ego is not deeply involved with their reactions to her. Her aim is a harmonious working relationship which will expedite the achievement of legislative goals.

Role and personality type are clearly linked in problem solvers. Their deep interest in specific policy areas makes the committee the center of their legislative world; they gravitate to the structural roles of substantive expert and committee chairman.

Over half the women in this study are problem solvers.

In the following pages each of these types is described and illustrated in some detail. Characteristic patterns of development are suggested and relations between value predispositions, goals, self-systems, interpersonal style and political role are delineated.

Leaders

Most of the work of a legislature takes place in subgroups—in party caucuses, committees, special interest groups. Most legislators, including the serious and effective ones, concentrate their attention and efforts on the work of some subgroup and make their contribution to the legislative process in so doing. A few—they are always a few—concern themselves with the whole business of the legislature and seek to play a significant role in government of the state. Because they interest themselves in the whole legislative task, for them to be as "effective" as they desire requires that they influence the whole of state government. People with such influence frequently occupy such titular positions of leadership as Speaker, Minority Leader, Majority Leader, and Whip. A few occupy key positions within central committees from which their influence radiates throughout the legislature and into the governor's offices. Leadership positions are not attained by accident nor retained without effort. Strong motivation and sustained effort are a prerequisite to the achievement of leadership.

Mrs. M has such drive and has succeeded in establishing herself as a power in the legislature of her state. In appearance and manner Mrs. M is far from the sterotype of an aggressive, powerful woman. Soft spoken, well-groomed, "lady-like" in every external respect, Mrs. M is now in her eighth term in the legislature of a border state. Her influence is recognized and felt throughout the government of the state—by her legislative colleagues, by the governor and his department heads, by the party leaders.

The only daughter of a widowed mother, Mrs. M's interest in politics developed early, before she went to college and law school. "I always knew that I would run for office someday," she comments quietly. "Twenty years before I ran for the legislature I asked the Dean of the Law School what he thought of a woman running. And yet," she muses, "if my first husband had lived, I doubt that I would have made the race."

Between the question to the Dean and the first race for legislature 20 years later, Mrs. M married, had three children, suffered a personal tragedy, remarried. When her oldest child was 12 and her youngest only 4, Mrs. M's husband and her 4-year-old son were killed in an automobile accident. She was left a widow with two children to support, a law degree, and no professional experience. "Naturally I went to work. I was able to enter the law firm of some associates of my late husband. This put me out into the business world, where I met many people." Including, she adds, her present husband. Mrs. M herself relates the tragic loss of husband and child to her late political career. Speaking of her first husband, she comments, "Our marriage was so beautiful, but, yet again, I question that I would have ever run for the legislature if he had lived. Our life was so . . . harmonious; each day was so perfect. Even though I had talked of politics, I doubt that I would ever have done a thing. It was just so harmonious. Why do anything else?" Her insights and questions are important ones: Would a woman with a "perfect," happy, harmonious marriage pursue a political career? Is "perfect" satisfaction and joy in marriage compatible with the development of other talents? Mrs. M thinks not. Was the loss of this perfect relationship a necessary condition of her political career? Mrs. M thinks so.[4]

Years later, during her second term in the legislature, Mrs. M remarried. This marriage obviously provides her some significant satisfactions, but is far from "perfectly harmonious," and it is not the center of her life. The state legislature occupies that position.

When Mrs. M first decided to run for the legislature, she "had never spent more than two minutes in the state legislature and knew almost nothing about it." But running was her idea. She decided to run, despite the mixed reaction she encountered in local party officers. In that first race there was no primary opposition, and no serious contest in the general election. The next time was different. Five persons including a local party leader (male) filed for the primary; there was a run-off between the two of them. She was generally expected to lose. Mrs. M's description of that campaign reveals the intensity of her psychological investment in politics.

"I experienced the greatest drive that I have ever felt. I have never in my life had as compelling a drive—one that kept me working from 4:30 or 5:00 in the morning till 11:00 or 12:00 at night. Those two weeks were the most intensive two weeks of my life. And I had no control over it. It was really somewhat fantastic to me—as though I were possessed." The possibility of losing "never occurred" to her.

The same intense involvement characterizes Mrs. M's legislative performance. She "loves" all aspects of the job; she "eats, sleeps, and breathes it to the point that I have to catch myself" and "make room" for her family, and "not impose politics and government on them." She works long hours and is "usually the last person to leave the Capitol."

Such absorption, such concentration of energy occur only when an activity has compelling subjective significance. The feelings of being able to mobilize extraordinary energy, of being "beyond control" constitute evidence that politics has profound and compelling significance for her. The long days and nights at the State House, the difficulty in diverting attention from legislature to family attest that we are dealing here with a person for whom influence has displaced affection as a central value.

Family obligations are the duty; politics the passion. Still, Mrs. M is committed to a culture which defines family as the first duty of a woman. Talking to her, it becomes clear that though in her view family *ought* to be most important, politics *is*. In her determined effort to "catch herself," and *not* eat, sleep, and breathe politics, in her description of why the families of legislators are somewhat neglected—(because the legislators become too "absorbed" in the job), her subjective priorities are clear. There is a fascinating account, too, of what she calls the "temptation" of running for statewide office, which she badly *wanted* to do, but felt constrained not to by the conviction that it would mean the end of her marriage. "It was," she says, "like wrestling with the devil." The office (power) was the temptation; marriage, the obligation.

Value preferences are clear, too, in her appraisal of her legislative accomplishments. Her greatest accomplishment is having achieved "a position of influence with other legislators." Her descriptions of the legislative process emphasize accumulating influence. Mrs. M has serious policy commitments, and serious moral commitments—but she is not concerned about symbolic consistency or "purity." "I do not always vote my convictions on an issue," she explains. "Sometimes, when it is not a close vote, I give a courtesy vote to someone sponsoring a bill. For example, there was a man in the legislature who had only 20 votes for a bill he felt very strongly about, and I had voted against him so many times and on so many issues that I supported him on this particular roll call. I have done that on other occasions. My vote is not always indicative of what it would be on a close vote."

"I don't really like to oppose legislation. When a bill is introduced that I am very much against I usually work quietly against it. I don't take to the floor. I am not very good at defeating legislation; I am very good at passing it. I never openly oppose a bill unless it is a major issue; I feel that defeating unimportant legislation is often like winning a battle, but losing a war."

Mrs. M thinks of herself as desiring influence for the sake of good government. She is deeply involved in the substance of legislation in different areas—education, labor, banking, the judiciary, and in the effective use of the state's resources to achieve good government. For her, good government is representative government. She takes the job of representative seriously and is convinced of her obligation to be guided by the "needs and thinking of the people at home." "I think our job is not to follow our own personal desires and wishes, but that of a majority of our people at home—to do what they feel would be best and what they would like to have us do in their behalf." There is room in her conception for creativity and judgment, because the legislator acts or should act on the basis of an informed opinion. The representative's judgment should be informed by study and investigation; it is not a rubber stamp. A legislator must have "vision, and a broad outlook, take into account the consequences—not just the immediate consequences, but try to see years ahead."

She says of herself, "The things that I have really wanted, I have gone after." The things that she has really wanted include the chairmanship of a major committee, a position on the steering committee, and a top party office. For two of these it was necessary to exert herself, to "stand up and assert [my] rights." There is another, even more authoritative position that she would like to occupy, and already, two and a half years before it will become vacant, she is at work accumulating the support necessary to claim it.

The conviction that she can achieve what she desires—within the limits of her physical energy and stamina (and she is sensitive to the limits of her stamina)—is one evidence of Mrs. M's self-confidence and self-esteem. Quiet confidence in her abilities contributes to the force of her personality—a force she communicates to both voters and colleagues. The only limits she sees to her upward political mobility are physical stamina and self-imposed limits resulting from a sense of duty to family. She is not uncomfortable speaking about her influence and potential because she evinces detachment that enables her to speak of herself as though she were someone else, to coolly appraise her strength and weaknesses. In any case, she sees influence as a form of achievement, a deserved reward for application and hard work.

Mrs. M makes heavy demands on herself and knows it. She demands long hours, hard work; she defines the legislative job as a very demanding one, and then demands of herself that she be a good legislator. Hearing her speak of "working very early, working very late," it would be easy to mistake Mrs. M for a person driven by basic and unquenchable insecurity, but she does not work from a conviction of inadequacy. "I know that I do a very excellent job," she says with quiet conviction, and one understands that she means it.

Mrs. M is an extremely task-oriented person. Her interests and satisfactions are focused on the passage of legislation and the government of the state. She has little interest in the interpersonal dimensions of the legislative process, except insofar as they impringe on legislative outcomes. After hours socializing seems to her largely a waste of time, "a fatiguing distraction," and yet, during some periods when she has judged it useful, Mrs. M has gone out every night with fellow legislators—eating, talking, planning.

Toward others she expresses the same attitudes of acceptance and detachment that characterize feelings about herself. There is no evidence of either overt or veiled hostility toward men or other women. She describes her electoral opponents as nice people who would also do a good job. Indeed, she seems to have a policy of accentuating the positive in speaking of others. Speaking to her one does not feel that she is unfeeling, merely preoccupied with other matters. Her aim is not fellowship. Although Mrs. M has little proclivity for intimate relationships, she displays an open, inclusive ego which gives her empathy for colleagues and the state's population. Her personal manner is warm, soft-spoken, almost shy. Convinced that a woman must always be a lady, she exemplifies the gentle manners of a past generation. In talking to her, however, the determined eye and sudden steel in her voice make clear that inside the softly feminine exterior resides a strong woman of ability and great determination. Neither party nor ideology has emotional significance for her.

Mrs. M is, of course, active in her party's caucus, and through habit and realism she takes the party fully into account in describing the legislature. Yet it seems clear that party identification is not emotionally significant for her. It is not strong in the way that identification with her district and state are important. She does not approach a problem as a member of a party, but she would never neglect to take her party into account. In purposive role orientation Mrs. M is an inventor par excellence; a woman determined to find solutions to state problems through legislative process. Ideologically she embodies a kind of principled pragmatism that combines broad empathy, moderation, technology, ingenuity, and a strong concern for the acceptability of solutions to the state's population.

Mrs. M identifies with her job, her children, her district, the state, and with women of good character. But these identifications have only marginal significance for her political life. She "does not involve her family" in her political life. Her husband, she says, never participates because "he feels this is something I must do on my own." Her children are "proud" of her political career, but have never campaigned for her. She believes that children both suffer and profit by their mother's activities. They suffer neglect from time to time but in return have a mother who is "less demanding, less domineering."

There are other women in this sample who have achieved leadership roles. All are characterized by (1) concern with whole process rather than a part; (2) intense commitment exhibited in long hours, hard work, and in preoccupation with the business of the legislature; (3) a detached interpersonal style oriented to maintaining harmony and cooperation rather than winning affection; (4) heavy demands on the self; (5) a clear sense of self, and of one's place in the process; (6) a strong future orientation which includes well-defined personal goals; (7) a relatively low level of emotional involvement in family and other personal relationships; (8) a high level of political skills.

In Mrs. M, the relationship between personal qualities and a leadership role is clear. Legislative leadership requires skill, broad interests, an ability to see the whole; a sense of the future, ability to examine and evaluate one's performance; a relative detachment from interpersonal relations that frees energies for investment in impersonal goals. Mrs. M conforms to Lasswell's description of political man. She "1. accentuates power; 2. demands power (and other values for the self. . .); 3. accentuates expectations concerning power; 4. acquires at least a minimum proficiency in the skills of power."[5] But she is also a democratic politican who uses power to attain values for the community. She has an open, inclusive ego based on broad identifications with family, community, state. Her desire for power is tempered by respect and empathy. Her political goals postulate the sharing of values.

Other leaders in this sample demonstrate similar patterns of motivation and behavior. Now in her fifth term, Mrs. E has also reached the inner citadels where the major decisions are made by a few. The oldest daughter of a prairie state farmer, Mrs. E was graduated from her state university, married, and had two sons before she was twenty-five. For nearly fifteen years thereafter she devoted herself to children, husband, farm, and community. Active in the Farm Bureau, the PTA, and her church, she developed a reputation for community leadership. More and more she began to feel that her children were occupied with school and the farm. She decided to run for the legislature when an opening occurred. "It might be different," she says, "if I had had a girl, but the boys were always following their father around when they weren't in school. I felt I could run for office and that no one would be the worse for it. The boys were 13 and 15 then. My mother, who lived with us, could keep the house running better than I could anyway."

Not feeling needed at home, Mrs. E ran for office, won, and has since devoted herself intensively to the legislature. She, too, has a broad interest in the government of the state, and apart from making herself an expert on certain aspects of agriculture, she has moved about in committees, depending on the major issue of the session. "I like to see all aspects of the state's problems," she says, "not just one or two pieces of the jigsaw puzzle." Party is important to Mrs. E; she does not speak long on an issue without relating it to the party.

Although her state has sent more women to the legislature than most, Mrs. E is the first woman to achieve a leadership position in the majority party. She, too, had to exert herself to arrive at this position. Personal relations have been more important in her legislative career than in that of Mrs. M. She has developed close relationships with many legislators, and especially with her own party leaders, and has incorporated a busy work-oriented social life into her schedule. During the session and often in between she spends long evenings with colleagues talking about the business of days past and days up-coming. She regards such socializing as an indispensable part of the job; as important as the work on legislation, on which she spends other long evenings. One also senses that she enjoys the easy camaraderie.

The long drive, the pressure of legislative business, and a low level of involvement at home keep her in the Capitol many of the weekends during the session. "Sometimes," she says, "I think perhaps the legislature takes too much of my life, but what we do there matters so much to the people of the state." "And," she adds, "whenever I force myself to spend less time on legislative business, I feel even worse. I know I have an important contribution to make. I know I need to make that contribution." She feels needed in the legislature in a way that she rarely felt needed at home.

Mrs. E thinks that had she started in politics earlier she might have run for Congress. "I would have liked serving in the Congress. I am a legislator by temperament," but she has no regrets and today is determined to "stay in the legislature as long as the voters will have me."

Mrs. E says of herself that her ideology can be reduced to three principles: help the people who need help, take advantage of resources and opportunities, never lose sight of the future. On legislative questions she is creative, future-oriented, prepared to seek new solutions. Though she is much too careful a politician to neglect her district, her fundamental orientation is to the state. The state is her arena; its problems have become her problems. To solve them, she says, she seeks power. Mrs. E is frank about having worked deliberately to gain a position of influence; she is frank about wanting that position, and about her intention to preserve and expand her power. She smiles a little when she acknowledges that she likes feeling powerful.

Mrs. E reports no family problems. Her children have married, her husband is still "awfully busy with the farm." Occasionally he comes to the Capitol for a weekend. "But he says he feels in the way." She describes him as a "very understanding man who knows how important this work is to me." He is, she says, "a booster." One gets the feeling they enjoy a pleasant but rather distant relationship. Certainly, Mrs. E's most intense involvement is politics, not family. It is in legislature that she invests the largest part of her time, energy, and attention. She is not indifferent to her family; she speaks of her husband with fondness and even alludes vaguely to the possibility of retiring at some unspecified future time so that she and her husband can travel and "enjoy" themselves. It seems doubtful that this intensely work-oriented woman—who never feels the job is done—could enjoy a long period of leisure.

Politics is not the exclusive value of the "leaders" in this sample. The legislators described here value their marriages, and regularly spend time with their husbands and now grown children. When Mrs. M perceived a clear conflict between continuation of her imperfect marriage and running for a top statewide office, she chose the marriage despite the intense "temptation" of the office. Both Mrs. M and Mrs. E deferred their political careers until their children were older; that is, they gave priority to non-power values during a substantial part of their adult lives. It is interesting that the "leaders" in this group were less active in community affairs during these child-rearing years than were the "problem solvers," perhaps because they have less interest in social activity for its own sake, perhaps because the abstract sense of duty to participate is less important in motivating them. For the leaders politics is not a hobby, but a fascinating, consuming interest; a romance, not a duty.

The Moralizers

All political actors seek through their political activity some version of the public good, some goal which they endow with moral status. Genghis Khan wrecked havoc in the name of Mongol unity; Hitler in the name of the preservation of civilization; Joseph Stalin in the name of Marxism-Leninism; Lincoln went to war in the name of "union"; FDR promised a "New Deal"; DeGaulle a vision of France. The desire to reinforce rectitude with power and power with rectitude links politics to morals ineffably.

But while all political actors have purposes they conceive as moral, not all conceive life and politics as a battleground in a continuing moral struggle. Not all conceive their political activities as one phase of larger war between good and evil. Some, however, bring to politics a world view that endows all transactions with moral significance and links even the most apparently trivial and remote questions to major moral issues. For such actors morality is the guide to political action. Their ideological style can be recognized in their continued emphasis on "greater moral purposes" and their peculiar moral intensity; their habit of describing themselves as moral agents; and their intensely censorious judgments of political opponents.[6] Such types appear most frequently in times of rapid cultural change. They bring to political life a quality of intensity and, frequently, an intolerance which contrasts starkly with the politics of economic interests and compromise. Because their perspectives, goals, and interpersonal encounters are seen in terms of moral categories, I call them "moralizers."

Mrs. Y, now serving her second term in a southern State House, provides a clear example of this type. Mrs. Y had had little interest in politics until the civil rights movement dramatized for her the centrality of politics for achieving racial justice. Until that time, marriage, children and church had occupied her time and energy. Her husband, was an ex-minister turned counselling psychologist and she herself had academic degrees in social work and counselling and had worked at a church settlement house for five years after they married. Mrs. Y had been a serious Christian and active in the church since childhood. After five years of hoping for a family their first child was born, and another followed rapidly; their two children were supplemented from time to time by a succession of foster children (usually nonwhite). In the years while the children were very small, Mrs. Y still found time to be active in the Women's Church Federation, the Mission Circle, a prayer group, the choir, and a temperance group which worked with alcoholics. When the children were still quite young, her husband took a job at a Christian settlement house in a nearby city. Situated deep in an urban slum, inhabited by itinerant addicts, derelicts, the aged infirm, and the destitute, it was hardly an ideal environment for growing children; but Mrs. Y, looking at the bright side, thought that they could learn to serve others.

To Mrs. Y, her children seemed a part of her "personal" affairs, which could, really should, not be permitted to interfere with higher (impersonal) matters. Her moral system gave priority to larger, more remote duties; her conscience made heavier demands for service to "higher" causes.

The city to which they moved had an active civil rights group, closely connected to the ministerial association. It was only natural for her to get involved. Then her husband began to pay attention to local reform politics. Gradually politics took on a salience it had never had in her life. More and more she found herself dwelling on the government's role in racial injustice. Up to that point, her activities in politics had been limited to voting Republican. When she thinks back on that time she is amazed by how much she has changed. The civil rights movement "became [her] life for two or three years."

She describes it this way: "I managed the city office of the movement. I traveled. I just literally left a husband and two children at home for two months, but our whole family thought that civil rights

were more important, that the movement was our only hope." Then
came the Vietnam war. Almost imperceptibly her focus of attention
changed as the racial situation improved and the nation sunk deeper
in the Asian conflict.

She never intended to run for office. There was no reason to think
she could do anything about the war in the state government, and
that was "the only important thing." But, through the efforts of the
anti-war group to get control of the local Democratic party, she
became more and more involved, and soon people were asking her to
run for the legislature. About the same time she was feeling very
disgusted with the Congress for not "doing something" to stop the
war. "I realized they were impotent by their own design," she says;
"Then I decided we are moving into a period of repression and this is
a crazy world and we had better get ourselves every elected office
that we can . . . and I still feel this way. I feel it is a very bad period
in our history; the only job open was on the state level so I decided
to run."

Mrs. Y had a rough primary, fought against a local conservative
candidate (male); she won, and went on to win the general election.
Since then she has divided her time between the legislature, the
Reform movement, anti-war activities, with not too much left over
for family and private concerns. She thinks of herself as sacrificing
personal goals to larger, moral ones. The language that she uses in
describing her life is steeped in Christian symbolism. It features the
concept of personal sacrifice. She speaks of "giving my blood" to the
movement, of "dedication," of "draining herself" for the causes in
which she believes.

Listening to Mrs. Y speak of the moral imperatives that so dominate her life, hearing her language of personal sacrifice, her need to
feel worthy becomes clear. There is also aggression and guilt in her
ideology and in her dedication. Mrs. Y has a military bearing, she sits
straight, head high, and moves like a combat-ready sergeant. Combat
against immorality mobilizes her and the supply of evil in the environment is adequate to keep her perpetually on duty. Ideology provides her with impersonal, permissible targets of aggression. Temptation, sin, weakness, alcohol were once such targets; they have been
replaced by the war, the military-industrial complex, the ecological

crisis. The psychological dynamics of self-sacrifice permit her to see aggression sanctioned by ideology as sacrifice. The sacrifice "pays" for the aggression and enhances other convictions of dedication to a higher cause.

Mrs. Y knows that others, especially her children, are involved in these sacrifices to larger causes. For the period of her most intense involvement in civil rights activities, she says, "I don't imagine I cooked two meals a month. I literally just lived that job. . ." and the children "picked up the tab at home." Mrs. Y feels that she has not spent as much time at home in recent years as she should. Her interest in politics has become "such an absorbing thing." She, too, says of herself, "I just eat, sleep, breathe politics." "Nothing interests me as much as politics," she says. "Politics is my center of gravity." Still, she thinks, she should have "disciplined" herself to spend more time at home. The marriage is not without problems. Her sex life suffers because she "comes home late and tired." Her children have "paid a price," but for this woman the moral imperatives associated with husband and children are rarely if ever as powerful as those of ideology. The big issues seem more compelling; reforming the "sick" priorities of the society more urgent than purely personal obligations. "Urgency" is a key component of her world view. The issues will not wait, the hour of decision is always at hand, the need is to act now.

Mrs. Y conceives herself as an agent for moral elevation; she is not reticent in attributing virtue to her motives and actions. She describes her campaign as "very exemplary," herself as "very nice," and "inspiring" to others, and very "educational" for the voters. The educator role is one she enjoys; carrying the message mobilizes her energy and enthusiasm. Furthermore, she enjoys contests. "I have come to see," she says, "that politics is between a social revolution and a tea party, and that the contest is as invigorating as a good tennis match. The contest is half the fun in politics."

So, there is fun in politics for Mrs. Y as well as inspired moral combat. Mrs. Y is not a fanatic. Moral categories dominate but do not preempt her political and her personal life. There are other values and these are nonideological bonds with other people. She has found that she can respect colleagues with whom she disagrees. Mrs. Y was surprised during her first term at "how hard the job of legislator is, and how much the members give to it." Nonetheless her relations with others are always affected by her moral mission. Most of her colleagues think of her as a crusader, she says, and as too unrealistic to have an impact on the world. She herself thinks she is "too frank" and "very judgmental." The leadership sometimes finds that she "doesn't play ball," that she "crusades too intently on an issue," or is "too much of a preacher." Commenting on this aspect of her style she says, "I have got to get over that, but I do it even from the floor. They incense me so that even though I know better, I stand up and lecture them anyway."

Life seems too short and her purposes too urgent for investing much time in interpersonal relations. After hours socializing is repugnant to her even though "I know it helps to get your bills through. I don't drink and I don't smoke and I'd rather be at home with my family than in a bar near the Capitol." The desire to be effective is not so powerful as the desire to express her positions (even when she knows they will alienate others), nor is it strong enough to overcome her distaste for "wasting time" in socializing. Although she sees knowledge as the key to legislative success, commitments to "the movement" are frequently so heavy that she does not "have time" to read and understand legislative issues thoroughly. And, she is "too purist" to go along with those whose votes she may need later. "Dealing"—swapping support for support—seems reprehensible; compromising a position in committee or going along with a majority seems reprehensible. She has, she says, "been very stubborn," and predicts "I have to pay a price for consulting my conscience on every vote. So far the price has not been too high."

Fundamentally Mrs. Y sees herself too pure for the politics of the state legislature. Her mind tells her to preach less and work harder; to be more friendly, and less "judgmental"; to "go along" more frequently and so "get along" better—become more effective in the legislature. But her moral preferences are too compelling to yield to pragmatic counsel. She finds it virtually impossible to stifle disapproval and forego expressions of disdain.

The issues that mobilize Mrs. Y are rarely dealt with at the state level, a fact which leads Mrs. Y to think she would like to be in

Congress. "The war, the credibility gap, the FBI, repression, the Wallace trend, youth—it is the big 'new politics' issues" that engage her. These issues are also notably compatible with her moral style. It is harder to function as an agent of the "movement" in the State House. Abortion and ERA have involved her since the women's movement captured her attention. Environment seems to her a worthy field of endeavor, but state government pales beside her commitment to national renewal through "new politics" reform.

Mrs. Y's concern with her district is tangential to her basic commitments. She sees herself as a representative of causes rather than people, a "tribune" who believes that her chief obligation is "to do the right thing" regardless of the views of constituents. Mrs. Y's moral mission and comprehensive moral categories limit the legislative roles available to her; her "certainty" is fundamentally incompatible with the norms of modesty and compromise; her unwillingness to "deal," to "go along," cause her to be regularly bypassed by leadership; her tendency to lecture colleagues from the floor violates both interpersonal and legislative norms. Her involvement with "bigger" issues diverts time and prevents her from becoming an authority on legislative matters. A moralizer is almost certain to be a "maverick" vis-à-vis both party and legislature. Mavericks may play an important role in a political body—reminding members of the moral implications of their positions, recalling them to principles. They may win the respect of colleagues even as they are shunned. Mrs. Y is such a legislator; in two terms she feels she has made an impact. Measured in terms of laws passed, her accomplishments are less impressive than those of other legislative sophomores but when her impact in the legislature is added to her extra-legislative activities, the sum is not negligible.

Mrs. Y is a "new politics" activist, but there are Moralizers of other persuasions. In this sample there are conservative and even moderate Moralizers. Mrs. X is an example of the former. The conviction that moral decay is progressively sapping the roots of the nation led Mrs. X first to become a Republican volunteer, second, to become an activist in the Goldwater campaign, and third, to seek public office. There are some interesting and suggestive parallels in the political histories of Mrs. X and Mrs. Y. Both left their traditional and heredi-

tary party identifications and joined the opposite party in pursuit of
their ideological goals. Mrs. Y deserted her Republican voting habits
to throw in her lot with "new politics" Democrats. Mrs. X, a life-long
Democrat, became a Republican when she was convinced that that
party was more dedicated to the traditional values of the nation.
Both have a long history of church activity. Mrs. X and her husband
were both active church members who have always taken their religion very seriously and devoted a great deal of time to church affairs.
Both women left rather young children at home while they pursued
their moral causes. In style, there are also striking similarities: both
are rather large, energetic women with a positive manner and a habit
of stating positions with great certainty. Both came to politics rather
late in life after years of involvement in religious causes. The similarities in ideological style are multiple. Both have an enormous sense of
urgency about impending dangers: Mrs. Y sees the country on the
verge of an era of repression; Mrs. X believes the nation is endangered
by progressive moral decay, decadence, and erosion of basic values.
Both went to the legislature as a step in counteracting the urgent
danger. Both state their missions in terms of Christian symbolism:
stewardship, dedication, personal sacrifice.

Mrs. X was the daughter of a high school principal, a devout man
who served for many years as superintendent of the Sunday School
in their downtown Protestant church. Growing up, Mrs. X learned
through town, church, school and family to identify with the problems of others. She learned, too, that in almost any situation there
are forces of good and forces of evil, and that she had a duty to add
her weight to the good side. Her sensitivity to the moral dimension
grew, and her commitment grew with it. It seemed to her that most
people cared less than they should about their duty and she began to
feel that there must have been deterioration. She thought most
people were too easy on themselves; and she determined to always
set high standards for herself. When her father died, shortly before
she finished high school, Mrs. X knew that her place was at home
with a bereaved mother and two younger siblings. She took some
college courses in an extension program, and has always made it a
point to read widely. After her children were born she took courses
in child psychology; in spare time she taught herself two languages.

Of her lack of formal education, she says, "This feeling that just because you didn't go to college you can't become an educated person—good grief, that's ridiculous."

The same feeling that you can change things if you try led her into politics. She decries the notion that "you are just a little pebble on the beach so what's the use." A sense of efficacy reinforced a sense of mission, and led her first into party volunteer work, then to candidacy for the state legislature. Running for office was her idea— and had the wholehearted support of her politically active husband, who agreed to take the responsibility of their three children, ages 10 to 16, while she ran and served.

As she describes the campaign, the odds were three or four to one against her. The district was predominantly Democratic. Her opponent was an incumbent. "They thought I would be a pushover," she says, with relish. No one counted on her indefatigable campaigning which began six months before the election and continued down to the wire. Mrs. X is a positive thinker. "It never once crossed my mind that I would be defeated, even with the odds. Never once did I or any one of my campaign people entertain a negative thought."

In her first term, Mrs. X played a conventional freshman role, but showed a certain talent for "getting into the middle" of things. The opposition in her second campaign was, if anything, tougher than the first, but she increased her margin, partly because of excellent service rendered her constituents, partly because she had spoken all over the district in the intervening two years. Mrs. X's ideology emphasizes the return of government to the people. It is only natural that she should take very seriously the job of representing constituents. Mrs. X has a poor opinion of "partisan politics"; her partisanship is based, she says, "on principle not on parties." She tends to categorize her legislative colleagues in terms of these principles as good guys and bad guys. She finds a good deal of corruption in politics and strongly disapproves patronage of any kind.

Mrs. X has a special interest in youth and has sought out committees that specialize in education, child care, and medical services for minors. She sees youth as the future that must be safeguarded. She is an indefatigable worker, but a good deal of her energy is spent outside the legislature, speaking before groups all over the state.

"Awakening" the people to their duties is a major preoccupation. In the legislature she "tries hard" to be pleasant, and get along well "with colleagues." But her standards of personal conduct are incompatible with easy socializing. The need to "lead a proper life and not ever put ourselves in a compromising position" means, in her view, that women cannot spend their time in the bar after the session. She is, furthermore, prone to lecturing her colleagues from the floor and in committee, exhorting them to care more for the public and to disdain the company of lobbyists. Her self-confidence and extraordinary sense of efficacy convince her that there are no obstacles she cannot overcome, no goals she cannot achieve. She thinks of running for higher office, and does not doubt that she could "overcome the influence of the interests" and achieve victory.

Both Mrs. X and Mrs. Y are somewhat insensitive in interpersonal relations, more given to exhortation than to accommodation. Occasionally, Mrs. X has travelled about the state, publicly berating a colleague for his position on some piece of legislation: "When I go into their respective districts—and I go very often—I speak all the time and I let the people in their communities know what they do. I will say: 'Now, I know your representative is an excellent representative. He is the very best that I have seen and he must have an awfully good reason for not supporting child care, and you must be interested in child care because you have me here talking about it. I don't know what his reason is, but I think you ought to find out.'" Both women think of themselves as effective. They think that the force of their conviction, dedication and perserverance make them women who must be taken into account. Both are agitators as well as legislators. Neither can accomplish their goals within the legislature because those goals involve nothing less than moral renewal of the population.

In a legislative context, the moralist almost inevitably fills the role of maverick. Moralistic mavericks speak a great deal and often do less homework than is required for a high degree of effectiveness. Her preoccupation with the big moral questions diverts her from concentration on the details of legislation; and reputations are built on the mastery of these details. Her dogged insistence on making decisions on the basis of her "priorities of conscience" disqualifies her as a reliable team player and effectively prevents her developing organizational influence. The tendency to preach, and the aura of self-righteousness surrounding the moralizer is likely to seem tiresome to peers, and to impede the development of the wide friendships which expand legislative influence. The moralizers in this sample understand their "outsider" status. They understand that their moral zeal prevents them from being as effective in the legislature as they might otherwise be, but they accept this as part of the wages of virtue. It becomes yet another proof that they are maintaining integrity in spite of the pressures of political life.

In her relations with others, the moralizer is leader, follower, teacher, disciple, but rarely an equal. Her close associations (what she calls friendships) are based on devotion to a common cause rather than on personal qualities. The moralizer is not deeply involved in interpersonal relations with concrete persons. The marriages of the moralizers in this sample seem also to be a kind of ideological alliance. In all cases the husband shares the moral perspective and enthusiasms of the wife. However, though he works in local organizations and takes on extra household responsibilities, it is the wife who carries the battle into elective politics. One gets the feeling that these marriages involve ideology as much as intimacy. The "moralizer" orientation tends to depersonalize both self and others, to replace people with positions. The moralizer demands of others the same ideological enthusiasm and dedication she asks of herself. This requirement that others share her opinions and conform to her high standards makes all personal relations alliances. "Personal" factors are subordinated to moral goals even in personal relations.

Because rectitude is measured only in relation to internalized moral standards, the moralizer is relatively invulnerable to the opinions and attitudes of others. The power seeker, whose influence depends on the responses of others, is necessarily alert to the values, preferences, and cues of those with whom she deals. A problem solver, too, is dependent on the cooperation of others to achieve her goals. The personalizer is, of course, continually involved with the responses of others. But the moralizer uses her principles as armor against the judgments of others. The expectation that it will prove necessary to suffer for her convictions is an important part of the psychology of the moralizer in politics. It arms her against defeat and rejection, provides an all-purpose explanation for failure, and transforms defeat into a source of reassurance and renewal.

None of the moralizers in this sample expect to be fully accepted or successful. "I am about as effective as a liberal could be in my legislature," says one in explaining her failure to achieve several objectives. "I won't go along. I have to pay the price," comments another.[7] Moralizers are likely to think of themselves as not "really" suited to politics because of their uncompromising idealism. The conviction of virtue which is both the strength and weakness of the moralizer is the psychological cornerstone of fanaticism. None, however, of the moralizers in this sample is a fanatic nor is a fanatic likely to be elected to public office in a system of democratic elections. Most voters demand representatives with multiple values, representatives whose moral principles are tempered by experience, common sense, and a decent respect for human frailty. The moralizer must take pains not to bore and offend the voters with her claims to purity. Once in the legislature she must keep a tight rein on her censoriousness.

Of the four types of political actor in this sample, the moralizer is most interested in words and in symbolic action. It is very important to her to *state* her principles, to *dispute* the false principles of others. She finds ideological affirmation a most satisfying form of political action, a fact that explains her enjoyment of campaigns, her tendency to speak too long and too often, her volubility in interviews. For her, talk is action. Words are more flexible, more yielding, more satisfying a medium than public policy which deals with complicated and often unyielding problems.

Many of the women—suffragettes, temperance leaders, social workers—who have made a mark on American politics were moralizers, renowned for their inflexible devotion to principle. Perhaps the reason lies in the tendency of traditional American culture to define women as specialists in virtue, custodians of the nation's conscience. Perhaps the reason is that the moralizer-agitator-"outsider" role was the only one available to women seeking to make an impact on the political scenes. (Moral symbols are frequently the best if not the only political weapon available for doing battle against a much more powerful adversary.) Perhaps the reason is that women *qua* women *are* the moral sex, fit by nature to bring morals into politics. A good many women have claimed—and still claim—as much. But is is significant in this regard that only four of the legislators in this group are moralizers.

The Personalizer

The political type whom I have termed a personalizer brings to politics a preoccupation with interpersonal relations and especially with the reactions of others to her. Her main satisfactions come from feeling approved, appreciated, and respected by her associates. Her activities as legislator are dominated by the pursuit of favorable responses. The personalizer is distinguished from her colleagues not by her concern for the opinion of others, but by the intensity of that concern and by its centrality in her psychic life and activities.

The legislative process involves legislators in continuous interaction with others—in committees, on the floor, in party caucuses, in informal encounters outside the legislature. Success as a legislator requires success in relating to one's colleagues; there are few legislative tasks which do not require the cooperation and support of others. The effective legislator is therefore concerned with the reactions of others; she tries not to irritate or alienate colleagues (who knows when their support may be needed?); she conforms her behavior to the informal norms that smooth interpersonal relations; she obliges colleagues where practical and attempts in various ways to build a reservoir of good will which can be drawn on as need arises. The average legislator (male and female) is a gregarious, sociable person with a high opinion of others. Most take pleasure from winning the respect and approval of colleagues. But, for most legislators in this sample, the high opinion of others is not a central value nor the major satisfaction in legislative activity. The personalizer is distinguished from her gregarious colleagues by the centrality of her concern with the attitudes, evaluations, feelings, and responses of others. For her, the greatest satisfactions and pleasures of legislative life are winning respect, approval, and affection from her colleagues. Although prevailing stereotypes suggest that preoccupation with interpersonal relations is characteristic of women, there are only four personalizers in this sample. (Presumably personalizers are more numerous among both males and females at lower levels where "being active" may consist almost exclusively of socializing.)

A pervasive orientation to the responses of others is frequently believed to be a symptom of low self-esteem. And it is true that the personalizers in this study seem to have less self-confidence and more doubts about themselves than the leaders or the moralizers (both of whom have enormous confidence in their rectitude and abilities) and than most of the problem solvers. The personalizers describe having initial doubts about their ability to make good legislators; all of them believed they might lose the election; all describe themselves as needing reassurance from others about their performance. However, they do run, they do win elections, and they do come to think of themselves as good legislators. They have a relatively lower sense of self-confidence and self-esteem than the other type of political actor, but this does not indicate neurotically low esteem. Orientation to interpersonal relations does not necessarily involve an exaggerated concern for the responses of others, nor pathological anxiety, nor debilitating, persisting self-doubt, any more than a concern with rectitude necessarily indicates fanaticism or concern with influence indicates being "power mad."[8]

There is no necessary association between a pathologically low self-estimate and a preoccupation with personal relations. Such preoccupation may reflect nothing more than prevailing patterns of socialization and role expectations. Women are socialized to be specialists in interpersonal relations. Bardwick and Douvan, for example, note that "In the absence of independent and objective achievements, girls and women know their worth only from others responses, know their identities only from their relationships as daughters, girl friends, wives, or mothers and, in a literal sense, personalize the world."[9] The nurturing functions associated with traditional female roles require a high degree of sensitivity and responsiveness to others. Because early in childhood little girls develop special sensitivity to interpersonal cues, it is neither surprising nor pathological that regardless of their fundamental self-esteem they come to especially value, enjoy, and pursue favorable responses from others, nor that we should find some orienting themselves to interpersonal relations in politics as in other spheres.

The point is emphasized because some prevailing cultural stereotypes denigrate an orientation to affection as somehow more petty or more base than a preoccupation with, for example, rectitude. In such a perspective the personal is less exalted than the impersonal, the local than the national, the concrete than the abstract. This hierarchy of preferences is characteristic of the rationalist style in politics and morals and is accounted for in part by the distaste for variable personal factors, the preference for depersonalizing politics and the related attraction to comprehensive deductive ideologies. [10] It is by no means clear that an orientation to interpersonal relations is less functional or less worthy than a preoccupation with rectitude.

An important distinguishing characteristic of the personalizer is the scope of her concern with the opinions of others. She does not necessarily care more than problem solvers do about the views of husband or children, but she cares more about the views of *more* "others" in her environment, whether or not she is intimately related to them. The personalizer orients herself vis-à-vis the wishes and responses of others *whether or not* she is related to them by ties of intimacy.

In interpersonal relations the personalizer is more likely to await cues from others before committing herself and so rarely initiates a course of action. Without exception, the personalizers were recruited as candidates for political office, making the decision to run only after being approached and persuaded by others in the party.

Affiliation needs are more important than power needs in motivating the personalizer's decision to run. [11] I do not mean to imply that personalizers are women without internal ballast, or that they are entirely passive. A completely passive person would not be elected for public office through competitive processes. Personalizers are not without initiative, but, in any situation, they will be more sensitive to the views of their associates, more responsive to encouragement and discouragement, and less likely to take initiative without advance informance on the attitude of others.

Among the women in this study the personalizers are the least inner-directed, the most easily influenced. For this reason, once in the legislature they become followers, not leaders. As followers they can and do make important contributions to the work of the legislature—doing invaluable staff work, serving as "lieutenants" to the leaders. The personalizer may become a subject matter expert, if she has an encouraging committee chairman. She may become an assistant whip or a member of the speaker's cabinet and work tirelessly to help achieve the leader's goals. Because of her sensitivity to others and her desire for approval, she dislikes conflict and is often quite skillful in smoothing over personal differences and patching up disagreements. She is not an expert in causing others to do her will, but in creating good feelings.

Mrs. Z is an interesting example of a personalizer. A highly competent woman, she had managed a professional organization for several years before local Republican party leaders, impressed by her quiet efficiency and her pleasant personality, decided she was just what they needed to round out their ticket—particularly since the Democrats had a woman on their slate. The county chairman was particularly active in his efforts to persuade her to run. He encouraged her, and spoke to her husband, who then also encouraged her to run. "They both told me that I could do it," she recounts, "but I asked myself whether I had the background necessary to do the job well." And, too, she was concerned about what others would think.

There never had been a woman representing this district before and I didn't know how people were going to accept a woman. Secondly, I think that sometimes we all acknowledge the fact that sometimes those who are nearest to us—our neighbors and townspeople—are kind of surprised when their next-door neighbors run for something like this.

What will people think, Mrs. Z asks herself before she undertakes a course of action. Will they understand? Will they approve? Will they think less of me? To answer these questions she solicits opinions. "The editor of the paper is a former legislator and he is also a very powerful man in the community and I went in and talked to him. And I went and talked to the former representative. I felt good when I found that I had very good support from all the party, and I decided to run."

For people who care a great deal about the responses and opinions of others, social activities can be very tiring. Listening and watching for cues, explaining and responding require close attention and sustained effort. It is tempting to avoid the effort by avoiding people. Obviously one who has run for office has not succumbed to this temptation. Still, Mrs. Z thinks of herself as "not an outgoing person," "not someone who meets lots of other people easily." She doesn't enjoy campaigning much, though sometimes finds it interesting.

She worries some about how to deal with others in the role of campaigner. She is "very careful not to be overfriendly with men," not to be "too chatty," not to be "seen around with one man too much," not to be "too personal in conversations." In the legislature these concerns persist. She tries to be "friendly but not too friendly"; she is concerned not to be "too loud," not to "talk too much." She worries about arousing disapproval among her constituents and among legislative colleagues. People, she says, are "quick to criticize," and finds it "discouraging, when I have worked real hard and they just don't understand." She finds it difficult, too, to make choices between people's needs—"you would like to help them all, and you just don't have the money and other resources." So you choose to satisfy one group's needs and not those of another. This is, she says, "the aspect I dislike the most."

Now in her third term, Mrs. Z is on the education, local government, and tax committees. She works hard in committees, always tries to be well-informed about the ramifications and implications of a bill before she speaks up. Knowledge is important to winning the respect of one's colleagues. Mrs. Z sees reputation as the key component of legislative influence and effectiveness. If people "like you and respect you," you are a good legislator. To this end Mrs. Z tries hard to win acceptance. She spends time almost every evening socializing with members of her party and committees. She tries to be helpful and agreeable and "not to live up to the unpleasant stereotypes about women." This effort leads her to dissociate herself from "women's interests" such as the Equal Rights Amendment. Her chief accomplishment (she thinks) is having won the respect of her colleagues.

Mrs. Z is an effective legislator who does her homework and meticulously attends to her obligations. She does not cause things to happen in the legislature, but she contributes conscientious work to the legislative process. In her approach to legislative problems, as to politics more generally, Mrs. Z is conservative. Her conservatism is both visceral and cognitive. A resident of a normally Republican

state, and member of a conservative legislature, and a Republican
herself, she acquired the beliefs about self-reliance, initiative, bureaucracy, and centralized power that, in combination, comprise a conservative orientation to the world. This orientation is reinforced by
her cautious attitude vis-à-vis other people and the world. All the
personalizers are relatively conservative (though not all are Republican) and in all, one can see the extension to politics in their cautious
approach to others. It is not that they find the world hostile
(moralizers tend more to the paranoid vision of the government); it is
that care and concern about the attitudes of others breeds a cautious
approach to problems—an approach characterized by timidity and
skepticism. For the personalizer, to act is always as hazardous as not
to act, and each action must be tested against the potential reactions
of those affected. The inner security of righteous intention is not
available to the personalizer. She has no blueprint for solving public
problems. The test of policy lies in the responses of others. So she is
tentative, cautious, more likely to take on the small problems than
the major ones. Mrs. Z is especially interested in legislation affecting
handicapped children and in a single detail of reform of the property
tax. She has already achieved some significant improvements in state
policies providing education to the handicapped and aims at further
reforms. "I do not expect to accomplish great things," she says,
describing her legislative achievements to date, "but I do hope I will
be able to make a contribution to some handicapped persons and
their families."

Mrs. Z understands her need for approval and expresses it more
clearly in speaking of her husband. He is her "strongest supporter."
She says of herself, "I need confidence. I am a person that needs lots
of confidence and I always feel I have an inferiority complex. He is
always there to give me the encouragement that I need and give me
the confidence." He helps her campaign, keeps up on the legislative
activities, discusses the work and the problems with her. He comes
down to the legislature one day every week and she goes home on
weekends. Without his sustenance, she says, "I wouldn't be there."

Regardless of how hard they work, the personalizers do not have
the commitment to the legislature characteristic of leaders or problem solvers. They tend more to see the legislature as a hobby, "an

avocation," as one put it, to which they would prefer not to devote too much time. They serve as much for personal enjoyment as for public service.

Mrs. E is another such woman. A Democratic legislator in a small, one-party state, she was recruited for the nomination by family friends who, like her husband, thought she needed something else to do. Initially reluctant, she decided to run only after being assured there would be no serious contest for the office. "The possibility of losing scared me to death. I had never been on a ballot, or run for any office at all. And I have a lot of pride." Campaigning is very disagreeable for her. "The newspapers misconstrue what you say. Your opponents and their friends twist your words. Frankly I hate it. I like the work in the legislature, but I don't like campaigning at all." "It is," she says, interpreting a campaign as a purely interpersonal encounter, "just a popularity contest." Despite her negative feelings she usually manages to lead her ticket.

Mrs. E, like Mrs. Z and the other personalizers, dislikes campaigning because the responses of voters are too important, too personal. Meeting people and seeking their support involves a level of personal risk which creates real discomfort. Their reaction reminds us that the level of risk (and of discomfort) in a campaign is determined by its meaning to the candidate. Many candidates interpret negative reactions and loss impersonally; they do not *feel* it as personal failure or rejection, but as a consequence of party, issues, the mood of the electorate, the failure of their supporters—or some other impersonal non-threatening cause. Because their egos are not at stake in the contest, they are not vulnerable to an adverse reaction; because they are not vulnerable they can enjoy the many and varied contacts that characterize a campaign. There is another equally important explanation of the personalizers' dislike of campaigning. Because they meet a large number of people in a campaign, the attitudes and responses of others, on which the personalizer relies, are jumbled, blurred, confused and frequently contradictory. The disapproval of some—journalists who "twist words," "opponents and their followers"—is inevitable. From the perspective of the personalizer for whom approval and appreciation is so very important, the campaign is a bad scene—because a certain amount of disapproval, discomfort and pain is inevitable. The fact that they run, and run again, is proof that the psychological price is not *too* high, but it is higher than for the other types of political actor considered in this study. In estimating the price it is very significant that the personalizers in this sample come from areas in which their party is clearly dominant.

Mrs. E continues to run because the pleasures of the legislature outweigh the frustrations of campaigning. But her commitment to the legislature is limited, contingent more on the feeling that she is needed than on moral imperatives or legislative goals. The personalizer is not only deeply involved with the others, she is also more involved with herself than are leaders or problem solvers, both of whom can measure their accomplishment against events in the external world. The personalizer has public goals with which she explains to herself and others her activities in the public sphere, but these goals are less salient for her than private goals. In this she resembles the moralizer whose actions are measured by internalized ideological goals rather than by public events.

Because she is an energetic and intelligent woman, eager to please and ingenious in doing so, Mrs. E attracted the attention of the majority leader not long after she arrived in the legislature. She made herself helpful in various ways and during her second term was rewarded with a lower level leadership post in the leader's cabinet. After three years in that post, she decided to step down. "I decided," she said, "I didn't want to beat my brains out any longer. So I asked for a committee where there wouldn't be too much work, and I resigned the party post. In fact, I found myself working very hard on the new committee anyway. It isn't really because I like to work that hard. It's that people keep asking you to do things. And then, I tend to be a perfectionist in everything I do. My house has to be so clean and my clothes have to be just so. Everything I do, I do this way, and I have followed through with this pattern in the legislature."

Besides the long hours and hard work, there is another reason that Mrs. E wanted out of the leadership. She found that "a great deal of animosity" was associated with an authoritative position. "There is always a little bit of jealousy," she says. "Other people want the job, they don't see why you should have it and they should not and this creates resentment." Hearing her speak, one realizes that for her the pleasures of leadership do not equal the discomforts of occupying an "exposed" position. "I could have been chairman of Appropriations last term, if I had wanted," she explains. "It is, of course, one of the most important committees in the House. I pleaded with the Speaker not to make me chairman. It's a tremendous job, at the center of many pressures. Finally I persuaded him." Leadership positions are not attractive to Mrs. E, though one can understand why the party leaders would be happy to have key spots filled by such an accommodating, noncompetitive, unambitious woman. This reaction reminds us that leadership not only promises deference and influence but also entails stimulating rivalries and incurring disapproval. Leadership roles are unattractive to those who dislike disapproval more than they enjoy influence.

Like Mrs. Z, Mrs. E has a realistic picture of herself. She understands her own priorities, she thinks of herself as a woman who is good at "personal" relations. Gaining acceptance in the legislature posed no problem, she said, it was just a matter of getting to know the members on a "person-to-person basis." She describes her successes and failures in interpersonal terms; her greatest satisfaction, she says, is in having gained the respect of other members; her effectiveness, in committee and elsewhere, is chiefly on a "person-to-person basis." "I am less persuasive at the mike," she says, "than I am on a person-to-person basis."

In spite of this conviction that she is "good" with other people in spite of her sensitivity to the opinions of others and her efforts to win them over (she never misses a committee meeting, even the very dull and boring ones, out of concern for the opinion of the leadership), she nonetheless has doubts about whether she is "really" liked and approved. "I feel I am accepted," she says, "but when you come right down to it, how do you know. Know, really and truly. People can be very nice to you but how do you actually know how they really feel about you?" Then she answers herself:

> You really don't. You can assume that they like you or that they think that you are bright or attractive, but how do you actually know how somebody else feels about you really. You're always the last to know how people actually feel about you.

The same doubt about whether people "really" approve of her or only "appear to" haunts her campaigns. "I think it is very hard to tell how you are doing, really. People will say, 'I hope you make it,' but you often wonder if the same people are voting for you in the polls. You have no way of knowing, really. . . .I have gone to the polls myself and wished every one of them good luck, knowing I would only vote for one." Because personalizers cannot be certain of the feelings of others, they cannot relax their efforts to win approval. Uncertainty about the "true" feelings of others keeps them working at interpersonal relations. All that practice may make them very adept at ingratiation. But the preoccupation distracts attention from other activities. Mrs. E rates herself a good, but not an outstanding, legislator. "I don't think I have the ambition that a real good legislator should have." Her ambitions lie elsewhere.

In the personalizer, personal predispositions are clearly reflected in political behavior at every level of the political process: in the manner of her nomination, the legislative role, political goals, and satisfactions. We have already discussed what brings the personalizer into politics and what keeps her there, but have not raised a question about why a woman preoccupied with interpersonal relations, who dislikes campaigning, and has no overriding political goals runs for elective office at all. The answer is that such a woman doubtless does not run for office except when there is a conjunction of several circumstances: involvement in a local party which offers companionship, a vacancy in the legislature, the lack of a candidate, persuasive party leaders, and an agreeable husband. Given these circumstances, the personalizer's usual desire to oblige takes over and, with misgivings, she agrees to run. Once in the legislature the personalizer's desire to please leads her to do a good job, for which she wins approval from her peers and applause from the party leaders back home. Assuming that her husband continues to support her political career, her success creates the probability that she will continue to serve even though she feels no strong commitment to a legislative career.

The personalizer's pleasant, unaggressive manner, her dislike of conflict, sensitivity and skill in dealing with others, make her an asset in committees, party affairs, and other legislative activities. Her only demand on others is that they accept and approve her, and even that is as much a demand on herself as on them. It is her responsibility to make herself agreeable. The personalizer brings more anxiety than hostility to politics. This anxiety inhibits but does not paralyze her. Rather more preoccupied with personal than political goals, the personalizer may nonetheless be a constructive, conscientious legislator. For her, however, legislation remains the by-product of a search for reassurance.

The Problem Solvers

Most of the women in this study are "problem solvers"; multi-value citizen lawmakers, motivated by a commitment to community service and deeply interested in the substance of legislation.

Less concerned with power than the leader, less preoccupied with rectitude than the moralizer, less pervasively concerned with personal relations than the personalizer, the problem solver is nonetheless deeply involved with all those values. A woman committed to the traditional roles of wife, mother, community activist, the problem solver also has broad identifications with her community and feels its needs as personal problems. Having long ago internalized a sense of responsibility for the community as a demand on the self, she has a career of community service and/or party activity behind her before she moves into the legislature. She therefore brings to legislative service broad experience in public affairs and a strong concern with public policy. She makes the move to the legislature because she sees the State House as a more effective forum in which to work on state and community problems. She moves into the legislature with the desire and intent of using the power of state government to achieve public policy goals.

In interests and satisfactions the problem solver is much like Barber's "Lawmaker";[12] she is differentiated from him chiefly by her longer legislative service. Barber dealt only with freshmen legislators and, therefore, had no opportunity to see the Lawmaker make lasting choices among institutional roles. Because the problem solvers in this sample have longer legislative service there is a greater opportunity to observe the relations between personal predisposition and legislative roles. We can watch them become "politicos," "inventors," subject matter experts and committee chairmen. Although the problem solver has deep roots and identifications with her local community and district, her areal perspective is readily expanded (not abstracted) to embrace the whole state. Because her goals involve using the legislature to map new solutions to problems, and to find new pathways to a better life for the community, her purposive role orientation is that of inventor. Because she is motivated and sustained by interest in policy outcomes, she gravitates to the structural role of subject matter expert and, seniority permitting, committee chairman.

Mrs. N is a good example of a problem solver. Like so many other legislators in this study she grew up in a single community. Later, she attended her state's university where she studied elementary education, married, and moved to a medium-sized city in another part of the state. After only two years of teaching, the first of her two children was born and she retired from teaching, never to reenter that profession. But her interests in education never declined. They were expressed in many years of activity in the PTA, and the school board (for which she ran after the second child was in junior high school), and later in extensive work on the education committee of the state legislature. She sees the experience of running for and serving on the school board as a prerequisite to becoming a candidate for the state legislature. It was there that she "made the connections" between public power and public policy, and came to think of herself as someone who might run for office. Because of this experience "I went to the party leader, whom I knew through other community affairs, and told him that I thought I would like to run for the legislature. Then I just left it there."

Two years later she became part of the Republican slate as candidate for the legislature. Her husband, very occupied by his business, was for it.

By the time she ran for office, Mrs. N "knew everybody in town," and having twice run for school board, she knew something about being a candidate. Campaigning involved just the kind of casual friendliness that came naturally for her, and in addition she found that she enjoyed expressing her views and explaining public issues at coffees and elsewhere. "I like it all," she says of campaigning, "meeting people, expressing myself, working hard at it. . .and," she adds,

"I have to admit I also like the contest, especially the winning."

In the legislature she felt her way, learning "who, what, where, why, and how" during her first session. She asked for assignment to the education committee and got it, with "elections" as her second committee. Now she finds she is almost as interested in the second as the first, having seen the importance to the state of reapportionment, regulation of primaries, and the like. Commenting on her technique for winning acceptance in the legislature, Mrs. N says, "I am the kind of person who likes to really *know* what I am doing when it comes to public policy. So I made it a point to research the bills before the committee, to try to map their various facets and to see the consequences of their enactment in different kinds of communities. I worked very hard on the whole subject and when I spoke, I knew what I was talking about. Before long, I came to be known as a serious committee member who could be counted on to do the job."

At the same time, she made it a point to get acquainted with party leaders and fellow committee members, Republican and Democratic. "You need friends on both sides," she emphasizes, "the support you need to pass your bills is found on both sides of the aisles." Many of the issues in which she is most interested turn out to get support and opposition in both parties. "What's important is to know the people you work with; know their interests and learn to work with them." Mrs. N has never felt that she was discriminated against in the legislature—on grounds of sex or anything else.

Part of the explanation for this feeling is found in her purposiveness; she seeks only cooperation from her colleagues. A sociable woman who enjoys the company of others, the problem solver nonetheless distinguishes between the people with whom she works and from whom she wants cooperation, and those whom she loves (such as husband and children) from whom she desires approval, reassurance, and love. Her style of interpersonal relations in the legislature is "friendly," considerate, fundamentally impersonal. She is an expert in purposive socializing, in frictionless, cooperative effort.

Problem solvers say that they have good relations with their colleagues, male and female, that they spend some time with them outside the legislature, that they feel free to take the initiative in proposing lunch or dinner to male colleagues, and they pay their own way, that they feel like "one of the boys" in the sense that their relations with colleagues are relaxed and inclusive. The problem solver's *style* of interpersonal relations is very similar to that of the leader, but her *goals* are different. Where the leader desires to establish a personal alliance or recruit a supporter in addition to expediting the work of the house, the problem solver is satisfied with the latter.

The problem solver is the task–oriented legislator *par excellence.* For her, private and public goals are consonant; her strong identification with community well-being means that in a very real sense the public good has become her private goal. Within limits. The problem solver does not "eat, sleep, breathe" public policy after the fashion of the leader; she has a private life to which she is as deeply committed as she is to public service. That private life usually consists of husband, parents, children, grandchildren, and other close relatives. Mrs. N is fairly typical, too, in having a husband who shares her interest in politics and helps with campaigns. "Not every day, not all the time, but he will help out." It is characteristic of the problem solvers to organize their lives so that politics does not dominate all aspects of it, and to plan periods away from politics in which they "forget" the problems of the state and the legislature and just get away from it all. The multiple values of the problem solver make moderation easy to achieve and her practiced efficiency aids her in combining political and nonpolitical roles.

Withal, the problem solver's commitment to politics is very important, and with her children grown, a large share of her attention is absorbed by legislative problems. Mrs. N is not alone in her comments on "drifting away" from nonpolitical friends as the legislature and constituency relations take more and more of her time.

Constituents are important to the problem solver not just because she needs their votes in the next election, but because of her strong commitment to community service and to representing the needs of the community in the State House. Mrs. N describes in some detail the long weekend hours devoted to hearing constituent problems and complaints. She thinks perhaps people are more willing to talk to a woman about their problems than they would to a male legislator. In any event, they are eager to bring their complaints and needs to her.

"I think the ombudsman function is one of the most important things a legislator can do. Helping people find their way through the state bureaucracy, aiding them in the effort to get what they want from the government. That's an important part of my job." The big satisfactions, however, come when after months or even years of study, discussion, maneuver, and compromise, legislation is adopted that solves old problems and provides new opportunities.

Problem solvers are issue-oriented, task-oriented, pragmatic.[13] In political orientation they are moderate, progressive, and may be either Republicans or Democrats. Regardless of party, they are devoted to the system and the society, but they are not stand-patters. Like so many Americans, they take change for granted, and assume that social progress is the goal of legislation. Their inclusive orientations preclude them from developing exclusive identification with any subgroup—whether class, region, economic interest, or sex. Their "do-good" backgrounds orient them to questions of the quality of life in the community, their lack of extended occupational experience tends to reinforce a "humane" rather than an "economic" focus.

Doubtless a legislature needs members with varying backgrounds, perspectives, and ambitions. Doubtless the problem solvers' pragmatic, humanistic incrementalism has shortcomings; perhaps in scope or depth of vision, perhaps in realism about "the interests" and their stake in government. But problem solvers come close to being the ideal legislators for a democratic society in which the function of government is to safeguard the interests and secure the benefits of prosperity to all citizens. With problem solvers in positions of power, government is less a threat than an instrument of public purposes. Multiple value commitments, age, past experience, lack of further ambitions combine, making the problem solver a type of political actor who, being relatively free of private ambition, can concentrate her attention on seeking the public good.

Women, Men, and Legislative Types: An Overview

Are women legislators more likely than men to be "problem solvers," concerned with the substance of policy and legislation, motivated more by a sense of public duty than the hope of private gain? Obviously nothing definitive can be learned from this study about sex and legislative role distribution. Sample selection guaranteed that only serious, effective women would be included in the study. Presumably problem solvers would also be numerous in a group of male legislators chosen by the same criteria. But these data nonetheless provide the basis for drawing some inferences about males, females,

Legislative Types: Four Female Variants

LEADER		PROBLEM SOLVER	
Value preference:	influence	Value preference:	multi-value
Structural role:	leader	Structural role:	subject matter expert, committee chairman
Purposive role:	broker/ inventor	Purposive role:	inventor
Areal role:	politico	Areal role:	politico
Orientation to conflict:	negative	Orientation to conflict:	indifferent
Interpersonal style:	eclectic	Interpersonal style:	purposive socializing
Recruitment:	office seeker	Recruitment:	indeterminant
Competing values:	affection	Competing values:	influence, affection rectitude

PERSONALIZER		MORALIZER	
Value preference:	affection	Value preference:	rectitude
Structural role:	committee-woman, friend	Structural role:	maverick
		Purposive role:	tribune
Purposive role:	ambiguous	Areal role:	trustee
Areal role:	district	Orientation to conflict:	positive
Orientation to conflict:	negative	Interpersonal style:	ideological
Interpersonal style:	ingratiating	Recruitment:	office seeker
Recruitment:	recruited by others	Competing values:	power
Competing values:	no close competitors		

and role distributions.[14]   There are, for example, no female equivalents in this sample of Barber's "Advertisers,"[15] young men on the make, bent on using a stint in the legislature to advance a career; there are also no representatives of "the interests." Their absence is made more significant because it is consistent with many other aspects of the socialization and experience of women, especially with differences in the economic roles of the sexes.

The expectation that they will hold remunerative jobs throughout their adult lives is communicated to boys while they are still quite young. Various types of indoctrination, education, and apprenticeship prepare the young male to assume chief responsibility for the support of himself and any dependents he may acquire. This breadwinning function is expected to end only in death or retirement, and is a principal, if not *the* principal, responsibility of the adult male. Should the young man become interested in politics, he must seek ways of expressing that interest that are compatible with his economic role. He might, for example, attempt to make a "career" of elective office, seeking only those offices which pay a "living wage." In this case, he will probably be interested in career advancement, which would mean election to ever higher offices. Another alternative open to the young provider interested in politics is not to attempt to support himself through politics, but to engage only in those activities or hold only those offices which are compatible with the practice of his principal (income earning) occupation. He is not free to forget or abandon his economic responsibilities in the pursuit of an avocation. Therefore, if he goes to the state legislature as a young man, it is likely that he will either be alert for possibilities to use the legislature as a stepping stone to a more exalted political position, or will give most of his attention to his principal economic role while serving in the legislature (where he will also be alert to opportunities for enhancing his occupational status or earnings or both). Either way, his tenure in the legislature will probably be short; he will move on or at least move out before he has fully mastered the job of legislator. Some version of this scenario is followed by a high percentage of the males elected to the legislature.

As a result, the legislature has a rather large number of young men on the way up—Advertisers who run and serve with an eye to the nonpolitical occupational benefits of political activity; political careerists who see legislative office as a low rung on the ladder; representatives of special interests who see public office as an opportunity to lobby for private interests. Another result is the high rate of turnover and persistent amateurism which characterize American state legislatures.[16] The resultant institutional weakness makes legislatures more vulnerable to the demands and maneuvers of "the interests," and less well-equipped intellectually and politically to discover and agree on policies serving the public interest.

It is not female chauvinism to point out that traditional role distributions protect women from many of the temptations associated with public officeholding. The woman who is supported by her husband enters the legislature without further career ambitions or hope of gain, untainted by association with special interests. As one of the legislators put it, "We women supported by our husbands are free to be virtuous." It is unlikely, furthermore, that she harbors hopes for higher political office, first, because she is probably too old by the time she enters the legislature to embark on a full-fledged political career; second, because most steps up would take her into a full-time job which might well conflict with her wifely role (e.g., by requiring her presence in the Capitol full time). Therefore, traditional women elected to the legislature are rather more likely to concentrate on the job of legislator, rather less likely to exploit legislative office for careerist goals. There are likely to be relatively more inventors and relatively fewer advertisers among female than among male legislators. But, and here's the irony, *the same traditional roles which make women legislators more public spirited discourage them from becoming legislators at all.*

Traditional roles permit, even encourage, women to focus attention on people, on duty, service, and the "higher" aspects of life. They lay the groundwork for the development of personalizers and moralizers, and multi-value problem solvers; but traditional roles also orient women's attentions to churches, schools, community services—to institutions other than politics. These traditional roles permit and even encourage women to take a disinterested view of the clash of economic interests, to see politics as public service. Rearing children and nurturing a family reinforce "humane," disinterested perspectives. These perspectives are carried into the public sphere via volunteer "service" activities which become the "jumping off point" for the few women who decide to seek election to the legislature. Such experience is especially well suited to the production of "problem solvers" because both the past and the future of contemporary women legislators predispose them to concentrate their attention on producing legislation that will serve the public good.

Therefore, it seems only reasonable that problem solvers would be *relatively* more numerous among the few women who make it to the legislature than among the many more numerous male legislators. As long as the culture supports the traditional patterns of value specialization and role distribution, one can expect to find a high percentage of problem solvers and few advertisers and brokers among the few women who make their way into legislatures.

NOTES

1. Harold D. Lasswell,, *Power and Personality* (New York: Viking [Compass Books], 1962) pp. 17-57.

2. The work of Harold D. Lasswell has had a crucial impact on the study of personality and politics, especially his *Psychopathology and Politics* (Chicago: University of Chicago Press, 1930), *Power and Personality* (New York: W.W. Norton, 1948),, *Politics: Who Get What, When, How* (New York: McGraw-Hill, 1936), and *World Politics and Personal Insecurity* (New York: McGraw-Hill, 1935). The best single discussion of the literature linking personality and politics is, of course, Fred I. Greenstein, *Personality and Politics* (Chicago: Markham, 1969). Also outstanding among the literature linking personality to political behavior is the work of Herbert McClosky and his collaborators. See McClosky, "Personality and Attitude Correlates of Foreign Policy Orientation" and McClosky and John H. Schaar, "Psychological Dimensions of Anomie" both in Herbert McClosky, *Political Inquiry: The Nature and Uses of Survey Research* (New York: Macmillan, 1969), pp. 70-125, 126-163. See also Herbert McClosky, "Conservatism and Personality," *American Political Science Review* 52 (March 1958): 27-45; Guiseppe DiPalma and Herbert McClosky "Personality and Conformity: The Learning of Political Attitudes," *American Political Science Review* 64 (December 1970): 1054-1073; Paul M. Sniderman, "Personality and Democratic Politics: Correlates of Self-Esteem" (Ph.D. diss., University of California, Berkeley, 1971); Paul M. Sniderman and Jack Citrin, "Psychological Sources of Political Belief: Self-Esteem and Isolationist Attitudes," *American Political Science Review* 63 (June 1971): 401-417. Also significant is Milton Rokeach, *The Open and Closed Mind* (New York: Basic Books, 1960), and the large literature on the authoritarian personality stimulated by Theodore W. Adono, Else Frenkel-Brunwik, Daniel J. Levinson, and R. Nevitt Sanford, *The Authoritarian Personality* (New York: Harper & Row, 1950). For a review of the literature that has developed around this seminal study see John P. Kirscht and Ronald C. Dillehay, *Dimensions of Authoritarianism: A Review of Research and Theory* (Lexington: University of Kentucky Press, 1967).

3. James D. Barber, *The Lawmakers: Recruitment and Adaptation to Legislative Life* (New Haven: Yale University Press, 1965), pp. 23-66.

4. For a discussion of cases in which a "Severe deprivation relatively late in life has led to furious concentration upon power" see Lasswell, *Power and Personality*, p. 51.

5. Ibid., p. 57.

6. This conception of the ideological style is consistent with that of Edward Shils, "Ideology and Civility: On the Politics of the Intellectual," *Sewanee Review* 66 (1958): 450-480, and "The Concept and Function of Ideology," *The International Encyclopedia of the Social Sciences* vol. 7 (New York: Crowell-Collier and Macmillan, 1968) pp. 66-75. See also Giovanni Sartori, "Politics, Ideology and Belief Systems," *American Political Science Review* 63 (June 1969): 398-411. The moralizer described here has much in common with

the "purist" delineated in Nelson W. Polsby and Aaron B. Wildavsky, *Presidential Elections* (New York: Scribner's, 1971), pp. 35-59.

7. The penalties for being a "maverick" are fairly clear to them. For a recent discussion of these penalites in a state legislature see Wayne R. Swanson with Allan H. Rouse, *Lawmaking in Connecticut: The General Assembly* (Washington, D.C.: American Political Science Assn., 1972), pp. 21-22.

8. For a good discussion of the consequences of *over*preoccupation with the various values see Harold D. Lasswell, "The Democratic Character," in *The Political Writings of Harold D. Lasswell* (New York: Free Press, 1951), pp. 498-502.

9. Judith M. Bardwick and Elizabeth Douvan, "Ambivalence: The Socialization of Women," in *Readings on the Psychology of Women*, ed. Judith M. Bardwick (New York: Harper & Row, 1972), p. 54.

10. Giovanni Sartori's discussion of the rationalist style in politics is germane. See Sartori, "Politics, Ideology and Belief Systems." See also Robert D. Putnam, "Studying Elite Political Culture: The Case of Ideology," *American Political Science Review*, 65 (September 1971).

11. This finding is consistent with Sears' finding that among girls, more frequently than among boys, achievement efforts can be motivated by the need for approval. Pauline Sears, *Final Report,* Cooperative Research Project N. 873, Stanford University.

12. Barber, *The Lawmakers,* pp. 163-211.

13. Problem solvers tend strongly to the "disjointed incrementalism" decision model. See Charles E. Lindblom, *The Intelligence of Democracy* (New York: Free Press, 1965), pp. 143-151.

14. On the relations among personality, role, and social structure see, *inter alia,* Daniel J. Levinson, "Role, Personality, and Social Structure in the Organizational Setting," *Journal of Abnormal and Social Psychology* 58 (1959): 170-180. See also C. Argyris, *Personality and Organization* (New York: Harper & Row, 1957), and Alex Inkeles and Daniel J. Levinson, "The Personal System and the Sociocultural System in Large-Scale Organizations," *Sociometry* 26 (1963): 217-229.

15. Barber, *The Lawmakers,* pp. 67-111.

16. It is the high rate of turnover which in large measure accounts for the amateur character of state legislatures. Although turnover rates differ significantly among the states and are declining somewhat, they remain very high. In 1965, for example, 66% of the Delaware house, 48% of Michigan, and 42% of the Illinois house were serving their first terms (as compared with 12% in California, 2% in Alabama, and 1% in Connecticut). William J. Keefe and Morris S. Ogul, *The American Legislative Process: Congress and the States,* 2nd ed. (Englewood Cliffs, N.J.: Prentice-Hall, 1968), p. 136. See also Charles S. Hyneman, "Tenure and Turnover of Legislative Personnel," *The Annuals* 395 (January 1938): 22; Malcolm E. Jewell and Samuel C. Patterson, *The Legislative Process in the United States,* 2nd ed. (New York: Random House, 1966), pp.118-121.

Chapter IX

Political Woman

WHAT have we learned about political woman—about whom we know so little—from our long look at these legislators? How does political woman compare with political man, about whom we know so much more? What have we learned from these political women about the constraints which inhibit women's participation in power? The time has come for a summing up.

The most important finding of this study is that political woman exists. Even if the "political" personality is defined, as Lasswell recommends, to include only persons who consistently emphasize power in their relations with others, and who consistently make choices aimed at maximizing power relative to other values, there are political women in this sample. I have called them leaders, and they conform in all crucial respects to the male model. If they are few in this sample, they are also few in other studies of state legislatures and political participation. Evidence is accumulating that "homo politicus" is a very rare type in democratic political systems and is found only at the upper levels of the political system where power is greatest and access most difficult. A growing number of studies suggest that, at least in democracies, other personality types find their way into political roles. That a majority of the women in this sample should *not* be consistent power maximizers who prefer power to all other values, could have been predicted from previous studies.

If we modify the definition of political personality to include the multi-value types more common in democratic politics, we can define as "political women" all those who:

1. desire to influence public events;
2. possess skills necessary to exercising influence;
3. seek influence;
4. wield influence; and
5. desire to preserve influence.[1]

Most of the women in this study conform to such a conception of "political woman."

That such women exist, not only in exotic times and places (Cleopatra and Elizabeth I, for example), but are found now in the small towns and the cities, on the farms and ranches of America, must be emphasized because there is a continuing tendency to deny that "normal" women can and do have an interest in politics, government and power strong enough to motivate sustained activity, and/or that "normal" women can in fact develop the skills necessary for effective functioning in institutions oriented to power.

Reluctance to admit the existence of political women is itself an interesting and significant attitude, one which requires discounting some aspects of reality. Such discounting takes three main forms. World leaders of the feminine sex—such as Elizabeth I, Catherine the Great, Isabella, Victoria, Golda Meir, Indira Gandhi—who clearly desire, seek, wield and enjoy power are discounted as extraordinary exceptions so unlike other women that they should hardly be considered women at all. Some other women holding political office are frequently discounted on grounds that they are not *genuine* political actors in their own right. It is often emphasized that this or that Congresswoman ran for office only after her incumbent husband died, as though that made her—two or three or ten terms later—some sort of surrogate. In the course of this study, I was asked again and again by friendly female interrogators, "Yes, but how many of your women were appointed to the legislature to fill out their husband's terms?" the implication being that a woman could not have made it on her own. Curiously, this implication of ineptitude and incompetence often hangs on even though the women may have won five subsequent elections. The fact that Margaret Chase Smith was initially appointed to serve out her husband's term seems more important to many than the fact that Walter Mondale was first appointed to the Senate to finish out the term of then Vice President Hubert Humphrey. Why? Because stereotypes persist, especially stereotypes that involve fundamental notions about the nature of reality—such as what women are like and what they want. Seeing political women as husbands' surrogates is a way of denying that they are *really* political actors in their own right.

A third way of denying the existence of political women is to deny that their influence is *real*. Comments such as these are common: "Sure. There are a few women in Congress and some women in state government. But they don't have *real* power." It is, of course, true that no woman is President, Governor, Speaker, Majority Leader. However, the fact that political women are not among the five or ten most influential actors in their arena does not mean that they are without power in matters of public policy. Power is not only divisible but divided; every legislator has the possibility of influencing public policy; effective legislators have a *real* impact on *real* decisions.

If we define political women as members of the female sex who *desire* significant influence in the process of determining public policy, acquire the *skills* necessary to achieve influence, *wield* the influence in institutions where decisions are made, and seek to preserve influence through continued participation in power processes, then there is no question that political woman exists—and exists in this sample.

An implication of this finding is that *"political woman" is not grossly deviant from her female peers.* She is not necessarily "masculine" in appearance or manner; she has not necessarily rejected traditional female roles and interests. Quite the contrary. The political women on whom this book is based are, as I have emphasized, women who accept and embody the tradional role definitions—in all respects save one. Almost all are wives and mothers and, in addition, most concur in the traditional view that these roles have priority at various times over other commitments. Well-groomed, well-mannered, decorous in speech and action, these are "feminine" women in the traditional sex-stereotyped sense of that word. Clearly they are not biological or social sports with deviant endocrine functions and emotional structures. These quite conventional "feminine" political women illustrate the point: *"normal" women who marry, have chil-*

dren, nurture their families, love their husbands, like their male asso-
ciates, can and do develop interest in winning and exercising political
power; develop skills needed for political success; face competition
without shrinking or collapsing; function effectively in legislative
bodies.

A third finding is that political woman bears many close resem-
blances to the more familiar male politican. There is a striking and
significant similarity in social backgrounds. Like the men studied by
others, these women are most likely to have been born and reared in
a small town or rural area; to have lived for many years in the same
place; to have more education, higher income and social status than
their parents; to have parents active in community affairs. This pattern of geographical stability and upward social mobility is strongly
associated with social and political participation in males and females
alike.

Both male and female participants tended to come from homes
where concern with community affairs was a normal part of adult
life, where the expectation of participation was internalized early as
a demand on the self. No accident then that most were active in
extracurricular affairs in high school and college.

Psychological similarities between political woman and her male
counterparts are many. Like most of the men who participate in
democratic politics, these women have:

Strong egos
High self-esteem
A high sense of personal effectiveness and political efficacy
A well-integrated self-system with low guilt, anxiety and aggression
Broad identifications
Habits of participationn
A persistant need for achievement
Realistic expectations
Pragmatic orientations.[2]

At this level of politics both males and females are most likely to
be multi-value types who seek limited power to achieve public goals.
A career in state legislative politics does not necessarily require
single-minded concentration, but leaves room for other interests and
activities. Practicing law, running a business, sustaining a marriage
and household are compatible with service in state legislatures. Many
effective lawmakers of both sexes pursue multiple values.

The similarities of male and female legislators is reflected, too, in their like perceptions of norms and roles: the legislative patterns described by women in this sample are nearly identical with the descriptions provided by males in other studies of state legislatures. There is no evidence in this study of distinctively feminine perceptions of the political world. They may and do frequently fill different legislative roles, but they operate in the same social world as male legislators.

A fourth finding of this study is that physiological constraints, male resistance, and even cultural constraints are less inhibiting to women's participation in decision-making than are traditional sex roles requirements. The women in this study differ from a comparable group of male legislators principally with regard to *economic role, occupational experience,* and *age of entry into the legislature.* All these sex specific characteristics derive from traditional role definitions which cast women as nurturers.[3]

Physiological Constraints

That political woman exists at all has important implications because it demonstrates that biological characteristics do not render all females too instinctively submissive to engage in competitive politics— at least in our time and place. It seems possible, even likely, that being "the weaker sex" effectively deterred women from taking part in political competition when policy was decided by physical combat, but no one today argues that a woman's musculature is politically disabling. The contention that female physiology is politically disabling is, in the contemporary context, an argument from psychology: it asserts that the basic psychological characteristics of the sexes are grounded in their distinctive physiologies; that biology is destiny.

We have seen that there are two principal variants of this argument: (1) that because of endocrine functions and/or anatomy, and/or reproductive functions women seek to avoid activities that involve (actually or potentially) competition and/or conflict with men; and/or (2) that males are physiologically programmed to exclude females from certain crucial activities, especially those that concern power and force.

The data of this study are relevant to both these arguments. Obviously, no single set of cases can definitively disprove a generalization concerning a whole sex (since such generalizations state probabilities); however, when taken in conjunction with other data on women's political behavior, they cast serious doubt on the notion that women are physiologically disqualified from seeking or exercising power or from developing skills required to do so. It perhaps should be noted, too, that the various ages at which these legislators developed an interest in running for office (their pre-legislative careers) and the varying ages at which they first ran for office preclude explaining their political behavior as post-menopausal, that is, as a function of lowered estrogen levels. It is significant, too, that three-fourths of these women explicitly disagree with the notion that men are better suited emotionally for politics than women.

The study provides no direct evidence on the biological programming of males, nor on the sources of male exclusiveness, however, data on the extent of efforts to exclude females was presented throughout the study. Some women encountered resistance from male party leaders when they sought nomination, others did not. Almost all were met with doubts and reservations when they first entered the legislature; most feel that their performance overcame male misgivings about distaff legislators. The women who rose into leadership roles report male efforts to freeze them out; and they report overcoming these obstacles. Most of the women legislators feel that members of their sex would be barred from the top offices, e.g., Speaker, Majority Leader; male legislators interviewed in this study agree.

What are we to make of these findings? Do they constitute prima facie evidence of male "bonding"? Do male legislators react to a woman's leadership ambitions like a rooster whose barnyard hegemony is challenged by a hen? Perhaps. But it seems equally plausible that resistance and reluctance are rooted in culture and social structure—in convention rather than nature. The ease with which males accept women as legislative colleagues once the women have demonstrated a capacity to live by the rules and do the job, suggests that their initial resistance is relatively superficial. Still, in all the legislatures represented in this study, there is a male monopoly of the top positions. Perhaps control of these positions satisfies male needs for exclusive control of governing functions. It will be a very long time before we are able to judge. If men are "programmed" for dominance in collective affairs, then the drive to maintain dominance will prove stronger than the belief in equality, or in political "affirmative action" programs. Testing this hypothesis must await greater commitment and greater effort to "open" the political system to women.

Male Conspiracy

The notion that men consciously and deliberately seek to keep women in positions of subordination suggests concert among males; a consciousness and a determination to protect by all effective means this privileged position, and an attempt to rebuff the efforts of the subordinate caste (women) to share power. It seems clear that no conscious conspiracy of males exists. Indeed part of the woman's problem is the male's unawareness of both his privilege and his tendency to exclude females. That there is a tendency, if not a conspiracy, to resist sharing power with women, is suggested again and again in these pages. There is some resistance to nominating women, voting for them, accepting them as legislative colleagues, admitting them to leadership positions. Perhaps it is true that "Because men typically have more power, they suspect and fear encroachment on that power." [4] However, the existence of these women legislators testifies to the willingness of some males to share political power with some females. Men stand at all the gateways to political power through which these women passed. Women could run for office and be elected only if some men assisted in their effort. They can function effectively in the legislature only with the cooperation of males. The existence of a male "party" consciously dedicated to preserving the male monopoly on power is not reflected in the experience of these women. The existence of male reluctance to share that power is.

Cultural Constraints

To what extent did cultural norms and sex stereotypes of masculinity and femininity inhibit the political careers of these women? At one level the answer is obvious. Every culture provides definitions, directs attention, channels energies, gives permissions, establishes limits. By its nature, culture constrains and culture permits. The significant question is not whether culture limits women—it limits everyone and enables everyone; the significant question is how much *this* culture impedes women's participation in power.

Obviously, cultural norms did not bar these women from desiring, seeking, and winning public office. The notion that politics is "men's" business was never internalized by them. Nor were various other purported requirements of femininity. Talking to these women, probing their views about femininity, politics and the expectations of the electorate, it became clear that most of them failed to acquire as girls the "understandings" about femininity which are believed to be most disabling for women.[5]

Culture has its most profound effects on women (as on men) at the level of expectations. These women have not internalized the expectation that women will eschew public service and public careers in favor of purely private (family centered) goals. With perhaps two exceptions, the women legislators do not perceive the prevailing definitions of "femininity" as constraining. They do not believe that culture forbids women to be serious, persistent and achievement-oriented. They do not believe it denies them possibilities for self-expression and self-assertion. They do not believe that women are denied the means and opportunities to influence public events, or are condemned for the effort. Apparently they never "learned" that "active, nonconformist, achievement-oriented women" were "castrating females, horrendous creatures."[6]

Most of them disagree, too, with Cynthia Fuchs Epstein's assertion that ". . .the core of attributes found in most professional and occupational roles is considered masculine: persistance and drive, personal dedication, aggressiveness, emotional detachment, and a kind of sexless matter-of-factness equated with intellectual performance."[7] The overwhelming majority of these women simply does not interpret the culture in this way. They deny that persistence, dedication, aggressiveness, objectivity, are male characteristics; they deny that most people so conceive them; they deny that voters, party associates, legislative colleagues believe that femininity includes "lack of aggressiveness, lack of personal involvement and egotism, lack of persistence. . . and lack of ambitious drive."[8] Their experience does not confirm the existence of such requirements; they have been success-ful in marriage and career behaving otherwise; they have not encoun-tered disabling penalites. Their understanding of femininity is crucial to the unconflicted pursuit of a political career. Apparently these women never received or never believed (never internalized) defini-tions of femininity that prohibited competence, persistence, asser-tion, dedication. Neither do they associate public achievement with masculinity. Unlike the various women described by Horner and others, these achievement-oriented women do not fear success, are not made anxious by competition with males, or by the prospect of winning.[9] *All* of them disagree with the notion that "Women who succeed in politics usually have to sacrifice their femininity to get there." They see no incompatibility between the requirements of femininity and those of politics. The extent to which their concep-tion of femininity differs from the more restrictive, more common conception is found in the following table. That they have an un-usually high regard for women is, as already suggested, consistent with secure sexual identifications and high self-esteem.

AGREE	WOMEN (%) LEGISLATORS	WOMEN (%) NATIONALLY*
Most men are better suited emotionally for politics than are most women	18	63
Women in public office can be just as logical and rational as men	100	74
A woman in politics will usual-ly be more idealistic than a man	61	46
Women in politics usually are more hard-nosed and aggressive than men	9	31
Women who succeed in politics usually have to sacrifice their femininity to get there	0	26

*These data are from the *1972 Virginia Slims American Women's Opinion Poll: A Survey of the Attitudes of Women on their roles in Politics and the Economy* (Conducted by Louis Harris and Associates, Inc.), pp. 29-31.

Yet the lives of these women legislators demonstrate that their socialization was comprehensive and successful. Furthermore, they argue persuasively that winning elections constitutes impressive evidence that *their understanding of the requirements of femininity is not regarded as unacceptably deviant or idiosyncratic in their communities.* This point is crucial to an assessment of the cultural constraints limiting women in the political sphere. One cannot infer generalized acceptance of character and personality from the success of a sculptor, a poet, or a physician, but election to public office constitutes a kind of public certification of acceptability. The fact that these women (and others like them) are elected to public office at least means that a majority of voters were not repelled by their competence, perserverance, dedication, and effectiveness. The fact that most have long-standing marriages indicates that they were also able to find husbands who could accept (and perhaps enjoy) such traits.

Why do these legislators understand the requirements of femininity so differently than so many other women and so many contemporary feminist writers? The answer lies in part in the pluralism and cultural heterogeneity which characterizes this society. Religion, ethnic background, location, class, and other broad conditioning factors no doubt affect sex-role definitions in much the same manner as they affect other social characteristics. Competence, perseverance, hard work were obviously welcome in the frontier woman and the black female head of family.[10] Perhaps it is no accident that most of the women in this study (like most of the women who have served in Congress) have Protestant backgrounds; that religion traditionally defines hard work and perseverance as human rather than male virtues.

Ego strength and self–esteem can also influence a person's understanding of sex–role requirements. Women are believed by many to suffer from "generally low evaluations of themselves,"[11] to have low self–esteem and an especially intense need for approval and reassurance. The need for approval may lead to a restless search to please. It may be that some women feel "accepted," and "approved" only when they feel desired and admired. The women in this study claim no such needs. Most are more concerned with their own goals and purposes than with the evaluation of others. Not given to introspection, not seeking in interpersonal relations an affirmation of their basic worth, they ask less, care less, settle for less from others than would a woman (or a man) with intense self-doubts. But their style and character is not so different from community norms as to render them unacceptable to a majority of their neighbors.[12]

Because they are full members of their communities, because they have internalized the norms associated with their roles, because they are fully mature adults who have accepted their time and place, they share most of the expectations of their communities.[13] *They feel free.* With few exceptions they accept as reasonable the prevailing relations between the sexes and, therefore, feel few resentments against the status quo. Culture can inhibit where it does not prohibit and, even though these women have sought public office and enjoy it, their political aspirations are low, their regrets are few; their priorities emphasize obligation to home and family. Even the leaders, for whom politics is the most intense interest of their lives, feel their families should come first. Expectations concerning relations within the family also reflect the dominant culture. For the most part, they expect that a woman will run for office only after the children are grown. They expect that a husband's wishes should be dominant. They expect to be financially supported by their husbands; and they expect little else. Husbands are not expected to accompany their wives to the capital or to come down weekends, even after retirement; wives are expected to shield their spouse's egos especially from possible damage due to the wife's prominence.

Listening to these women discuss the impact of politics on their own marriages it becomes clear that few would run for office if they did not have their husband's approval. In this sense all but two of the married women can be said to "put their marriages first." A good many of these women expect little, ask little, and get little help from their spouses. They neither expect nor get the kind of service many male legislators' wives provide.

"Their wives come up with them," said one woman of her male colleagues, "and (their wives) do everything for them. The men have their clothes laid out, they have their food ready; the men then send their wives off to sit very loyally all during the sessions and committee meetings where they look back and forth and are fascinated by their husbands' activities. Women don't have this. The woman is up there in the legislature, her husband is back home working and I tell the fellows all the time, 'You really have it made.' They have lovely wives and the wife's whole life revolves around her husband and his desires. Sometimes I wonder. But it must be a very good feeling for them."

By feminist standards, the level of demands made by these women on their husbands is very low. And the lower the expectations, the fewer the frustrations. Still, the point to be emphasized is that these women feel free. They feel that their legislative careers and political successes demonstrate that a woman is free to seek office and participate in public decisions if she chooses and if she works hard. The fact that they have "made it" to where they want to be in politics seems to them more significant than any obstacles encountered along the way. Determined, achievement-oriented women, they emphasize the positive: "I think I can"; "I think I can"; "I think I can"; "I thought I could." And, as with the little engine that could, determination, perseverance, optimism serves them well. It is no accident that among this group few think about whether the cost of their achievements has been unnecessarily high, whether others have it easier, whether their achievement is as high as it might have been. The focus is on coping with existing realities rather than on judging or changing them. Women's political role is not as large as these women wish it were nor expect it to become but this does not lead them to the conclusion that women are an exploited group. Four-fifths of them believe that women will play a larger role in the future.

Their feeling of freedom is closely related to the sense of efficacy, which in turn underlies the reality of accomplishment.

In sum, these women reflect and embody a version of the dominant culture. They have experienced and internalized many of its constraints and most of its permissions. In the process, they have profited and lost. The same socialization which prepared them to give priority to nurturing roles prepared them to participate in public affairs. Low political ambitions and a high sense of efficacy are similar cultural products. Self–confident, multi-valued, service-oriented perspectives are a product of the same culture which limits their aspirations and acceptability. These legislators constitute evidence of women's freedom and possibility, and, simultaneously evidence of the constraints which hedge their full participation in power.

Most of these women understate and minimize the extent of their deviance from conventional behavior and emphasize their acquiescence in conventional values. In this manner they assure themselves (and doubless also their constituents) that in all fundamental respects they are what a woman ought to be. Their success derives in part from the fact that they have respected conventional norms, have been good wives, mothers, homemakers as well as office-holders. Measured by conventional norms they are virtuous and successful and have worked their way to the top of the female status hierarchy.[14] Their conformity to fundamental cultural requirements may be a prerequisite to success in their unconventional political careers.

In a sense these women embody the dominant culture's ambiguities and ambivalences about women. Achievement and participant orientations, political skills and self-confidence were acquired in the socialization process; so were priorities that emphasized family roles. These few women worked out the contradictions in the role contemporary culture assigns to women, and more or less harmonized the conflicting roles. It is to the problem of conflicting roles we now turn.

Role Constraints

Culture and role are aspects of a single social whole. Culture explains, justifies and protects role distributions. Traditional culture underpins traditional roles and the relations among them. The roles of wife, mother and community volunteer are compatible with each other and with cultural norms; all are women's roles. Like all other major political roles, that of state legislator is traditionally a man's role; one not easily combined with the roles of wife and mother. Earlier in this study we examined how women gained acceptability as legislators; we have still to consider how they managed to combine legislative and other roles.

Can a good legislator find happiness in marriage? Can a good wife devote the time to politics necessary to be an effective legislator?

These are questions rarely raised about male politicians. Most discussions of sex and politics concern powerful men, beautiful secretaries and neglected wives. The wife who leaves behind husband and perhaps children when she goes down to the capital each week is a less likely character in a less familiar scenario.

The fact that she attempts to juggle and to harmonize roles normally considered incompatible means that she is an achievement-oriented nonconformist. Commenting on women in the legislature, one distaff legislator said, "You wear so many hats all the time. So, I think you have to be a special kind of woman to expose yourself to this and to these kinds of problems in the first place. You have to either have a great desire, great energy, or great something even to get into the melee in the first place. Trying to keep a house running, a husband happy, and a legislative career going isn't the easy way to spend one's life."

Whether a woman can keep a family happy while serving in the legislature obviously depends on the woman, the husband, and their respective and mutual needs and demands. The problem is different for a forty-five-year-old woman whose youngest child is in college, whose husband is preoccupied with a demanding business than for a thirty-five-year-old woman with three children at home in school and a husband who sees no real need for his wife to express herself in politics. It matters, too, whether the husband can tolerate having a well-known, influential wife. It is different in states with "full-time" legislatures than in states where the legislature meets 60 days every year (or two years).[15]

Strain and conflict (internal and external) are the normal result of attempting to combine noncongruent roles, as, for example, wife, mother and legislator. The culture provides a fairly clear-cut hierarchy of values in which women can make choices and allocate time: children come first, husbands second, careers last, if at all. Many of these legislators avoided the most intense role conflict by postponing a political career until their children had left home; others avoided the most intense conflict by waiting till the children were older and had less need for a mother at home. Only one attempted the toughest task: serving in the legislature while there were still preschool children at home.[16] Six of these legislators ran for office while their children were under 11, and eleven ran with children under 18.

Cross pressures are the chronic problem of the wife-mother-legislator. Learning to live with cross pressures is a prerequisite to professional survival for legislator-mothers as for professional women in other fields. And she can't do it alone.

All the married legislators agree that a cooperative husband is the first requirement for successfully juggling family and career. The importance of husband's approval is dramatically reflected in the fact that *only two legislators* say that their spouses do not approve their political activities. Four-fifths say their husbands "strongly approve" their political roles, as compared to about one-third of the male legislators. Liberal and conservative, Republican and Democratic, northern, southern, eastern, and western, the married women in this sample emphasized the importance of a husband's cooperation. It is not necessary that the husband take an active part in a wife's career, only that he acquiesce to her absence, her investment of time and energy. Most of the women expressed views like the following:

> I don't think a woman should even get into this if her husband isn't a secure person, confident of himself and his accomplishments and his ego and so on. If it is going to be a threat to your husband then you get into it with the risk of your marriage. If your husband is a strong man and self-confident and approves of your activities, it can be great.

Four types of husband–orientation toward the wife's legislative career are represented in this sample. There are *participant husbands* who play an active role in their wives' political career; *helpful husbands* who, though not personally active in politics, are willing to shoulder an extra burden at home; *acquiescent husbands* who approve their wives' activity but remain uninvolved; and *jealous husbands* who disapprove their wives' involvement and would like to end it.

Participant husbands encourage their wives' initial decision to run, actively help them campaign, and take an interest in legislative policy. In several cases the participant husband served as campaign manager and advisor to his legislator wife. Such husbands are apparently willing to have their wives in the limelight and to play the kind of supportive role that is more conventionally played by women. They are described as "putting aside their own work to spend full time on a campaign," as serving as "eyes and ears of the delegation." Though they sometimes seem formidable towers of strength, the wives of such husbands frequently attribute their success to their spouses' support, and insist, "I could never have done it without his help"; "His help is indispensable"; "I depend on him"; "He is my most valuable counselor"; "I could never have done it without him." There is a strong suggestion in these comments of the tributes husbands more frequently pay to their supportive wives. One feels that, within the marriage, credit for political accomplishment is shared almost equally between husband and wife, that the wife's reiterated dependence on the husband makes him a full partner in the enterprise. It is interesting and perhaps significant that such relationships are found exclusively among the older legislators, and occur in the marriages of both conservatives and liberals. Participant husbands in this sample are of different educational or professional backgrounds, geographical regions, and income levels. The participant husband turns out to be associated with mutually supportive interpersonal relationships rather than an egalitarian ideology.

Helpful husbands also encourage their wives to run for the legislature either because they share a political commitment (as with husbands of moralizers), or because they believe it important to their wives. The helpful husband does not merely approve his wife's legislative career, he takes on extra burdens in order to permit or facilitate it. The wife of one such husband reports that he has "taken over at home. He says that earlier, when he was away a lot, I did the lion's share with the children, and that now when I have this opportunity, it's only right that he should keep the home fires burning." Another comments, "My husband can handle it pretty much with the children (two junior high school age children) cooperating, but it puts an extra load on him." Such husbands must have time and energy as well as patience. They suffer deprivation of all the special services so frequently performed by wives, and, in addition, take on household responsibilities. There are not many in this sample. All ideological persuasions—from Goldwater conservatives to New Politics liberals—are represented among them. Again, the willingness of a husband to support a wife's career and to take over some aspects of the conventional wife's role is unrelated to any general beliefs about relations between the sexes. It should be noted that not all the women with children at home had helpful husbands ready to take over in their absence. The special role flexibility of the helpful husband is apparently very rare, even among the husbands of political women.

Acquiescent husbands are the most numerous in this sample. These are men who approve their wives' political career, who may give financial support or advice if it is solicited, but who have no further personal involvement. They do not campaign and mend fences; they do not take on the responsibility of running the home in the wife's absence, but in a general way, they approve the activity. The importance of giving approval should not be underestimated; most wives say they would not run without it. In essence the acquiescent husband agrees not to protest (frequently or strenuously) against his wife's prolonged absences, her long hours, her preoccupation with the business of the legislature, her failure to provide many of the services husbands are usually accorded in this society. Acquiescent husbands seem to be of two types: those who, being very much involved in their own work, are happy to have their wives similarly engaged; and "good fellows" who though not especially busy themselves are willing to have their spouses involved in a time-consuming activity. Examples of the former are a traveling salesman home only on weekends, a businessman who "does a lot of entertaining, has many trips to make and lots of evening commitments," a rancher "busy all the time with the ranch." The acquiescent husband has less emotional investment in his wife's political career than the participant or helpful husband; is probably, though not necessarily, less committed to its success and continuation; is most likely to feel ambivalent and to develop intermittent resentments. Describing her "acquiescent" husband, one legislator put it this way, "Now, my husband has had ups and downs. The first campaign had his total blessing and we both enjoyed it, but the second campaign, which was horrendous anyway because I had a terrible opponent, took a lot out of both of us. We were both so drained—my husband had real doubts that it was worth it, and that I ought to go on." Another legislator, speaking of her acquiescent husband, commented, "He was all for it originally and now, to be perfectly honest, he is sometimes very disgusted. But he hasn't suggested I not run for reelection. And when I become very cross because I have too much pressure put on me, I say, 'All right, I just won't run next time.' and he says, 'No, no, don't do that.' Still it takes so much of my time, and I'm away from home a lot, he barks sometimes. It's a problem."

The fourth type, the *jealous husband* is represented twice in this sample. In both instances, the marriage is shaky, a separation and divorce is in the offing; and the wife believes her career to be a major factor in her marital problems. One husband, a former office holder, is described as very proud. "He feels hurt when people come to me and not to him. It is very hard on him." The other is also described as resentful of the attention and deference his wife receives. Both began as acquiescent husbands.

Even in the good relationships where the husband basically approves his wife's career, many feel that there are problems and potential problems. The danger of growing apart, "like being tuned to two different television channels"; the danger to the man's ego of having a wife in so much demand; the attenuation of the relationship ("You come home too tired for sex"); the possibilities of infidelity growing out of long separations; and, especially, the irritations to a husband of having a wife "whose mind is so much on other things," who "isn't free to go out" whenever he chooses; all these are pitfalls to successfully combining marriage and career.

Children are a more pressing but no more difficult problem. Well over half of these legislators bypassed the conflicts between the mother/legislator roles by running for legislator only after their children were grown. Those who did not wait so long were confronted by the multiple problems that face any working mother, not infrequently exacerbated by regular overnight absences from home. If the children are young they must either have a cooperative relative (a widowed mother or aunt is ideal) or they must have the money and luck to hire an acceptable mother surrogate. In addition, they must confront the question of whether they are justified in leaving the child—a question which may be difficult in a culture where mothering is considered a full-time occupation, where theories of childrearing take a dim view of absentee parenthood. Finally, they must persuade voters that in seeking public office they are not neglecting their responsibilities to family. Here we are concerned with only the first two of these problems.

There is near unanimity among these women about the difficulties of pursuing a political career when one's children are under six. Only one of the women in this sample attempted it, and most assert that they regard it as undesirable. "To be very frank," said one in a comment echoed by many, "I couldn't have done it. I really couldn't have been an effective legislator if my children were little. I'm just not of that temperament. I would have carried too much of a load of guilt." And quickly added, "It depends on a woman's personality and circumstances. If you have an aunt, a mother, or a mother-in-law, it works—a permanent, loving, stable person there to keep things together, it works. There are some delightful young women in the legislature now who have small children. But it wouldn't have worked for me."

The one woman in the sample who first ran for the legislature when her youngest child was one-and-a-half years old, describes her experience this way. A mother of four, she was, she says, virtually drafted to run. Having demonstrated campaigning skills in several successful contests for the school board, she was approached by party leaders convinced that they needed a woman to round out a slate. The idea seemed interesting but impractical, and she used her husband as an excuse for not running. This excuse evaporated when her husband expressed his enthusiasm to the party leaders. A nearby widowed aunt was pressed into service and three terms later the situation seems to the legislator to have worked out reasonably well. The children help in campaigns and visit the legislature; they are, she says, both impatient and proud. "They want me around to provide services but they are very proud of me and they do get a lot of extras. They love to brag about going to the legislature. Still they have some resentful periods. Without the aunt, I couldn't have done it."

Once the children are in school, the problem is less acute. More women feel that it is possible to find satisfactory helpers for school-age children, especially where there is a cooperative husband and older siblings to help.

Many believe that older children benefit from their mother's political careers. These putative benefits are of several kinds. (1) Older children are believed to profit by their mother's broader interests and experience: "I know I'm much more interesting now, and that my kids are proud of me." (2) It saves the children from the unreasonable demands of a domineering mother: "The children get freedom from your ever-watchful eyes, from your apron strings. When a woman like me is at home with our families as our only concern, we have a tendency to be overbearing. I was constantly pressing my point of view on them." Another put it more gently, "You are less domineering and demanding, you are more giving and outgoing, more forgetting. You give more and you take more." (3) Children have an opportunity to become self-reliant. "I think we pamper our children too much. Since I have been in the legislature my two children are much more responsible, and more independent! It's very good for them." (4) Children learn from their mother's political life. "My children come down to the capital. They listen. They spend time on the floor and in committee sessions. They hear the conversations at home. They help me campaign. I know that they have learned a lot not just about politics—about people and their needs, too."

All factors considered, these legislators do not believe that the demands of motherhood and politics are necessarily incompatible. More than other women, more than men in general, more than male legislators, they believe that the roles of wife, mother, and legislator can be harmonized.

A woman's effort to harmonize potentially conflicting family roles makes demands, then, on everyone; demands for flexibility from her husband, for greater responsibility from her children, for empathy and understanding from both. And it offers rewards as well as frustrations. Many of the legislators say of their husbands, "He says that I am a much more interesting person to him because I have gone out into public life. He says that my career adds excitement to our life, that he looks forward to hearing about the legislature from me." And there are personal psychological benefits: the feeling of doing a useful job, the feeling of *being* a useful and interesting person.

All too frequently those who consider the strains and role conflicts that beset the women who juggle noncongruent roles overlook the

Role Incompatibility

DISAGREE	WOMEN (%) LEGIS-LATORS	WOMEN (%) NATION-ALLY	MEN (%) LEGIS-LATORS	MEN (%) NATION-ALLY
1. It is almost impossible to be a good wife and mother and hold public office, too.	85	57	66	50
2. To be really active in politics women have to neglect their husbands and children.	71	41	41	35

The data on men and women in the national population are drawn from the 1972 Virginia Slims Poll. The first item was worded slightly differently in that poll: "No woman can be a good wife and mother and be active in politics, too."

problems structured into conventional roles, especially the problems that afflict a conventional family-centered woman once her children no longer need (or want) much of her time and attention. The woman who feels superfluous, who knows that her productive career as a mother is behind her suffers existential traumas which are still neither fully appreciated nor understood. Several of the legislators addressed the problems growing out of the fact that, given contemporary life expectancy, mothering is not a full-time, lifetime job.

"At my age," said a woman of 47, "you get that emptiness syndrome. Among my contemporaries some have gone back to work or are doing interesting volunteer work. These are the creative, constructive ones. Others, many others, are filling up their time with bridge, tennis, golf, needlework, flowers and the like—all beautiful activities, but these women don't still feel they have a mission to accomplish in the world, and some of them are becoming alcoholics, and some are having nervous breakdowns. I think of the women that I know personally, the ones who are not in public office are having many more marital problems than those of us who are. You know, one point you shouldn't overlook when you think about women in legislative careers—we all probably have a certain amount of aggression and hostility within us and if we express these fighting the man who is opposing our bill, or fighting the speaker or governor or somebody, then we can be little pussycats with our husbands. This is," she added, "the flip side of the record."

Among the women in this sample, only two make explicit reference to "needing something to do" as a reason for first running for the legislature. But many more communicate subliminal anxieties about how they would fill their time and their lives in the absence of a political career. One does not doubt that being strong, energetic, involved women, they would have found something to do with themselves in the years when mothering was no longer a full-time occupation. Neither does one doubt that they would have needed challenging and time-consuming jobs through which to express themselves.

The distribution of roles in society affects the political careers of these women in many ways. In all stable societies education and socialization are linked to adult roles. Potential farmers get educations that will equip them for farming; future engineers get training in engineering. Future homemakers are rarely trained to be lawyers, insurance agents, farmers, businesswomen, or to enter other occupations from which men typically move into public life and elective politics by other, less direct routes. Volunteer service is the most common route. Volunteer roles are convergent with traditional nurturing roles and can provide training and experience during the years a woman is principally involved with the wife-mother role.

Not all conventional role distributions inhibit women's political activity. Since breadwinning is conventionally assigned to the male, his wife is frequently freed from the necessity of remunerative employment. Being free not to work for money gives a woman more control over the disposition of her own time—once the children are on their own a large part of the day. In deciding whether or not to run for the legislature, for example, a woman financially supported by her husband need not be concerned about loss of income from other pursuits or about the low salaries of state legislators. The significance of this freedom to spend time in nonremunerative activities is frequently underestimated in these times when attention is focused on women's disadvantages. A woman supported by her husband need not balance her commitment to political or civic activity against the need for increased income. She need not justify the decision to devote large blocs of time to nonremunerative activities. In the legis-

lature she is freed from the necessity of juggling economic and legislative roles—of supporting a family while developing a political
career. Given the fact that being a state legislator is a part-time, low-
paid job in most states, women probably provide the best source of
high talent to fill the jobs. That so few women take advantage of this
freedom to build a career in public service testifies to the power of
cultural constraints.

Still, the principal constraints that impede women's full participation in the power processes of society appear to be rooted in
prevailing role distributions rather than in anatomy, physiology, male
conspiracy, or even in the basic values of society. Education, occupational experience, place of residence, average age of entry into a
legislative career are all products of the sex-role system.

The women in this study are remarkable not only because they
have gained entry into a "man's world" and made a place for themselves in it, but also because they manage to harmonize their political
roles with conventional women's roles. Refusing to choose between
"women's" roles and participation in the "man's" world of politics,
they have worked out successful combinations. Their management of
conventionally incompatible roles is characterized by unusual
amounts of empathy, flexibility and self-knowledge. Empathy
enables the woman to see the situation from another's point of view;
to understand the husband's need for reassurance of the continued
centrality of the marriage in her life; to protect him from the threatening aspects of her job; to provide compensation and appreciation
to spouse and children; to maximize or minimize their roles in her
career depending on which is most appropriate. Being able to see
herself as a husband with a wife in politics makes for more accommodation, fewer demands, more appreciation. Desirable or undesirable
as these attitudes may be (as measured against egalitarian norms)
they are highly functional in helping to sustain marriage and a political career. Flexibility is an equally important characteristic of this
style of role management. The ability to doff one demanding role
and enter another, and to do so without anxiety and trauma is
required of all politicians, but is especially vital to women. The flexibility required of her is greater than that of the legislator/lawyer/hus-
band/father because the roles of wife and mother involve less asser-

tion and more accommodation to the needs and moods of others. Greater empathy is needed because the role requirements are more disparate. Self-knowledge is needed because it helps to keep priorities clear, and to guide one through complex choices.

If these women can do it, why can't/don't others? Perhaps because they lack high self-esteem and broad identifications, habits of participation, a desire to influence public policy, political skills needed to do so, a husband willing to cooperate, the empathy, flexibility, self-knowledge, and energy needed to live a busy and complicated life when so many less demanding alternatives are so readily available.

NOTES

1. The conception is, of course, Harold D. Lasswell's. See especially "Psychopathology and Politics," in *The Political Writings of Harold D. Lasswell* (New York: Free Press, 1951), pp. 38-64; idem, *Power and Personality* (New York: Viking [Compass Books], 1962), pp. 39-58.

2. This list of characteristics bears a marked resemblance to Lasswell's description of the "democratic character." Harold D. Lasswell, "The Democratic Character" in *Political Writings*, esp. pp. 495-514. It is also consistent with Lane's discussion of democratic leaders. Robert E. Lane, *Political Life* (New York: Free Press, 1959), p. 128. An interesting discussion of the relation among personality, recruitment, and types of political systems is Rufus P. Browning and Herbert Jacob, "Power Motivation and the Political Personality," *Public Opinion Quarterly* 28 (1964): 75-90.

3. This finding is consistent with studies of women's nonparticipation in other aspects of professional life. See, *inter alia*, Cynthia Fuchs Epstein, *Women's Place: Options and Limits in Professional Careers* (Los Angeles and Berkeley: University of California Press, 1970); *Special Report on Women and Graduate Study*, Resources for Medical Research Report No. 13, June 1968 (Washington, D.C.: U.S. Department of Health, Education, and Welfare, National Institutes of Health, 1968), pp. 5-7; Viola Klein, *The Feminine Character* (New York: International Universities Press, 1946), pp. 169-170.

4. Epstein, *Women's Place*, p. 117. This view, that the possessors of power are *necessarily* jealous of it, is based on Hobbesian assumptions about human nature which would *not* be acceptable to most women.

5. Rossi emphasizes the importance to women's professional futures of internalizing such "feminine" traits as submission, conformity, and seeking to please. Alice Rossi, "Who Wants Women in the Scientific Professions?" in *Women in the Scientific Professions,* ed. Jacqueline A. Mattfeld and Carol G. Van Aken (Cambridge: MIT Press, 1965), p. 13.

6. Jessie Bernard describes this as the dominant stereotype until recently. Jessie Bernard, *Women and Public Interest* (Chicago: Aldine · Atherton, 1971), p. 13.

7. Epstein, *Women's Place,* pp. 22-23.

8. Another Epstein list of the requirements of femininity. Ibid., p. 22.

9. Matina S. Horner, "Femininity and Successful Achievement: A Basic Inconsistency," in *Feminine Personality and Conflict* (Belmont, Calif.: Brooks/Cole, 1970), p. 45. They do *not* feel "anxious, guilty, unfeminine and selfish." They do not "pay a price in anxiety" for

this success. Eleanor E. Maccoby, "Women's Intellect," in *The Potential of Women,* ed. S. M. Farber and R. H. L. Wilson (New York: McGraw-Hill 1963), pp. 24-39.

10. Germaine Greer, among others, emphasizes this point in *The Female Eunuch* (New York: Bantam Books, 1970), pp. 209-231.

11. Though it should be noted that in her study of women lawyers, such women "rated themselves highly and felt that others in their profession thought highly of them." Epstein, *Women's Place,* p. 25.

12. High self-esteem is associated with effective learning of social norms, e.g., Guiseppe Di-Palma and Herbert McClosky, "Personality and Conformity: The Learning of Political Attitudes," *American Political Science Review* 64 (December 1970): 1054-1073.

13. Such identification with one's time and place is identified by Erikson, and others, with maturity. Erik Erikson, *Childhood and Society,* 2nd ed. (New York: W. W. Norton, 1963), pp. 268-269.

14. They illustrate Epstein's assertion that "Women who choose careers react to the cultural expectations of femininity by trying to prove themselves in all spheres. They accept all the role expectations attached to their female status, feeling that to lack any is to deny that they are feminine." Epstein, *Women's Place,* p. 32.

15. In 1971, 37 states had provisions for annual sessions. Two-thirds of all the states imposed a constitutional limit on the length of the sessions, most setting these limits at 60-90 days. Elimination of constitutional limitations and increase in the frequency and length of legislative sessions is an important item on the agenda of proponents of legislative reform. See, *inter alia,* Donald G. Herzberg and Alan Rosenthal, *Strengthening the States: Essays on Legislative Reform* (Garden City, N.Y.: Doubleday, 1971), p. 4; Citizens Conference on State Legislatures, "Legislatures Move to Improve their Effectiveness," Research Memorandum No. 15 (Kansas City: The Citizens Conference on State Legislatures, April 1972), p. 6. Note also that the amount of time devoted to legislative duties tends to increase with years of service. Many of the women in "part-time" legislatures report working "full time" or more.

16. All agree that most voter resistance is generated when a mother of young children runs for office.

Chapter X

Epilogue: Futures for Women in Politics

MUST it ever be thus? Is male dominance of power processes written in the stars and underwritten by human biology? I doubt it. The fact that all modern societies — democratic and communist, eastern and western — are governed by men (even in India and Israel where women hold the top job) does not settle the question. Even the fact that women have occupied a subordinate status in most societies does not guarantee continuing male dominance of power processes. Past and present provide data on probabilities; the future involves possibility as well. The future need not reproduce the past, particularly in contemporary times when the principle of equality dominates political culture, when technology has transformed the relation between physical strength and political power, when electronic communications render culture more manipulable than ever before, when pharmacology can alter mood, when medicine has provided longer life expectancy and the possibility of multiple careers. But social scientist and citizen alike are more concerned with probable rather than possible changes. (Though conceptions of the possible have obvious importance for the formulation of goals and strategies.) In ·assessing the probable political future of American women it will be useful to examine the direction in which we are headed and the conditions that may facilitate and limit change.

It is clear to all observers that the nonparticipation of women in high politics is supported by the traditional role system and by norms and expectations of the traditional character-culture manifold.[1] Further, "the obvious fact is that terms like character and culture are attempts to refer to recurring features of the same process, namely the interpersonal relationships of man."[2] That is, the nonparticipation of women is supported by complex webs of interpersonal relations. In principle, all aspects of interpersonal relations not biologically determined are subject to change; modal personality types do, in fact, vary through time and space,[3] responding both to the external environment and to human intentions.

In functioning societies there is always some "fit" between personality and society, but the extent of that congruity is an empirical question which should be investigated rather than assumed.[4] The more stable the society the higher the degree of congruence between modal personality and social structure. In large social units such as modern nations, there is both cultural pluralism and personality pluralism. At any given time there exists a range of personality types, some of which diverge in important respects from the modal personality. Obviously, there is always a poor fit between the existing role system and nonmodal personalities.[5] For this reason, persons with deviant personalities constitute an important source of social change.

Furthermore, as Levinson points out, "both personality structure and social structure inevitably have their internal contradictions."[6] Those contradictions also constitute a potential source of change for existing cultural and psychological patterns and social practices.

The women in this study are examples of character-culture deviance. Like most other women now found in traditionally male professions they are nonmodal feminine types whose existence calls attention to alternative ways of being and affects expectations about what women are and may become.

If definitions of femininity, socialization practices, self-conceptions, family and economic role distributions and politics are part of a single social fabric, then major changes in one entail parallel changes in others. To serve in public office, women must leave husbands and children; they must spend one part of their lives in residence at the state capital and another part campaigning for office, mending fences, preparing for hearings; they run the risks of losing and incur the obligations of winning; they must be able to conceive of themselves as useful legislators; they must be persuasive, confident, effective, persistant. Large numbers of such women require large numbers of men to accept and love them, and even larger numbers of voters to cast ballots for them.

A great expansion of women's role in politics can occur only as such nonmodal types multiply, only as character-culture and roles change. For women to achieve de facto political equality, to enter political life in the same numbers as men and achieve the same levels of office as men — both a cultural and a social revolution is required. Social goals, beliefs about the identity and the role of men and women, practices concerning socialization, education, political recruitment and family: all must be altered to support the accession of women to full participation in political power.

A good many fundamental beliefs about the nature of men, women, children and government would have to be abandoned or revised. For example, it would be necessary to abandon the notion, still supported by some influential religious denominations, that men are the natural governors of society, that women are unfit for political (or religious or social) leadership, that men are inherently better suited to authoritative positions either because they are more rational and/or less emotional and/or more stable and/or better able to face forceful challenges. It would be necessary to abandon these beliefs as well: that there is something ineffably incompatible between femininity and the pursuit of power, that feminine women neither desire nor seek power, that femininity is inexorably associated with the submissiveness of female to male, that, in a woman, the desire for power is a signal of alienation from her true identity, that women who participate in power processes are, in fact, unfeminine women, that women are (and should be) less assertive, persistent, competitive, more private and less likely to engage in public affairs than men, that women will devote themselves largely to home and family, that children fare better if cared for by a full-time, natural mother, that normal women will find their principal satisfactions in family roles, as daughter, wife, mother, that the satisfactions available from the dutiful performance of these roles will be adequate to a lifetime, and that for all these reasons women will not develop the skills and careers most closely associated with politics. They will not become lawyers, businessmen, insurance and real estate agents, farmers, or enter other occupations from which candidates for office are typically recruited in this society.

Both men and women must abandon these and the many corollary beliefs associated with them before women can become full members of the political world. Nor is this all. Relations between men and women involve reciprocal understandings about rights and obligations. It is axiomatic that if women are to change, men too must change. Obviously, changes will be embodied in new institutional practices, in new role conceptions and demands. Conceptions of the good wife and the good husband will also change. Before competent, autonomous women arise in large numbers, men (and women) would have to give up the notion that such women make less desirable wives than dependent women who lack initiative, assertiveness and persistence. What must also go is the expectation that the male will have prime responsibility for the financial support of the family and the female for its nurturance. If women are to succeed in politics in the same numbers as men, they must acquire comparable professional skills and experience; if husbands are to follow wives to the capital, they cannot also be expected to shoulder the financial burdens of the family. And if wives are to reach the top in politics, then husbands must be willing to take on substantial responsibility for home and family.

Such changes constitute the minimum conditions for what might be termed the maximum change model.[7] Do I exaggerate in asserting that such comprehensive changes of society, culture and personality are prerequisites to the equal participation of women in political power? Do equal power roles entail a whole new pattern of interpersonal relations between the sexes? After all, the women in this study developed within traditional society and remained a part of it. For them political achievement was not contingent on the rejection of most traditional wife/mother roles; neither social nor cultural revolution was required to support their move into the public arena. But there are several reasons that these legislators may mislead us about the relation between contemporary society and the pursuit of power. The fact that they *are* deviants reminds us that changes would be necessary to mass produce such personality types. It should also be recognized that these women serve at the middle level of the political system, not at the top; to move on up the political ladder would require giving politics a higher priority than most of these women have been willing to do. Most, it will be recalled, undertook political careers after their children were half grown, most declined to move from the locality in which the husband had his professional base. Competition and demands escalate as one moves up the political ladder. To win nomination to the state legislature is an easier task than becoming a party's nominee for lieutenant governor, governor, Congress, or vice president. Nomination to these higher offices requires the approval of more party leaders, more voters; it requires more time, effort, and further abandonment of traditional family roles.

Because a working democracy involves competition and mass participation, it guarantees that the holders of power will not deviate widely from dominant (accepted) values and styles. Grounded in the prevailing culture-character manifold, role constraints will give way only as norms change and people change. But dominant values and styles *do* change. They change "naturally" in response to social and technical inventions and to changes in the natural environment; they also change in response to human intentions and goals.

To estimate how likely it is that women will achieve full (equal) participation in power, we need to know something more about current trends. In the United States (and elsewhere) cultural and social changes are already in progress; they have increased women's participation in all major social processes. These trends reflect the extension to the female sex of the same levelling, egalitarian tendencies which produced universal education (sharing of enlightenment and skills); adult suffrage (sharing in power); graduated income tax, inheritance taxes and other measures for redistribution of wealth (sharing of wealth); social security systems and national health plans (sharing well-being); religious and cultural freedom (sharing rectitude); and related developments. Equality is a major passion—perhaps *the* major passion—of the age. Its effects are observed on all continents in the most diverse political systems. The trends to inclusiveness and to the integration of masses into political systems are defining characteristics of political modernity. So is the practice of distributing roles on the basis of skills. The extension of the suffrage and of full political rights to women, the opening of professions, higher education, professional training to women, the definition of women as full citizens and social equals is but an extension of political and social equality to another group previously excluded from power because of some ascriptive characteristic, e.g., femaleness.

That there is a trend toward greater female participation in major social values can hardly be doubted. Women, who until this century were barely legal persons, have made their way into most areas of social life. Their education has risen and is continuing to rise. The numbers of women graduating from high school, from college, earning graduate and professional degrees have risen and are continuing to rise.[8] Their participation in voluntary associations, an important indicator of integration in the larger society, is up.[9] The number of women voting in elections has increased until it nearly equals that of men.[10] More women are becoming candidates for public office; and there is more encouragement of these candidacies. Progress in these and other areas has been uneven, but it has continued. The duration of these trends is, as historical trends go, brief and gives no grounds for concluding that we are dealing with some inexorable movement of history. But it is persistent enough to suggest that the progressive inclusion of women in the social life of society is a characteristic of the period.

Increased levels of education and social participation are paralleled by changes in other aspects of social life relevant to role distributions and, indirectly, to political behavior. The size and conception of family are, for obvious reasons, closely linked to women's role in other social activities. Everyone understands that the family has been affected by urbanization, mobility, changed life expectancy, changing norms, the development of contraception and greater ease of divorce. One clear-cut indicator of family change is the employment of mothers. Commenting on the rising number of women in the labor force, Ferris asserts, "Increases in the work rate of females are especially notable since 1964 in the younger, more vigorous ages—20-24 years, 25-34 years and 35-44 years . . . These ages, the same as the principal childbearing ages, bear witness to changes in the mother's role within marriage and the family."[11] There are many other straws in the wind. Birthrates began to decline in 1957;[12] and a recent Gallup report confirms the changing conceptions of family life with the news that the percentage of women desiring to have more than two children is down from 45% in 1960 to 20% in 1973.[13]

Changing attitudes about family size, changing patterns of employment, rising education, increasing participation in social and political life reflect changing conceptions of feminine identity and role. These are also reflected in surveys of the acceptibility of women in public office. One of the more dramatic indicators of change are responses to a Gallup question that has been regularly repeated. "If your party nominated a woman for President, would you vote for her if she qualified for the job?" In August 1939, 31% of a national sample said they would vote for a woman for President, compared to 65% who said they would not. In March 1969, the number responding affirmatively had increased to 54%; and in July, 1971, the percent who said they *would vote for a woman* had climbed to 66%.[14] The significance of these data does not depend on a literal interpretation. At a minimum they signify substantial change in the beliefs about what constitutes an acceptable answer to the question. (Note, too, that the fact that 29% still say they would not vote for a qualified woman for President represents a still insurmountable *political* barrier.) Apparently, the lower the office the greater the willingness to fill it with a woman. The 1972 Virginia Slims poll reports that 40% of women (and 49% of men) would be less likely to vote for an equally qualified woman for President, but only 25% of women (and 33% of men) would be less likely to vote for a woman as vice president.[15] In 1970, 84% of voters interviewed in the summer of 1970 said they would be willing to vote for a qualified woman for Congress.[16]

More significant than the general changes in attitudes concerning women are changes in women's attitudes toward themselves. These changes are of unusual magnitude and suggest that the women's liberation movement may be not so much a vanguard of revolution as the tip of an iceberg. Gallup reports, for example, that between 1969 and 1971 the willingness to support a woman for President went up 18% among women (as compared to 7% increase among men). The

1972 Virginia Slims poll revealed a similarly dramatic change: the number of women who said they favored "the efforts to strengthen or change women's status in society" was up from 40% in 1971 to 48% a year later.

There is a kind of "consciousness raising" going on among masses of women which results in rising self-esteem and an expanded sense of possibility. Changing self-conceptions are expressed in rising career expectations, increasing enrollments in colleges, graduate and professional schools, in new demands for a larger share of power, freedom and other values.[17] But so far there has been no mass revolution against marriage and the family, no mass uprising against the male ruling class. Nor any promise of either. To the contrary, most women seem content with their lot. According to the 1972 Virginia Slims study, more women than men feel "very satisfied" with their lives: 58% of women, 49% of men;[18] and a Gallup study of fall, 1970, reports that 65% of American women believe that "women in the U.S. get as good a break as men,"[19] while 46% believe that women have an easier life than men (as compared to 30% who believe men have an easier life).[20] A further indication of widespread female satisfaction is that 84% say they have never wished they belonged to the opposite sex.[21] The 1972 Virginia Slims study reports "The majority of women view their responsibilities as mothers to be as challenging and important as men's jobs and they are not about to risk their security at home for the uncertainties and rigors of a career. They are aware also that careers are less accessible to them than men, but this does not seem to distrub most of them."[22] Approximately half of all women are unsympathetic to "women's liberation groups."[23] Reflecting the same distaste for a women's liberation symbol, 89% of married women and 67% of single women reject the title of Ms. instead of the conventional Mrs. or Miss.[24] It seems likely that even if day-care facilities of high quality were available, even if greater tax deductions for child care were granted, even if more women attended graduate and professional schools, many women would still *prefer* to devote themselves to bearing and nuturing children and to homemaking. The 1971 Virginia Slims poll, for example, reports that 71% feel "taking care of a home and raising children is more rewarding for women than having a job,"[25] and the same study reports that, asked what they found most enjoyable about being a woman today, 53% said being a mother; 23% being a homemaker; 22% being a wife, as compared to 14% who referred to general rights and freedom, 7% to being able to have a career, 2% to having an increased say in world affairs, 2% to having increased job opportunities.[26]

Current trends in mass opinion suggest a continuing and increasing demand for progressive inclusion of women; they suggest larger numbers of professional women, increasing efforts to combine family and professional roles. Should they continue, increased numbers of women will be seeking public office. But the increase is likely to be gradual and partial. Taken by themselves, existing trends provide no grounds for expecting a revolution either in the numbers of women who run for public office or in attitudes toward them.

Preferences change slowly, but in our times change does not always follow the opinion of the masses, even in democracies. The national experience with desegregation seems to prove that, at least under certain circumstances, it is possible to legislate against mores. This experience seems to suggest that, at least under certain circumstances, coercion can be used to achieve goals (e.g., the end to school segregation) that do not have the support of public opinion. Can political power be used to bring about the full (equal) participation of women in power processes? Recently some men have used the power vested in their roles to procure a larger voice for women in politics. The "McGovern-Fraser guidelines" for the 1972 Democratic Convention decreed that there should be equal numbers of women and men in convention proceedings.[27] The various "Affirmative Action" programs of recent years provide examples of the deliberate use of public policy to achieve greater participation by women in various social processes from which they had been excluded. In their effort to establish employment "goals" (quotas), these programs reflect the belief that public policy can and should be used to expedite the rise of women in various high status professions.

What else could government do to expedite the greater participation of women in politics? There are many possibilities. I shall suggest only a few.

First, there are many opportunities for symbolic affirmation. It can be reiterated that political equality includes de facto equality of the sexes; that sexual discrimination in law, employment practices, education and elsewhere is intolerable. Opportunities can be made and seized to publicize respect for women's competence.

Second, government can aid and speed the development of women's participation in public life by the appointment of more women to conspicuous and high positions. Such appointments actually increase feminine input into the policy process and simultaneously, they affect the self-conception of girls and broaden the role choices available to them by dramatizing alternatives available to people like themselves.

Third, government policy can help women win equal access to the professions which are most closely related to politics by continuing to refuse public support to universities and related institutions that discriminate against girls and women in admissions policies, awarding of fellowships, scholarships and other types of student aid.

These and comparable policies can be adopted without serious violation of existing norms and would probably accelerate the trend toward increased participation of women in public power processes. But it is doubtful that they would bring about equal participation in political power in our times.

What else could government do? Establish quotas requiring equal numbers of female and male employees at all levels and in all branches of the civil service? Require that one Senator from each state and half of each Congressional delegation be female? Require sex balancing in state legislatures? city councils? rotation in mayors' offices? Adopt a system of compulsory voting to assure that at least half the electorate will be female? Such measures might accelerate women's participation in power but would surely involve the sacrifice of such other values as equal opportunity, intra-party democracy and self-government. They could not be enacted by majoritarian decision processes.

The obstacles to the achievement of de facto political equality of the sexes are enormous. They make its achievement in the near future very unlikely. Far more likely is the continuation of existing trends toward gradual inclusion of women in power processes, a continuing increase in the number of women who seek power, a continuing increase in the flexibility of sex roles in marriage and the economy, and a continuing decrease in male resistance to sharing power with women. The elimination of blatant sexism from TV, textbooks and public policy should help more girls grow up with greater self-confidence and self-esteem; the expansion of educational and professional opportunities should provide them skills and practice; the explicit affirmation of sexual equality by political parties should make politics more welcoming to women, and the existence of women like the legislators in this study should encourage those who come after by proving that it can be done.

NOTES

1. The term is Lasswell's. Harold D. Lasswell, "The Democratic Character" in *The Political Writings of Harold D. Lasswell* (New York: Free Press, 1951), pp. 487-989.

2. Ibid, p. 487. A good discussion of this concept is Heinz Eulau's, "The Maddening Methods of Harold D. Lasswell," in *Micro-Macro Political Analysis: Accent of Inquiry* (Chicago: Aldine · Atherton, 1969), pp. 119-137.

3. In his seminal study of American character, David Riesman notes a decline of "inner directed" personality types in America. See David Riesman and Nathan Glazer, *The Lonely Crowd* (New Haven: Yale University Press, 1950). Max Weber's *The Protestant Ethic and the Spirit of Capitalism,* trans. Talcott Parsons (New York: Scribner's, 1958), is, of course, a famous study of the rise of a new character type. One of the most insightful studies of the character/culture and politics remains Plato, *The Republic of Plato,* trans. Francis M. Cornford, books 8 and 9 (Oxford: Clarendon Press, 1941), pp. 259-313. Erik H. Erikson's work linking psyche to historical epoch is also persuasive. See, e.g., *Childhood and Society,* 2nd ed. (New York: W. W. Norton, 1963); *Young Man Luther: A Study in Psychoanalysis and History* (New York: W. W. Norton, 1958). See also Erik H. Erikson, "Identity and the Life Cycle," *Psychological Issues* 1, no. 1 (1959). Lasswell has examined the problem in Harold D. Lasswell, "Political Constitution and Character," *Psychoanalysis and the Psychoanalytic Review* 46 (1960): 1-18.

4. This point is emphasized in Daniel J. Levinson, "Role, Personality and Social Structure in the Organization Setting," *Journal of Abnormal and Social Psychology* 58 (1959): 170-180.

5. One of the challenges to a social system is to integrate deviant personalities into the system by providing institutions for their absorption (e.g., Shamans, "fools," hermits, lunatics and the various monastic alternatives which institutionalize withdrawal).

6. Levinson, "Role, Personality," p. 180.

7. I suppose the maximum change model should reverse the power positions of women and men. However, such a distribution of power is so far-fetched as to be frivolous.

8. Abbot L. Ferriss, *Indicators of Trends in the Status of American Women* (New York: Russell Sage Foundation, 1971), pp. 21-43.

9. Ibid., pp. 171-176.

10. Ibid., pp. 179-182.

11. Ibid., p. 118.

12. Ibid., p. 76.

13. *The Gallup Opinion Index,* Report No. 92 (February 1973): 17-18.

14. *The Gallup Opinion Index,* Report No. 74 (August 1971): 25-26. Note an even more dramatic rise in the number saying that they would vote for a black for President, from 38% yes in 1958 to 69% in 1971.

15. *The 1972 Virginia Slims American Women's Opinion Poll,* A Study Conducted by Louis Harris and Associates, pp. 36-37.

16. *The Gallup Opinion Index,* Report No. 63 (September 1970): 11.

17. Sharp rises in educational and professional aspirations are reported in *The Special Report on Women and Graduate Study,* U.S. Department of Health, Education and Welfare, National Institutes of Health (Resources for Medical Research, Report No. 13, June 1968).

18. *1972 Virginia Slims Poll,* p. 11.

19. *The Gallup Opinion Index,* Report No. 63 (September 1970): 4.

20. Ibid., p. 8.

21. Ibid., p. 9.

22. *1972 Virginia Slims Poll,* p. 12.

23. Ibid., p. 4.

24. *The Gallup Opinion Index,* Report No. 93 (March 1973): 22-23.

25. *1972 Virginia Slims Poll,* p. 10.

26. Ibid., p. 10.

27. Only 32% of women and 24% of men believed that half the delegates to national nominating conventions should be women. *1972 Virginia Slims Poll,* pp. 42-43.

Appendix:

A Methodological Note

Selection of Respondents

THE legislative representatives of the American Association of University Women, The National Federation of Business and Professional Women's Clubs and The League of Women Voters in twenty-six states were asked to recommend women of both parties who were effective in their own legislatures and who intended to seek reelection to the legislature or another elective office. A committee of the Center for the American Women and Politics then made selections from those recommended. Selections were guided by the desire to insure good geographic distribution, roughly equal representation of both parties, varying age groups and persons with an interest in the experience of women in politics. Fifty legislators attended the conference; of these, forty-six were interviewed and completed questionnaires.

Questionnaires

Questionnaires were distributed to the legislators prior to their arrival at the conference. Most of the questionnaires were returned by the legislators on arrival. Because they provided biographical data, the questionnaires were read by the interviewers in advance of the interviews.

Interviews

The following questions were covered in all interviews, but not necessarily in the order presented below. Respondents were encouraged to

254

speak freely, to mention whatever seemed relevant to the subject. Only the interviewer and the respondent were present at the interviews. All interviews were taped.

1. How many years have you been in the legislature?
2. That makes how many terms?

The Decision to Run

3. How did you happen to run for the state legislature?
4. Had you held any party or political office up to that time?
5. Do you remember when the idea first occurred to you? Did you get the idea by yourself or did someone else mention it first?
6. In making up your mind to run, what kinds of things did you take into account?
7. What did your family and friends think about it?
8. Did you worry about the possibility of losing?
9. Well, what kinds of things did you worry about? How did the local party leaders feel about your running?
10. Was there a contest for the nomination?
11. (If *yes*) Was your opponent in the party a man or a woman?
12. (If served more than one term) What about the next time you ran? Did you have any problem in being renominated?
13. Was the attitude of the party leadership any different than the first time you were nominated?

The Campaign

14. Who was your opponent in the election the first time you ran for the legislature, or did you run unopposed? (Be sure the answer makes clear the *sex* of the opponent.)
15. What kind of campaign was it?
16. How do you feel about campaigning? Do you like it or dislike it or what?
17. What types of activities do you do most of during a campaign? speeches? or coffees? or what?
18. Were other women running for public office at the same time you first ran?
19. Did you feel you enjoyed the full support of your party (or slate)?

20. Do you think people, in general, react differently to a woman campaigning than to a man?

21. In what ways?

22. Does a woman have any special assets in a campaign?

23. What are her chief liabilities?

24. Thinking about women generally, would you circle the *two* of the following qualities which are most useful to a woman running for public office. (CARD A)

INTERVIEWER: Make sure respondent's name is on each card. She should mark card. You should write her name on it immediately after the interviews.

    A.   A high degree of integrity and dedication

    B.   Many good friends and acquaintances

    C.   Social status in the community

    D.   An ability to enjoy contests and competition

    E.   Plenty of money

    F.   Broad knowledge of the issues

    G.   Lots of energy and stamina

    H.   Knowing your way around politics

25. Some people think that any woman who campaigns energetically will be regarded as "unfeminine." What do you think about this?

In the Legislature

26. How would you describe the job of being a state legislator — what are the most important things a legislator should do?

27. Thinking of these characteristics of the job, how would you rate yourself as a legislator?

28. What do you consider your chief accomplishments as a legislator?

29. In which aspects of the job have you been least successful?

30. Regardless of how well you do as a legislator, which parts of the job do you like the least?

31. Turning now to the committee work, are you satisfied with your committee assignments?

32. Were they your first, second, or third choices or what?

33. What does it take to do a *good* job in a committee?

34. Do most members take their committee work seriously?

35. Do you?

36. How does a legislator become influential in a committee?

Now I want to ask you some questions about women in the legislature.

37. How many women are there in your legislature?

38. How many of these are in your party?

39. Has the number of women in the legislature increased since you've been there?

40. Do any women hold leadership positions in the legislature?

41. What was the attitude of the male legislators toward you when you first arrived?

42. Has that attitude changed?

43. Does a woman have more difficulty than a man gaining acceptance in the legislature?

44. (If *yes*) In what ways?

45. Do the special problems confronting women in the legislature diminish their effectiveness?

46. (If *yes*) How?

47. (If *no*) Why not?

48. Is there a tendency to give women certain kinds of committee assignments?

49. (If *yes*) Which are these?

50. In the committees on which you sit, are you or any other women influential?

51. What about within the party caucus? Are you or other women influential?

52. And what about within the legislature as a whole—are you or any other women really influential in affecting the outcomes?

53. Are there limits to how influential a woman legislator may become?

54. What are they?

Social Situations

55. How often do you get together with other legislators outside of the regular sessions and committee meetings?

56. When you get together with other legislators *outside* the capitol, do you discuss legislative business?

57. Generally speaking, do you think such informal activities are important to the work of the legislature?

58. Are women likely to be frozen out of informal legislative contacts?

59. Are women fully included?

The Future

60. Now let's turn to the future. Do you plan to seek reelection to the legislature?

61. (If not) Why is that?

62. Is there any other public office you would like to run for?

63. (If yes) What's that?

64. Do you think you are likely to actually do so?

65. (If no) Why not?

66. (If yes) What problems do you think you will likely encounter in seeking to run for other offices?

67. Here is a card with some offices listed on it. Please indicate which of these you would *like* most to hold *regardless* of the realistic likelihood of your ever trying to achieve it. (Show CARD B)

    A.   President
    B.   Vice President
    C.   U.S. Senator
    D.   Congressman
    E.   Cabinet Member
    F.   Ambassador
    G.   Federal Judge
    H.   Federal Prosecutor
    I.   Other National Office
    J.   Governor
    K.   Lieutenant Governor
    L.   State Senator
    M.   State Representative
    N.   State Judge
    O.   Other State Office
    P.   Mayor
    Q.   Other Local Office

68. Thinking about political activity in general, which *two* of the

following things do you like *most* about political activity? (Show CARD C)

    A.   Helping defeat the opposition.

    B.   The chance to become a community leader.

    C.   Advancing my career.

    D.   Helping to educate the electorate.

    E.   The opportunity to meet many interesting people.

69. And which *two* of the following do you like *least* about political activity? (Show CARD D)

    A.   The necessity of compromising my convictions.

    B.   The time it takes from my family.

    C.   The possibility of losing.

    D.   The expense.

    E.   The competition and conflict with others.

70. What would you most like to accomplish through political activity?

71. Which *two* of the following characteristics do you believe to be most necessary to anyone—male or female—who wants to achieve political success? (Show CARD E)

    A.   A personal fortune.

    B.   Firm convictions about the issues.

    C.   A reputation for leadership.

    D.   Many good friends and acquaintances.

    E.   A desire to be influential.

    F.   Knowing your way around politics.

    G.   Broad knowledge of public problems.

    H.   Lots of energy and stamina.

72. What are your reactions to the women's liberation movement?

73. Do you expect that more women will become more influential in American politics and parties in the next decade?

74. Which *two* of the following traits are most *detrimental* to a woman running for office? (Show CARD F)

    A.   Being too competitive.

    B.   Lack of firm moral principles.

    C.   A bad reputation.

    D.   Lack of financial resources.

    E.   Inadequate understanding of the issues.

    F.   No reliable friends in the party.

Family

Now, I want to ask some questions about what your political activity and service in legislature have meant to your family life.

75. What is your present marital status?

76. How many children now live at home?

77. (*If married and living with husband*) Generally speaking, what has your husband's attitude been toward your political activity?

78. Has he played a role in your activities? (What is that?)

79. How much does serving in the legislature keep you away from home?

80. How does your husband feel about these absences?

81. How about your children?

82. How old were your children when you first got active in politics?

83. How old were they when you first ran for the legislature?

84. How difficult is it for a woman to balance the demands of home and family on the one hand and a political career on the other?

85. What are the main problems?

86. Do you think the children suffer when their mothers hold public office?

87. Would you mind telling me if you have ever been divorced or widowed?

88. Do you think marriage problems are more common among women who are active in politics than among the population as a whole?

89. Why is that?

90. What about men who are politically active—how do they handle their family obligations?

91. Do their children suffer?

92. Is it your impression that marriage problems are more common among men who hold public office than among others?

93. Why is that?

Legislative Reform

94. Many states are moving toward a full-time legislature. Is this true of your state?

95. Does your state have annual or biennial sessions at this time?

96. How long are the sessions?

97. Will more frequent or longer meetings be likely to discourage women from serving in the legislature?

98. Many states have been increasing the salaries of legislators. How are the current salaries in your legislature?

99. Would an increased salary make the job more attractive to women?

100. Would increased salaries make the job more attractive to men, and so make it harder for women to get nominated and elected?

101. Has your legislature adopted a code of ethics or statute relating to conflict of interest?

102. Have the women in the legislature played any special role in dealing with questions of ethics?

103. Do you think women legislators are less likely than men to be involved in conflicts of interest?

104. Finally, could you tell me what you believe to be the chief problems facing your state today?

Index

AAUW, 22, 87, 89, 254

Abortion issues, interest in, 161, 190

Achievement: cross cultural studies of, 16; lawyers as candidates and, 83; parent membership and children's orientation to, 36; as traditional value, 48, 49-50; upward mobile women and, 33

Acquiescent husbands, 231, 233-234

Adelson, Joseph, 33, 36

Adler, Alfred, 19

Advertiser style of legislators, 212, 213, 215

Affirmative action programs, 250

Age: of lawyers as candidates, 82-83; of children, participation by mother and, 67, 230-231, 235; of male legislators, 38; perceptions related to, 138; relations between women and men legislators related to, 114; of women legislators, 55, 222, 230-231

Aggression: campaigning and, 97; hormone levels and, 12; of moralizer style legislators, 188; women legislators and, 120-121, 224

Allocentric ego style, 50

Ambivalence among women legislators, 47

American Association of University Women (AAUW), 22, 87, 89, 254

American Federalism (Elazar), 142

American Voter, The (Campbell et al.), 52

Amudsen, Kirsten, 19

Animal studies of hormone level and aggression, 12

Argentina, 11

Aryan, as racial symbol, 5

Authority: as component of political power, 10; leader style legislator and, 174; parent membership and children's attitudes toward, 36;

physiological basis for, 12; sex differences in perceptions of, 138

Autocentric ego style, 50

Baboons, male group leadership among, 12

Barber, James David, 21, 97, 129, 134, 149, 152, 155, 175, 207, 212

Bardwick, Judith M., 47, 54, 62, 198

Biological constraints on political participation by women, 9-13, 221-223

Birth rates, 248

Blacks: campaigning and group demands of, 99; resemblance between situations of women and, 19; results of effective suffrage for, 7

Black women: legislative welcoming of, 108; qualities of, as family heads, 226

British Parliament, decorum in, 115

Broker role in legislature, 143, 155, 156, 215

Buchanan, William, 113, 146, 154

Buddy system, structural roles and, 159

Business: as background for legislators, 60, 140, 220, 244; as "man's world," 15

Business and Professional Women's Clubs, 22, 73, 99-100

Cabinet, women in, 3

California, 146

Campaigns, 85-105; accounts of, 86-90; civic activity compared with, 61-62; husbands and, 97, 103, 231, 233; leader style legislators and, 178-179; moralizer style legislators and, 193; personalizer style legislators and, 200-201, 202, 203, 205; presidential (1972), 94; problem solver style legislators and, 208; requisites of, 90-103

262